BAHAMIAN LANDSCAPES

An introduction to the physical geography of The Bahamas

NEIL E. SEALEY

MEDIA PUBLISHING

© Neil E. Sealey, 1985, 1994

All rights reserved. No part of this publication may be reproduced, stored in a retrieval system, or transmitted in any form or by any other means, electronic, mechanical, photocopying, recording, or otherwise, without the prior permission of the Copyright owner.

First published 1985
Second Edition 1994

ISBN 0-9643786-0-4

Computer typeset in Palatino 10.5 on 11pt by Media Enterprises, Ltd., Nassau, Bahamas
Printed by Star Printing, Tallahassee, Florida, USA

1st Edition published by Collins Caribbean, 8 Grafton Street, London W1X 3LA, United Kingdom
2nd Edition published by Media Publishing, a division of Media Enterprises Ltd., PO Box N-9240, Nassau, Bahamas. Tel (809) 325-8210

CONTENTS

	Acknowledgements	4
	Preface	5
	Introduction	6
1.	The origin and structure of The Bahamas Platform	8
2.	The banks - a story of sedimentation	18
3.	The canyons	31
4.	The islands and their recent geological history	38
5.	The ridgeland landscape	53
6.	The rockland landscape	60
7.	The wetland and coastal landscapes	69
8.	Natural resources	85
9.	The climate of The Bahamas	109
	Bibliography	126
	Index	128

ACKNOWLEDGEMENTS

As will be clear to the reader, much of this book is a compilation and presentation of the work of other people. Where their work has been quoted or their illustrations copied, they have been acknowledged in the usual way. In many cases, however, the nature of this book has not allowed detailed references, and for this the author apologises. Serious students and others wishing to follow up some of the many studies referred to are directed to a small bibliography at the end. This lists the most easily available local sources, and a few of the more academic papers. By starting with these, the reader will quickly be directed to the several hundred other papers on which much of this work is based.

On a more personal note, the author wishes to thank Dr Richard Cant, hydrogeologist with The Bahamas Ministry of Works, for making the first edition of this book possible. When the author arrived in The Bahamas it was Dr Cant who first explained the geology to him and took him around New Providence. Since then he has provided published papers from numerous sources, technical information, personal recollections and introductions to other workers in the field. He also read the manuscript and provided much advice on it. This is not surprising. Dr Cant was one of the authors of the multi-volume *Land Resource Study* (often quoted in this book), and has been the guide and mentor of scholars from all over the world who have come to study The Bahamas.

The author also wishes to thank all those who provided information and advice at the Department of Statistics, the Department of Economic Affairs, the Department of Meteorology, Morton Bahamas Limited, Marcona Ocean Industries Limited, the Comparative Sedimentology Laboratory at the Rosentiel School of Marine and Atmospheric Science, University of Miami, The Bahamas National Trust, Miss Paula Sweeting of the Ministry of Education, and Dr Steven Mitchell, of Bakersfield, California.

In the years leading up to the second edition there have been many others who have influenced the author and made contributions to the geology and geography of The Bahamas. Among these the author wishes to acknowledge Dr John Mylroie of Mississippi State University; Dr James Carew of Charleston University; Dr Donald Gerace of The Bahamian Field Station, San Salvador; Dr H Allen Curran of Smith College; Dr Mark Boardman of Miami University, Ohio; Dr William Keegan of the University of Florida; Dr Conrad Neumann of South Carolina State University; Dr Robert Ginsburg of Miami University; Dr Eugene Shinn of the US Geological Survey; Mr Rob Palmer of Technical Diving Ltd, UK; Drs Fiona Whitaker and Peter Smart of Bristol University, UK; Mr J Stephen Dowd of Marcona Industries Ltd.; Mr Philip Weech of the Water & Sewerage Corporation, Nassau; Drs John Sahota and Paul Hearty of The College of The Bahamas; Mr John Burrows of the Ministry of Education, Nassau; Michael Toogood of Toogood's Photography, Nassau; Ms Florence Bryden of St Andrew's School, Nassau; Mr Ivan Sealey of Imperial College, London; and Joanne and Larry Smith and the staff of Media Enterprises.

Where known the sources of illustrations have been acknowledged in the caption or text. The publishers would appreciate the appropriate information where any illustration has not been properly credited. Photographs not provided by the author are acknowledged in the caption. The publishers are most grateful to these persons, and The **Bahamas Ministry of Tourism**, which provided the cover photograph.

PREFACE

1st Edition

Twenty-eight years ago Norman Newell and Keith Rigby published their *Geological Studies on the Great Bahama Bank*.[1] In it they quoted 99 references to the geology and other related areas of study of The Bahamas, some of these published over 100 years ago. Since that time there has been an enormous increase in the amount of research and in the number of articles written in this field. Every year, teams of experts, individuals and students, especially from the United States, come into the country to study its unique marine and land environments. This activity is not, of course, particularly strange, and few countries have not been treated in a similar manner. What is unusual, however, is the absence of any publication, for the general public, for the student, or for the local teacher, on what all this work has achieved.

The purpose of this little book is to rectify, at least for the time being, this gap in our knowledge. Hopefully, in the not too distant future, a definitive work on the physical geography of The Bahamas will be written. In the meantime, this study is an attempt to collate from numerous sources, many of which are not available in The Bahamas, the considerable amount of material gathered over the years, and particularly in the last 25 years. The result is intended to be both a geological history and a geographical inventory which is intelligible to everyone with an enquiring mind. It cannot be completely comprehensive, nor entirely simple, for The Bahamas is a complex environment which still has to yield many of its secrets. Nevertheless, it is a most interesting story so far, and for most people should be an enjoyable and instructive study.

[1] Norman D. Newell and J. Keith Rigby: 'Geological Studies on the Great Bahama Bank.' *Society of Economic Palaeontologists and Mineralogists*, Special Publication No. 5, 1957, pp. 15-72.

2nd Edition

Soon after the publication of the first edition, Collins Caribbean was taken over by Longman Caribbean, and the book was then distributed by this firm until it went out of print in 1993. Longmans indicated that they did not wish to continue with the title and offered the rights back to the author. This created both a problem and an opportunity: the problem being how to keep *Bahamian Landscapes* in print, the opportunity being the ability to revise and add to the original edition.

Over the years a variety of errors and limitations had been identified in the text, and new research, such as the work on blue holes, stromatolites, caves, and stratigraphy needed to be included. New geological dates had become available and the economic data needed revision. The Ministry of Education had now made the study of Bahamian geography compulsory for their General Certificate of Secondary Education, and there was a need to make the book more accessible to secondary school students, and for a separate chapter on Climate to serve this market.

The author was most fortunate to find the solution in one company, Media Enterprises Ltd, a well known Bahamian communications company. Media, in association with the author, agreed to undertake the resetting of the text and its publication locally, and the result is the second edition presented here.

It is hoped that this book will be of value to all secondary and college level students. (Chapters 1, and 5 through 9, cover the relevant portions of the BGCSE and College Prep syllabuses in geography). Visitors to The Bahamas, and all those interested in the Bahamian environment who have enjoyed the first edition, should find this edition of interest and value.

INTRODUCTION

The place on the surface of the earth where The Bahamas is today did not always exist. Geologically, we must think of The Bahamas as a *platform* standing up from the sea-floor off the south-east coast of North America. The *islands* we know today, and call The Bahamas, are the exposed parts of this platform, a mere 30-60 metres (100-200 feet) of land compared with up to 6 100 metres (20 000 feet) beneath sea-level (Figure 1.1).

Our first task is to see what created this platform, how it grew and took shape, and to find how it relates to its neighbours, Florida and Cuba. The story, in fact, begins with nothing less than the creation of the Atlantic Ocean 200 million years ago!

Once a place for the platform had been created, the platform itself had to be built. Various investigations, such as by deep drilling, have shown that virtually all the rocks that make up the 6 100 metres (20 000 feet) or so thickness of The Bahamas Platform were formed in shallow water. As they were formed, they subsided under successively newer layers. This process is known as *sedimentation* because the rocks were, in fact, formed from hardened (lithified) *sediments*.

The sediments that took part in this process are still being formed today, and are quite varied. We must, therefore, examine their nature and formation, for it is the sediments themselves which hold the key to the present-day shallow water *banks*, that vast area that comprises 90% of Bahamian territory.

Around and within The Bahamas are various deep-water channels and straits including the Tongue of the Ocean. We must ask why do these exist at all? Why did they not fill up with sediments like the banks? The origin of these enormous under-water canyons is not properly understood even today, but there are several theories that we can discuss.

Once we have understood how the platform and its many features were formed, we must ask how it was that portions of the platform became land while others did not. The answer is a story of changing sea-level, the winds, and, above all, of the great *Ice Ages* that commenced about two million years ago.

Following the Ice Ages, the map of The Bahamas was more or less complete. Nevertheless, sedimentation on and around the banks has never stopped, while on land we can see both *erosion* and *deposition* actively at work. The landscape continues to change, and if we are to use it wisely we must know what is happening, how quickly, and why?

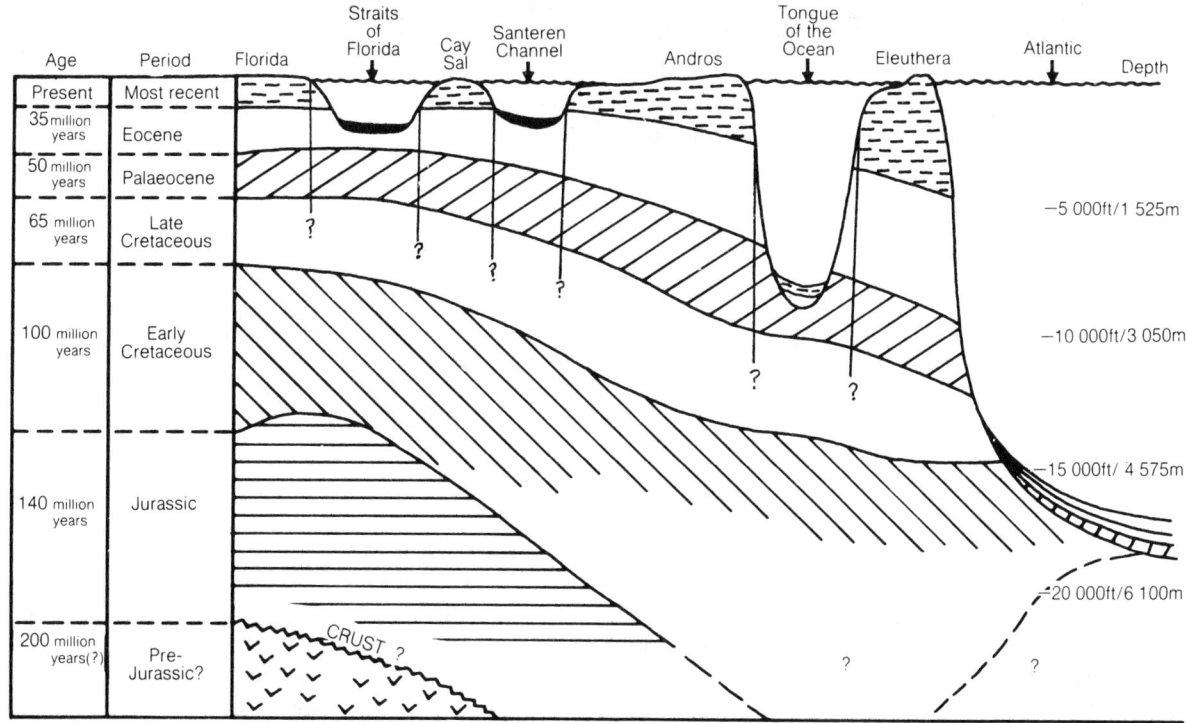

Figure 1.1 Geological view of the Bahamas Platform. As far as is known the geological structure of the platform is one of thick beds of limestone sloping towards the Atlantic where they are at their thickest. It is not known just how deep down the crust is, and the beds are believed to be faulted in their lower layers.

The key to deposition and erosion today is clearly the climate we are now experiencing. It is important that we understand the strength and direction of the winds that generate the waves that shape our coast. In particular the frequency of hurricanes is of considerable importance. The amount of weathering that occurs is directly related to the rainfall we receive. For these reasons, and others related to our soil development and water resources, it is necessary to have a sound knowledge of our local climate.

Today many are looking to the country, both onshore and offshore, to supply its own resources - oil, sand, coral, aragonite, salt and so on. There are some 13 000 square kilometres (5 000 square miles) of land and 130 000 square kilometres (50 000 square miles) of shallow water banks. Therefore, we must take a separate look at the natural resources of The Bahamas.

Finally we should ask what is the point of all this study, other than academic curiosity? Of the many answers the one that has the most relevance is that in an age of increasing pressure on our resources, it is only by understanding these resources thoroughly that they will be able to be used economically. It should become clear as the reader progresses through the book, that nothing in The Bahamas exists in isolation. Every impact in one place will have a multitude of repercussions, both there and elswhere. The study of these impacts and their anticipation is the province of students of Resource Management, or Environmental Management. Nevertheless, although these concerns have not been dealt with separately, they are implicit throughout the book, and many examples of environmental response will be noted.

1 THE ORIGIN AND STRUCTURE OF THE BAHAMAS PLATFORM

For over 100 years geologists have wondered about the origin of The Bahamas. Looking at the scatter of islands and shallow water led one observer to suggest that The Bahamas was a 'delta' at the mouth of the Gulf Stream. However, a study of the rocks clearly shows that The Bahamas are not made up of the kind of eroded particles which would be washed into a normal delta. In fact, The Bahamas is comprised of a variety of limestones such as coral, which have not been transported, but were formed where they are now.

THE BIRTH OF THE BAHAMAS

Other writers realised this and suggested origins similar to those for other islands found in the tropics, notably for the coral atolls of the Pacific Ocean. Most atolls consist of a layer or *cap* of coral built on top of a submerged volcano. Alternatively, the coral could have formed on a submerged mountain range. As coral can only survive in relatively shallow water it is usual to find it attached to some other submerged feature. However, geological investigations over the last 40 years have shown that this is an unlikely origin for The Bahamas. Firstly, despite drilling as deep as 5 800 metres (19 000 feet), volcanic material has never been encountered. Secondly, the rocks discovered below the surface are all of the same type, known geologically as *shallow water carbonates*, and these can only have formed near the surface.

There have been many other theories, but most of these had to be abandoned with the development of new ideas in the 1960s. At this time the old ideas on *continental*

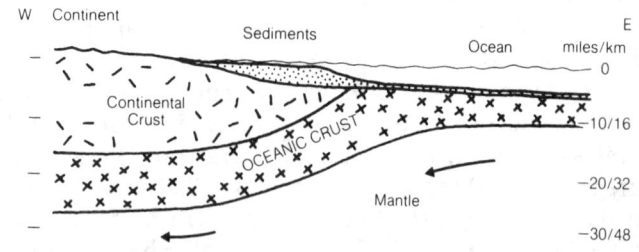

Figure 1.2 Relationship of Continental crust to Oceanic crust. This is believed to be the situation where North America and the Atlantic meet. Mantle currents are moving both crusts to the west, creating a shallow water area at their junction. It is here that carbonate sediments can form, and that the Continental crust is thin enough to be pushed down by their weight.

drift became more acceptable, and were included within the much bigger study of *plate tectonics*. Briefly, this is the theory that considers the Earth's crust to be of two basic types: an upper *continental* layer resting on a lower *oceanic* layer (Figure 1.1). The theory goes on to show that in the past there was just one huge piece of continental crust - a supercontinent - which rested on an oceanic crust which covered the whole Earth. About 200 million years ago this supercontinent started to break up as a result of *rifting* or splitting in the underlying oceanic crust. The pieces that drifted apart became the continents we know today, and between them new oceanic crust was formed. Over the new crust, new oceans were formed. One of these was the North Atlantic Ocean, located in the space created when North America drifted away from Africa and Europe (Figure 1.3).

Once this process had been understood, attempts were made to fit the continents back together, and when this was done a surprising situation developed - there was no room for the present-day Bahamas!

As a result of this geological detective work we have learnt something about The Bahamas: the Earth is approximately 4 500 million years old, but The Bahamas did not exist as recently as 200 million years ago; The Bahamas is not a part of the North American continent; its base must be part of either the newly formed oceanic crust or a stretched-out edge of the rifted North American crust - opinions vary.

GROWING UP

Theories like the above can be fascinating. In general, there is no doubt that The Bahamas was born a little less than 200 million years ago when the Atlantic was formed - at the time when dinosaurs roamed the Earth!

However, we need to know a lot more before we can tell the whole story. For instance, why did no other groups of islands

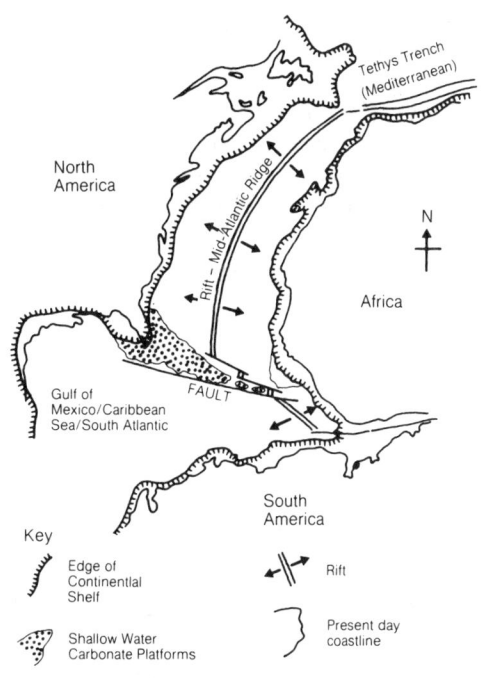

Figure 1.3 The Bahamas Platform was formed about 150 million years ago. It is seen here as a triangular projection off the south-east coast of North America. Only at its tip have small and isolated banks formed, and southern Florida and the Turks and Caicos Islands are all part of the Platform. The Caribbean Sea and West Indian Islands have not yet been formed. (R. S. Dietz et al, 1971)

form like The Bahamas, and why are they located just where they are now? Why is it that if we drill we only find rocks from shallow seas when The Bahamas goes down as deep as four miles, depths at which normally only the abyssal oozes of the oceans are formed?

The answers would all be known if we could simply have a look under The Bahamas, as far down as is necessary to come to the crust on which the platform is built. Then we could analyse all the rocks from the bottom to the top and reconstruct the geological history up to the present day.

Although this is impossible to do directly, we can at least get some samples by *drilling boreholes.* Over the years, several deep and a larger number of shallow holes have been drilled in many parts of the archipelago. The deepest of all reached 5 766 metres (18 906 feet) below Cay Sal, and about twelve others have gone deeper than 3 000 metres (10 000 feet). (See Figure 1.3). From these deep test wells several facts have emerged that help us to put together some of the jigsaw of evolution for The Bahamas:

- None of the wells reached the crustal rocks.

- Even in the deepest wells all the rocks found had actually been formed near the surface.

- No rock was found which was older than the Cretaceous Period, that is 135 million years old, with one exception. In the Great Isaac's well, limestones and marine shales from the earlier Jurassic Period were found, and also some volcanic debris. The latter may have come from the North American continent. It is possible that the lowest beds, known as the 'red beds', are in fact the surface of the crust on which The Bahamas is built. One authority considers them to be of Triassic Age, which would fit in with this theory.

- Virtually all the rocks are of marine

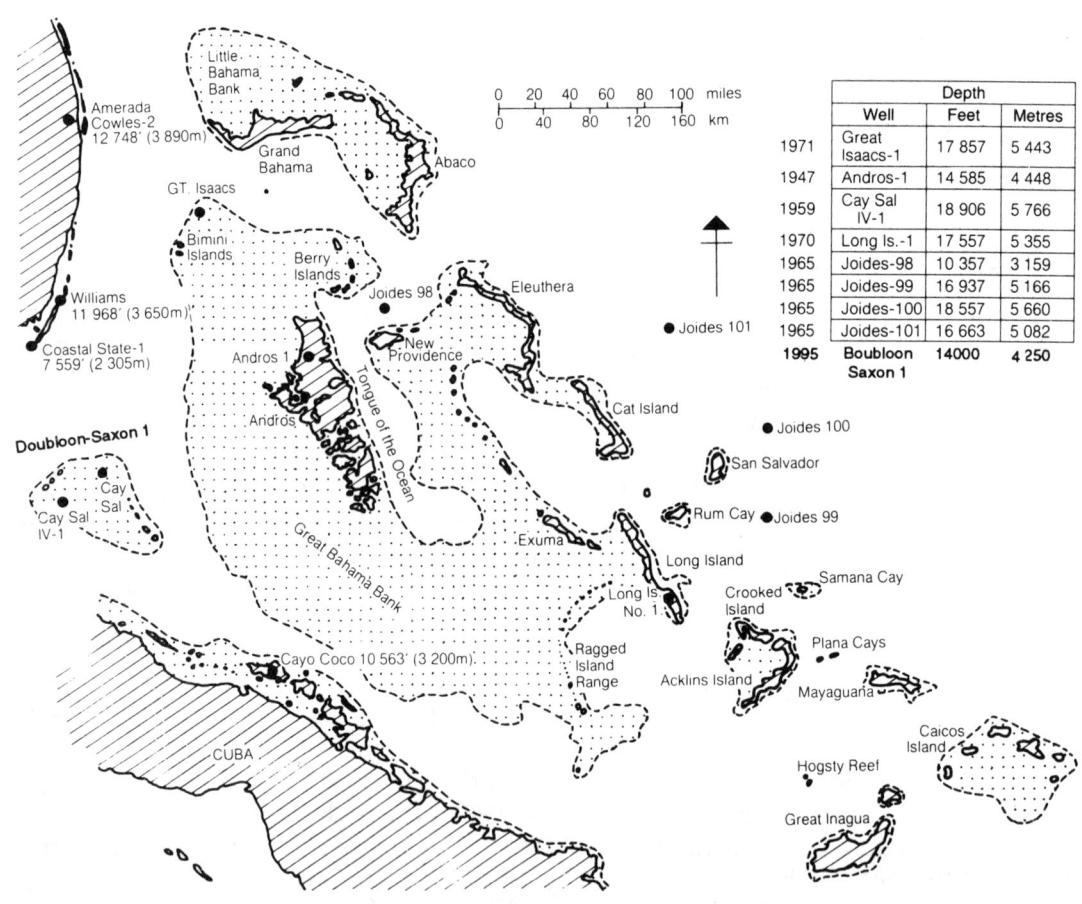

Figure 1.4 *Location of all deep bore holes in The Bahamas with depths in metres and feet.*

origin. The exceptions are the 'red beds' referred to above, fossil soils and sand-dune rock (aeolian limestone), which have been found in shallow wells and in the ridges. This suggests that The Bahamas has always had a marine environment from the time of its formation until the recent Ice Ages.

The age of the oldest rocks discovered is important, as it fits in with the theory that The Bahamas formed after the North Atlantic. Rocks found in North America date back thousands of millions of years, and show that this continent had a quite different origin.

The fact that all the rocks were originally formed in shallow water requires some explanation, but in practice this is not uncommon in geology. For example, coal was originally formed at the surface in swamps, but these swamps became buried and coal is now found deep underground. Nevertheless, in the case of The Bahamas, the great thicknesses and total absence of any other rocks is both remarkable and unique. To explain it we need to have had two things going on at once: the *production of sediment* at a fairly rapid rate in a shallow marine environment; and *subsidence of the crust* on which The Bahamas stands. The rate of subsidence had to be fairly slow so that the water did not get too deep for the processes to continue, but not so slow that sediments appeared above sea-level.

There is yet another feature of the Bahamian rocks - mainly limestones - that is unusual. Unlike almost anywhere else in the world, the rocks that were formed in the past, at depths down to at least 6 100 m (20 000 ft) (as deep as the ocean is today), are essentially the same as those that are found, and are actually forming, at the surface today. This means that geographical conditions at the surface have been more or less the same for the whole of The Bahamas' history. In other words, this has always been an area of shallow seas and banks, and it is clear that much is to be learned from a study of the rocks, and the sediments that have formed them.

Although drilling does give us actual contact with the rocks underground, it is still necessary for us to look beyond the limits of drilling. Fortunately there are several ways of doing this:

■ *By gravity measurements*

Any solid object exerts a force which we know as gravitational attraction. The Earth exerts a force which causes objects to fall towards it, and this force will be greater according to the *density* of the rocks in the crust. The rocks of the Earth have different densities, and, in particular, the rocks of the continental crust (granitic) have a lower density, i.e. they are lighter, than the rocks of the oceanic crust (basaltic). In fact, it may be said that the continents float on the oceanic crust.

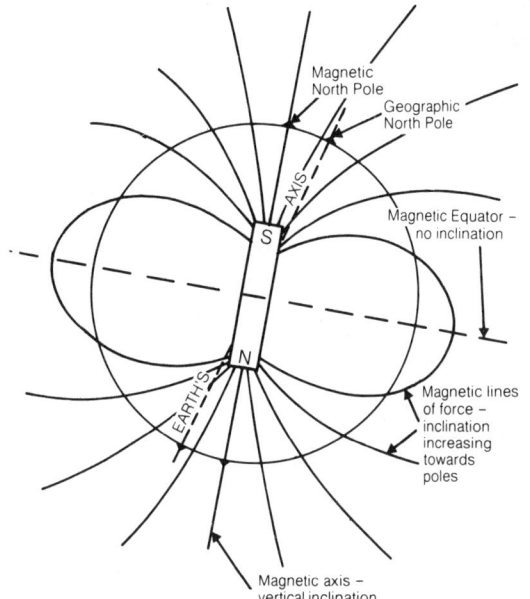

Figure 1.5 The true nature of the Earth's magnetism is not fully understood, but the effect is similar to having a short bar magnet located in the Earth's core. As a result, the magnetic lines of force have both direction and inclination - they cause a needle to dip towards the Earth's surface except at the magnetic equator. This property helps to locate rocks at the time of their formation.

Gravity can be measured very accurately with a *gravity meter,* which will give differing readings according to the different rocks beneath it. Several gravity surveys of The Bahamas have been made in recent years and have provided valuable information about the rocks and their structure at depths greater than 6 100 metres (20 000 feet).

■ By magnetic measurements

As we all know, the Earth has a magnetic field which causes a compass to line up with the North and South Magnetic Poles. This magnetism is believed to be generated from the iron content of the Earth's core, deep down inside the Earth. If a compass was taken to the North Pole, it would in fact point *down* into the ground. Similarly, at any other point on the Earth's surface, the needle would point *into* the Earth to some degree, except at the Magnetic Equator. This is because the Magnetic Poles are situated far below the surface (Figure 1.5).

Magnetism is a particularly useful property, because most rocks when formed, and especially *basaltic* rocks, have some iron particles in them that have aligned themselves with the Earth's magnetic field, and in doing so have become magnetized. As a result, magnetism from these rocks becomes *added* to the Earth's magnetic pull, and a *magnetometer* passed over these rocks gives a higher than average reading

Quite separate from this is the fact that in the past the Earth's magnetic polarity has frequently been *reversed,* meaning that the North Pole has become the South Pole and

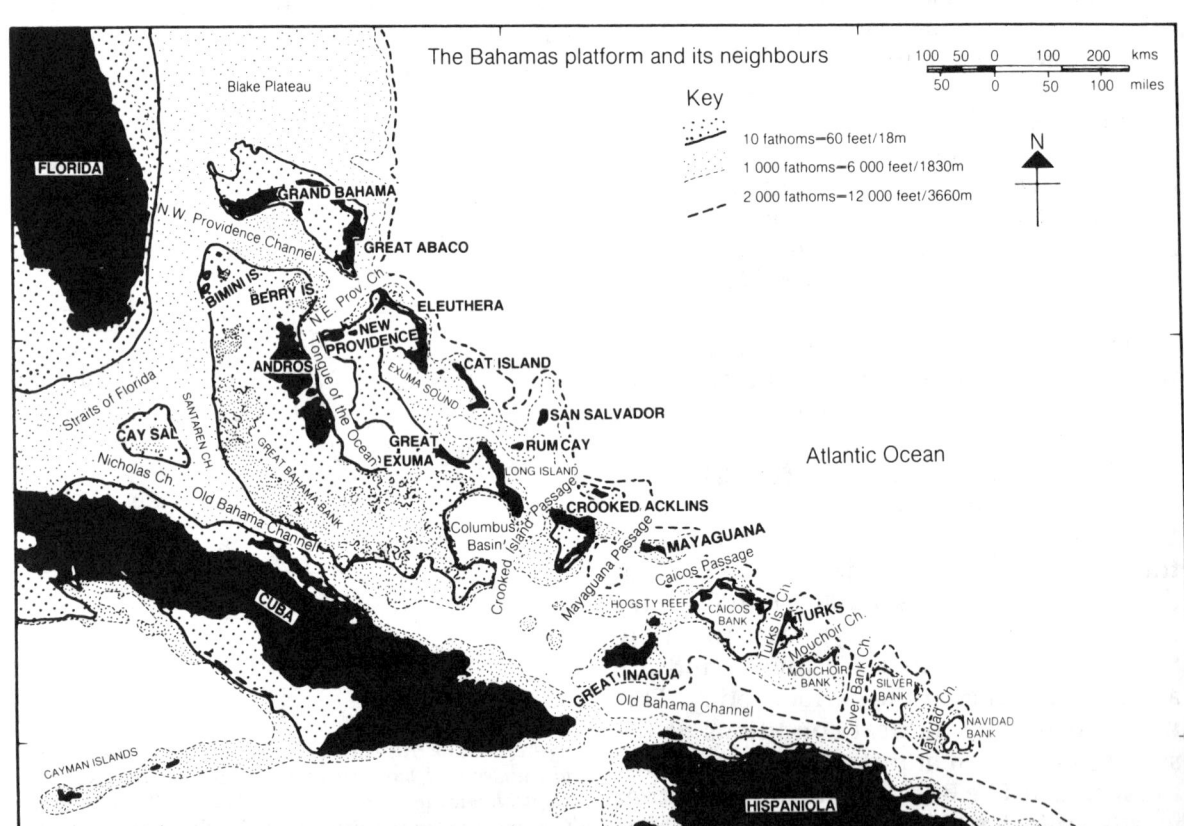

Figure 1.6 *If the depth shading is studied carefully, it will be seen that the 18 metres (60 feet) depth contour outlines the various banks, while the 3 660 metres (12 000 feet) depth outlines the whole platform, which includes The Bahamas' neighbours of the Turks and Caicos Islands and the Blake Plateau.*

vice versa. This means that any rocks which were formed at such a time will have acquired an opposite magnetism to the magnetic field of the Earth today. If a magnetometer is passed over these rocks it will give a low reading, as the rock's magnetism now counteracts the Earth's magnetism.

Several magnetic surveys of The Bahamas have been made to see if the underlying rocks resemble more closely the rocks of the continental or of the oceanic crusts.

■ By seismic measurements

Any noise transmitted in the sea will travel down through the water to the sea-floor and return to the surface. Since the speed of sound is known, the depth of the water can always be calculated if the time taken for sound to travel down and back up again is measured. Timing this *echo is* the principle of the *echo sounder* or depth recorder used by boats and ships. Seismic measurements use a similar principle. By varying the frequency of a sound-wave, the signal can be made to pass through some types of rocks but be reflected from others. The denser a rock is, the more likely it is to reflect a signal, whereas loose sediments, or sedimentary rocks (like limestones) are more likely to allow the signal to pass through them.

Seismic surveys of The Bahamas have been made in order to determine the thickness of both marine sediments and sedimentary rocks, and the depth of the harder basement rocks.

In 1985 a new set of seismic profiles were taken across about 700 kilometres (430 miles) of the north-western part of the Great Bahama Bank (Figure 1.7). To everyone's surprise the data revealed buried channels. It appears that the Great Bahama Bank had been split and infilled on more than one occasion in the past. (See also Chapter 3)

FORMATION OF THE PLATFORM

As a result of all these studies, a general picture of the development of The Bahamas can be pieced together. One of the first things to realise is that geologically The Bahamas

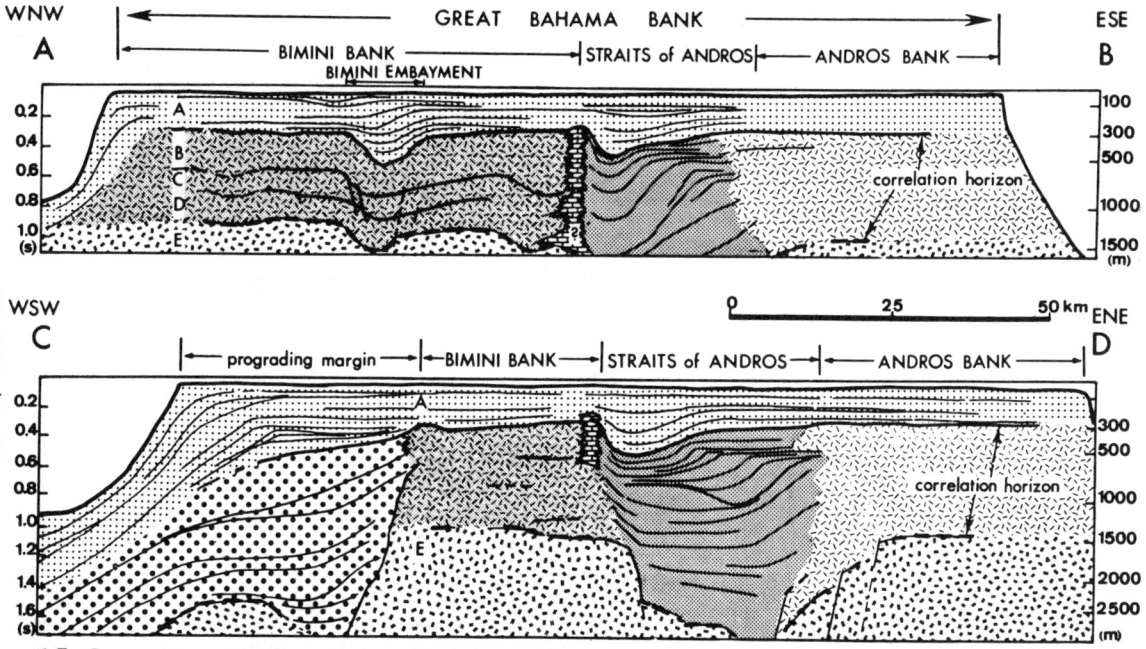

Figure 1.7. *Cross-section of the Great Bahama Bank, based on seismic surveys. (From Eberli and Ginsburg, 1987)*

is related to its neighbours - Florida, Northern Cuba, the Turks and Caicos Islands, and to the Blake Plateau to the north (Figure 1.6). Throughout this region similar conditions existed, and although at first sight the surrounding areas might appear very different, they really are quite similar when closely inspected. The Turks and Caicos Islands are very much an extension of the South-eastern Bahamas, and it is the south-eastern Bahamas which are rather different from the rest of The Bahamas, that is, from the Great and Little Bahama Banks. Southern Florida is really not much more than a large-scale version of Andros, although it does not have such a great thickness of sediments as Andros (Figure 1.1). The southern half of the Florida Keys is also very similar to the many chains of cays found in The Bahamas, such as the Exuma Cays or the Bimini chain. It is of interest that these cays could also be joined up by a system of roads and bridges in the same way as the Florida Keys are linked to Key West. (It should be noted that only the keys south of Big Pine Key are composed of oolitic limestone, the more northern keys being built of coral limestone (Figure 1.8).)

The Blake Plateau which lies to the north can be considered to be a submarine extension of The Bahamas that was drowned about 80 million years ago, but carried on sinking so that it is now under 900 metres (3 000 feet) of water.

Cuba is rather different from the other islands because it has been subjected to mountain building at its extremities, but virtually all of northern Cuba has had the same history as The Bahamas - shallow water carbonate deposition for 200 million years. Much of mainland Cuba is a flat limestone plain, and numerous islands fringe the northern shores.

Thus the story of the origin of The Bahamas involves its neighbours as well.

So far we have only found a place for The Bahamas, and a suggestion as to its foundations. Studies suggest that at the boundary of North America and the Atlantic Ocean the continental crust was stretched and thinned as Africa pulled away from it.

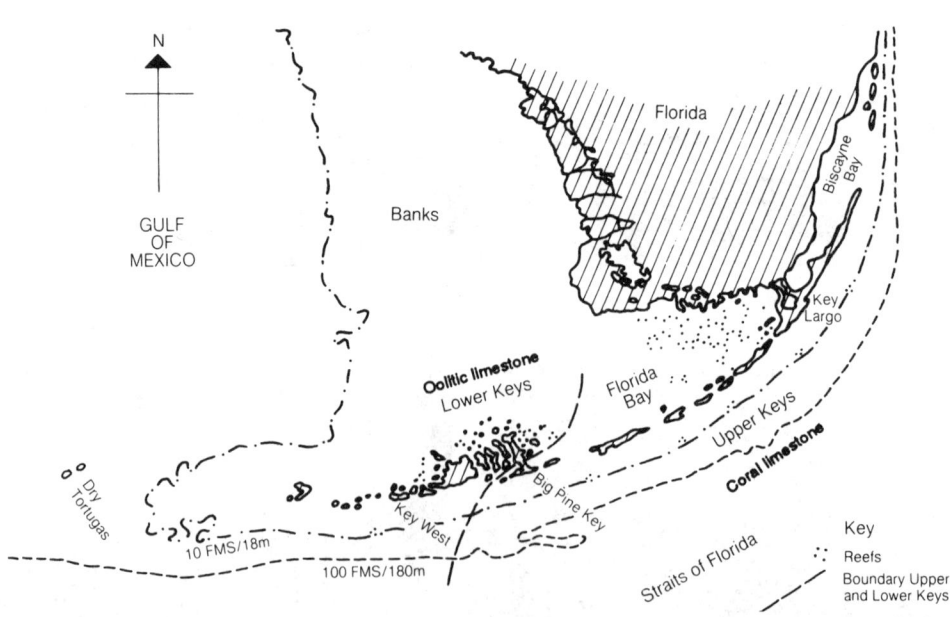

Figure 1.8 Florida and the Florida Keys have much in common with The Bahamas. The Lower Keys are mainly composed of marine oolitic limestone, as is most of the southern tip of Florida. They are broad and low-lying, cut by many tidal channels and are fronted by coral reefs and backed by banks.

Gradually this thinning crust began to be flooded by the new ocean, and a great variety of sediments were laid down in the shallow seas so formed. As the stretching went on, the crust got thinner and weaker. As the sediments got heavier they weighed down on the weakened crust, forcing it to sink. (The widening of the Atlantic is still going on today, although at a slower rate believed to be about 2.7 cms (1.1 inch) a year. The stretching of the crust has probably now stopped altogether.) All this time The Bahamas and its neighbours were nearly at sea-level, and probably formed a single vast marine plain dotted with islands. This situation only changed when in some areas the rate of adding sediment became less than the rate at which the crust below it was sinking.

About 80 million years ago there must have been a major change in the environment. Perhaps it was the creation of the Gulf of Mexico which led to the flooding of the Bahamian area by the waters of the Gulf Stream. If so, this strong current may have carried the sediments away, or the changing conditions may have stopped the production of sediment. In either case, the absence of a build-up of sediment in some parts of the sinking platform would have led to flooding and submergence. Perhaps there was an excess of sediment which smothered and killed the coral reefs. Whatever happened, the result was:

- the drowning of the Blake Plateau;

- the separation of The Bahamas from Cuba and Florida;

- the disintegration of the south-eastern Bahamas and the Turks and Caicos Islands into a series of small banks (with low islands on them), surrounded by a complex system of troughs and basins over 1 800 metres (6 000 feet) deep;

- the creation of troughs and channels within and between the Little and Great Bahama Banks (see Figure 1.6).

EVOLUTION OF THE BANKS

It was originally thought that these developments happened all at once, and that the map of the Bahama Banks that we see today was more or less established then. Research in the 1980's has shown that the picture is more complex. Seismic studies (P.13) have revealed buried channels on the scale of the Tongue of the Ocean, and submarine dives along the edges of the banks have shown 'scalloping' of the bank margins in some areas, and extensive sediment accumulation in others. Consequently the banks have undoubtedly been evolving since Cretaceous times, even if there was a single event that disrupted the original platform.

Work by Mullins and Hine in 1989[1] suggests that several processes are at work:

- step-faulting or rifting which creates troughs or channels. This lowers the sea bed below the depth at which shallow-water sedimentation can occur.

- in-filling of these troughs by lateral accretion. Sediment is swept into the channels from the adjacent banks to windward.

- scalloping of the bank margins which creates crescentic embayments. As this continues the bank is progressively destroyed. It has been suggested that this is what produced the fragmentation of the Southeastern Bahamas, perhaps because scalloping was more active in this area.

The scalloping theory needs further explanation. Observation of the bank margins from research submarines suggests that this kind of erosion is most active on the windward sides. Erosion takes the form of collapse of portions of the bank edge, in much the same way that a cliff face collapses. The collapsing leaves crescentic embayments in the platform edge (Figure 1.8). Successive collapses over millions of years create a progressive destruction of the bank, like the headward erosion of river valleys, and this may account for the large semi-circular embayments found in the Columbus Basin, and at the head of the Tongue of the Ocean, today.

In the case of the Tongue of the Ocean it, should be noted that its general alignment follows subterranean faults in NNW/SSE direction, but that the southern extension of the 'tongue' is a huge embayment oriented to the east. Even bigger is the Columbus Basin to the south-east of the Tongue of the Ocean, and it can be conjectured that if scalloping and headward erosion continue the Tongue and the Columbus Basin will join, and the Great Bahama Bank will be split in two.

In the case of the south-eastern Bahamas it has been suggested that this has already happened. This part of The Bahamas is much closer to the North American Plate margin than the northern Bahamas, and it is therefore more likely to be affected by plate movements. Earthquakes along the plate margin (in the vicinity of Cuba and Hispaniola), would provide just the right kind of shock-waves to trigger the collapse of unstable masses along the edge of the bank. As the Bahamas platform is much narrower in this region anyway, channels could have been cut through it more quickly than in the north, such as the Crooked Island Passage, the Mayaguana Passage and the Caicos Passage (Figure 1.6).

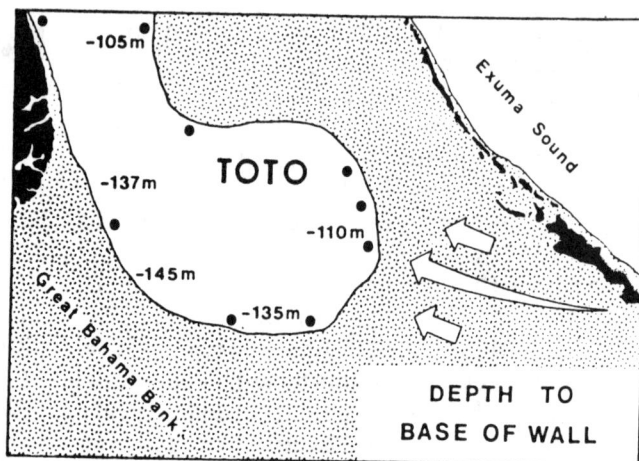

Figure 1.9 Headward erosion at the edge of the Tongue of the Ocean. Arrows show the prevailing wind, and depths are to the base of the drop-off (wall), and imply the increased deposition covering the windward slopes.

However they were formed, the deep water troughs and channels receive much less sediment than the shallow-water areas. Some sediment undoubtedly enters them from catastrophic collapses along the bank edge, and these avalanches have been identified as *turbidity currents* as they continue across the sea floor. In addition there is a continuous fine 'rain' of minute particles from the banks. This settles over the deep-water sea bed as an *ooze*, which is the only sediment found in areas far from land.

During the current geological era, known as the Quaternary Era, some 120 metres (400 feet) of sediments have been laid down over Andros, but only a metre-thick layer of ooze has been deposited in the adjacent Tongue of the Ocean and Providence Channel. Consequently, sedimentation in these areas did not keep up with the subsidence of their floors, which now lie well below the level of the banks, as Table 1.1 shows.

On the banks themselves, sedimentation continued, accumulating at a rate of about 2 cms (0.8 inches) per 1 000

Table 1.1 Depths in the Bahamian troughs and surrounding channels. Compare with Figure 1.1.

Trough or Channel	Depth (Metres/Feet)
Florida Straits	600/2 500
Blake Plateau	900/3 000
Exuma Sound	1 600/5 250
Tongue of the Ocean	1 500-1 800/5 000-6 000
Providence Channel	3 000-4 000/10 000-13 000
Atlantic Ocean	4 600-6 000/15 000-20 000

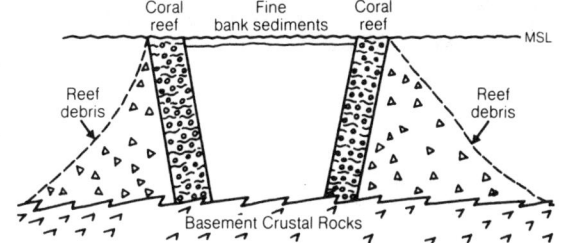

Figure 1.10 The bucket theory explains the way in which a coral reef wall grows vertically and retains the fine biological sediments produced within the rim. (E Shinn et al 1978)

years. Each bank is a self-contained system, usually referred to as an *atoll*. In it a variety of sediments are produced, but these would simply be washed away and lost were it not for the retaining walls of the atolls - the *coral reefs*. In many ways the atolls, whatever their shape, can be likened to a bucket of sand (the loose sediments) with the sides of the bucket (the coral reefs) holding it in (see Figure 1.10). (The term 'atoll' is not meant to imply the volcanic origin so common in Pacific atolls. Atolls are marine sedimentary structures whatever they are built on.)

The next part of the story is that of the production of the sediments. The Bahamas has been likened to a vast carbonate rock factory which produces many types of limestones. The various processes which produced the sediments, and which converted them to rocks, are the same ones as are active today. We thus pass from geological history to a reality that can be observed and studied in great detail. The sediments are also the materials that people most commonly come into contact with in their environment, and are therefore most important to them. For these reasons they are treated separately and in some detail.

[1] Mullins, Henry T, and Hines, Albert C, Scalloped bank margins: Beginning of the end for Carbonate Platforms? *Geology*, 1989, 17, p 30-33.

2 THE BANKS–A STORY OF SEDIMENTATION

We should now realise that the production of sediments is at the heart of the Bahamian environment. Although there are some signs of erosion, such as sea cliffs and sink holes, The Bahamas is essentially a *depositional* landscape, unlike the much more common eroded landscapes of the continents, or even of large islands such as Jamaica.

Sediments can be, and are, produced in many ways, such as:

- chemically – by evaporation and precipitation of the salts in sea water
- biologically – by *photosynthesis* in marine plants
  – from the bodies and skeletons of marine animals
- physically – by erosion of the coasts or coral reefs

Ultimately these will be converted to solid rock by *cementation* in a variety of ways, a process known as *lithification* - rock-making. This will probably be after some sorting, mixing and transportation has taken place. In addition we must not forget that coral builds itself directly into a solid form - *coral limestone.*

In The Bahamas, there is no volcanic material or any other igneous rock, nor are there any metamorphic rocks. Of the sedimentary rocks, only *limestones*, and their relatives the *evaporites,* all products of the ocean, are found. Other sedimentary rocks such as sandstones[1], shales, chalk or coal are totally absent, although some peat has been found in a few areas.

Probably the greatest mistake that can be made is to believe that the Bahamian islands are coral islands. It is true that occasionally fossil patch reefs can be found on land, but most of the islands contain insignificant amounts of coral (Mayaguana is an exception). For the same reasons they are not made of *coralgal limestone*, which is derived from a mixture of coral and algal sediments, although this is more common in many islands. As we shall see, it is another type altogether, *oolitic limestone*, which is the basis for much of the land, and certainly all of the higher land.

In a borehole in New Providence, the first 38 metres (125 feet) penetrated was found to be entirely oolitic limestone, but below that corals became quite common. Possibly in earlier times - the *Tertiary Era* - climatic conditions were more favourable for coral growth.

THE PRODUCTION OF SEDIMENT

Although most of the actual sediment found in any one place is a mixture of several types, it makes sense first of all to see just what produces sediment.

The *coral reef* is an obvious source of material, but surprisingly coral itself is often a minor part of the sand and mud produced

Figure 2.1 Halimeda *and* Penicillus *growing among* Thalassa *sea grass. (See Figure 2.2 for identification) Photograph courtesy of Robert N Ginsburg.*

Table 2.1 Composition of sediment from the coral reef area

Sediment	Percentage
Skeletal debris	41
Cryptocrystalline grains	21
Grapestone	14
Clay	11
Oolite	6
Pellets	5
Eroded coastal rock	2

This is an average of 33 samples taken from the outer edge of the banks. Source: E. G. Purdy, 1963, p. 474.

on and around a reef.(Table 2.2)

Before studying each of these in turn, we should first define some of the more unusual terms:

- *Skeletal* This is fairly easy to understand. It refers to any whole skeleton or part of an animal or a plant - for instance a piece of coral, a tiny shell, a sea urchin spine, or a piece of calcareous algae. A more scientific name used by geologists is **'bioclastic'** - 'bio', from living things; 'clastic' for eroded material.

In this particular study other skeletal grains identified in the coral reef area included the *calcareous green algae*, which will be discussed later, and the *foraminifera*, which are minute single-celled marine creatures. These live in all the oceans and make up over half of the sediments found on the *ocean* floors. However, in shallow water they rarely account for more than 20% of the sand, and more usually about 5%. It is the presence of two coloured varieties of foraminifera that give the attractive colour to the pink sands of Eleuthera and Abaco.

- *Cryptocrystalline grains* are more difficult to explain. Basically this is a general term which includes all grains which apparently became converted from any original type into a new crystalline form. Calcium carbonate has a common crystal form called *calcite*, but in the sea most calcium carbonate is produced in a slightly different crystal form known as *aragonite*. Aragonite is still calcium carbonate ($CaCO_3$), but is slightly heavier and denser than calcite. Eventually it will change into calcite.

Any sediment produced in the sea can lose its original form and in time just appear as crystals of aragonite. These are what are known as cryptocrystalline grains. The 'crypto' part of the word means that the crystals can only be seen under the microscope.

- *Grapestone* occurs when *ooids* are stuck together in a lump. (Ooids are described on page 24)

- *Clay* is the finest possible sediment - individual particles cannot be seen and the

Table 2.2 Composition of skeletal grains from coral reef area

Sedimentary particles	Percentage
Parts of the green calcareous algae *Halimeda*.	10
Parts of other green calcareous algae	2
Molluscs such as the conch, and many others	7
Corals	6
The shells of foraminifera *peneroplidae*	7
Miscellaneous	9
Total	**41**

particles stick together like flour. It is often described as 'mud'.

- *Oolite* will be discussed later. It is a pure sediment of rounded grains precipitated directly from sea water. An individual grain is known as an *ooid*.

- *Pellets* are the cemented faecal product of worms and possibly a few other minute sea creatures.

- *Eroded coastal rock* is simply the product of coastal erosion. It is also known as *cay rock*.

THE SKELETAL SEDIMENTS

■ Algal sediment

Although we have been looking at the coral reef area, we have in fact discovered all the main types of sediment produced in The Bahamas. Only the percentages differ from place to place. In the vicinity of the coral reefs, skeletal material is the most important. Such a sediment is usually called *coralgal* ('coral' + 'algal'). In our analysis of the skeletal material in Table 2.1 we noted that algal debris made up 12% of the skeletal grains. Let us now look at a single particularly suitable area, the east coast of Andros just inside the fringing reef.

The sand is nearly all skeletal here, as illustrated in Table 2.3:

Table 2.3 Composition of skeletal grains, east coast of Andros

Sedimentary particles	Percentage
Calcareous algae	27
Foraminifera	23
Molluscs	15
Coral	14
Other skeletal remains	12
Other grains	9

Source: N D Newell & J K Rigby, 1967, p. 49

Figure 2.2 Two of the algae that build the Banks. Halimeda (left) is by far the most important. Its little plate-like 'foliage' eventually breaks down to form the larger fragments of skeletal sand, some of which is seen around the root. Penicillus (right) is a 'hairy' alga and breaks down into a fine mud. In both cases note how the root binds the sand together.

We can see that here the green calcareous algae account for over one-quarter of the sediment, and in some places it may even be higher. A study of sedimentation in the Bight of Abaco showed that algae have been largely responsible for the 2 metres (6 feet) thick layer of calcareous muddy sand

Table 2.4 *The distribution of sediment types according to bank environment (in percentages).*

Sediment	Outer Edge	Inner Edge	Interior 1	Interior 2	Interior 3[a]
Skeletal[b]	41	6	13	11	17
Cryptocyrstalline	21	7	27	2	2
Oolite	6	67	15	6	2
Pellets	5	7	5	33	13
Grapestone lumps	14	8	36	6	5
Clay	11	5	5	43	62
Cay rock	2	0	0	0	1
Dominant sediment	Coralgal	Oolite	Grapestone	Pellet mud	Mud

[a] *Although there is no guaranteed progression, these three interior types are usually found progressively further in to the centre of the bank.*
[b] *Virtually all algal, except at the Outer edge.*

on the sea-floor, producing sediment at a rate of 12.5 cms (5 inches) per 1 000 years. In addition, as much again has been produced and washed off the bank.

Although many algae are present on the sea floor, as well as on and around coral reefs, there are four genera that are far more important than any of the others. These are:

- *Halimeda*
- *Penicillus*
- *Udotea*
- *Rhipocephalus*

All are members of the family *Codiaceae*, and there are various *species* of each of the *genera* shown in Figure 2.2.

Algae can grow on almost any surface and may be collected with ease off any Bahamian shore. In the Bight of Abaco they occur at a density of about 22 plants/square metre (18 plants/square yard), and a plant such as *Penicillus* could have 6-12 crops a year.

Calcareous green algae are simple marine plants. They use sunlight by the process of *photosynthesis* to produce *chlorophyll* and to extract calcium carbonate from the sea water. Eighteen genera have been identified as capable of doing this, but the four named are the most important, with *Halimeda* being the most important of all. In some areas it has been found that *Halimeda* accounts for as much as 40% of all the sediment produced. About half of the plant's weight may be $CaCO_3$ when it dies (the actual figure varies from 25%-90%), and this becomes sediment. In the case of *Halimeda* the debris is initially the large segments of which it is made, but these soon break up into less distinctive sand grains. It has been shown that plants of the *Halimeda* genus can produce $CaCO_3$ from one-and-a-half to ten times faster than the reef-building corals. *Penicillus* has very fine needles of aragonite in its brush-like fibres, and these form a calcium carbonate mud.

Algal sediment is found everywhere on the banks, as shown in Table 2.4

In addition much of the cryptocrystalline grains and the clay may have been of algal origin. If any single thing can be called the builders of The Bahamas, it must truly be the calcareous green algae.

■ Coral

Although we have played down the role of coral as a sediment, we must not neglect its great importance to The Bahamas:
- It is the bulwark that protects and contains the sediments of the banks - the 'rim of the bucket' (see Figure 1.10).
- It is a host to many other sediment producers such as grazing fish like the parrot fish;

Table 2.5 Sediment contributors and other producers in the coral reef zone

Common name	Scientific name	Contribution
Corals		
Elkhorn coral	*Acropora palmata*	Frame (massive*) and rubble
Staghorn coral	*Acropora cervicornis*	Rubble and frame
Mountainous star coral	*Montastrea*	Frame
Brain coral	*Diploria*	Frame
Mustard hill coral	*Porites astreoides*	Frame
Club finger coral	*Porites porites*	Rubble and frame
Leaf and sheet coral	*Agaricia*	Rubble and frame
Starlet coral	*Siderastrea*	Frame
Hydrocorals		
Stinging coral	*Millepora*	Frame
Coralline algae		
Red algae	*Corallinaceae*	Encrustations and sediment
Sponges		
Sclerosponge	*Ceratoporella*	Frame
Green calcareous algae	*Halimeda*	Sediment
Sea urchins		
Long spined sea urchin	*Diadema*	Sediment

Source: in part: **Carbonate Rock Environments**, by H.G. Multer, p. 200.
*The term 'massive' is used to describe sedimentary rocks that originate as a massive structure, and not as sedimentary particles.

various algae like the coralline algae; and a great variety of other animal and plant communities, such as molluscs, sea urchins, sponges, and foraminifera.
• It is an important sediment producer itself.

Although the figure for coral grains in skeletal sand is only 14% (see Table 2.3), this is somewhat misleading. Much of the debris from coral reefs remains in large pieces such as boulders, and in fact if the weight of material was to be considered coral would be first (and molluscs second) in the amount of material produced in the reef zone. Coral rubble is a common feature of back reefs, flats and storm beaches, and of the living reefs themselves. Much of the massive coral types (such as brain coral) are never broken up but remain as a solid base for further coral growth. It has been calculated that coral reefs on the edge of the banks produce as much as 5.5 kilograms/sq. metre (10 lbs/square yard) of coral every year, and about 1.5 kilograms/square metre (2.5 lbs/square yard) on patch reefs in the bank interiors or inner margins. This is a combined figure and includes corals, coralline algae and calcareous green algae, and would amount to a thickness of 2.5-5 cms (1-2 inches) of sediment per year. At this rate the coral reef would soon reach the surface. The main producers on the reef are shown in Table 2.5.

Only the algae are producing sediment independently of the coral. Sea urchins and parrot fish destroy the surface by grazing it, and one study has shown that a single sea urchin can produce 450 grams (1 lb) of sediment in a year. A similar study of parrot fish showed that they could be responsible for about 440 grams of sand per square metre (13 oz/square yard) in a year.

The *coralline algae* must not be confused with the green calcareous algae. They are a red encrusting algae and in most parts

Figure 2.3 A typical sea floor view, showing a variety of corals and marine plants growing on a shallow reef. Photograph courtesy of Sally Varani.

of The Bahamas they are eaten faster (by parrot fish, sea urchins, etc.) than they can build up a surface. It has been shown, however, that in surf and other conditions which prevent grazing, these algae can build up a ridge at 2.5-5 cms (1-2 inches) per year, thus producing an algal reef.

The coral itself breaks off in lumps, particularly branches of staghorn, elkhorn and finger corals, and especially under storm conditions. The lumps are further reduced by *attrition*, that is wear and tear as they are moved about on the sea-floor, or are rubbed against other fragments. In this way a true coral sediment is produced. That the reef is a sediment producer is clearly seen in the ring of unvegetated sand around patch reefs. This is renewed continuously and so turtle grass, etc., does not have time to form on it (Figure 2.3).

It is appropriate to add a few words about the *sclerosponge* which can grow up to one metre in diameter and is unusual in having an aragonite body. It lives in caves or deep water, and below 60 metres (200 feet) it replaces coral as the main reef builder. Apart from this particular species, *sponges* are more noted for their destructive boring activities on the reef, and for their one unique property, which is to be the only producer of *silica* particles, this mineral being the main constituent of their spicules.

Bahamian coral reefs are not as well developed as they might be, or as well developed as in the Pacific, for instance. The water temperatures are near the limit for coral growth, which is 18°C (65°F), with an optimum between 25°C (77°F) and 29°C (84°F).

Average *sea surface* temperatures off Abaco, range from 23°C (74°F) to 28°C (83°F). If the water is clear, coral can live in depths of up to 100 metres (300 feet), although corals are only significant reef builders down to half that depth. The clarity of water in The Bahamas is such that they rarely grow at depths greater than 15 metres (50 feet). As a result most Bahamian reefs are discontinuous, as is the case even with Andros's renowned fringing reef.

Interruptions in coral reef growth can come about due to:

• *Cold water* - caused by climatic change; cold fronts lasting several days; cold ocean currents.

• *Sediment* - which chokes the polyps. This can be brought in by currents, stirred up by rough weather, or can be precipitated from sea water.

Man-made activities such as dredging and marine construction must also be taken into account.

• *Lack of sunlight* - caused by cloudiness due to sedimentation, or cloudy skies. Once there is less than 1% of the available sunlight, coral cannot receive enough energy to live.[2]

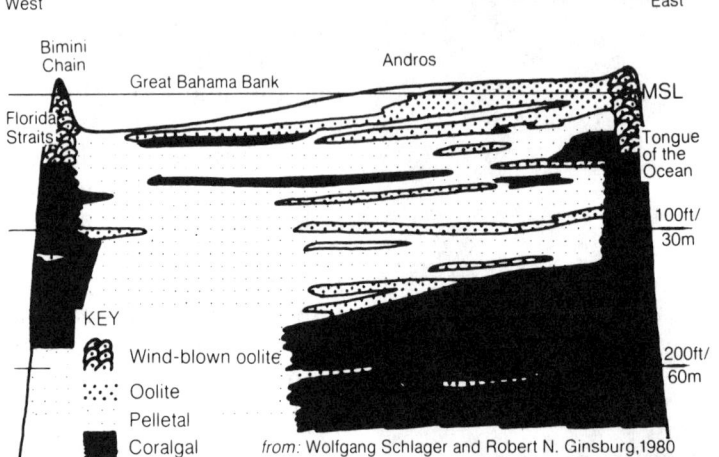

Figure 2.4 Coral and bank-type sediments, mapped from boreholes on the Great Bahama Bank and in Andros, show how far the reality matches the theory. Coral deposits dominate the wall-like edges with finer, mainly pelletal sediments in the interior.
Note *(a) Below 36 metres (120 feet) coralgal deposits are much more abundant, possibly due to a change in climate.*
(b) Above 15 metres (50 feet) wind-blown oolite replaces the coral. This coincides with the start of the Ice Ages and a fall in sea-level.

- *Submergence* - due to a rise in sea-level at a faster rate than the coral can grow upwards. This would be at a rate of more than 2.5-5 cms (1-2 inches) per year. This has certainly been exceeded in recent geological times, as in the Pleistocene Ice Ages.

Thus there are a variety of reasons for the uneven line of reefs around The Bahamas today. In fact the main reef lies about half a kilometre seaward of the present one, and about 30 metres (100 feet) below sea-level, but it is inactive and extinct. There is some evidence to suggest that corals were once more widespread, and that the reef was once continuous and much wider, before the Ice Ages. To this date, there has been no drilling through the reef area, so there is still much to be learned about this zone (Figure 2.4).

OOLITIC SEDIMENT

Although this seems a strange name, it is an appropriate one. 'Oo' is the Greek word for 'egg' and 'lite' (or any suffix like 'lith(ic)' refers to anything of rock or stone, such as 'palaeolithic' for 'Old Stone' Age. Thus we have an 'eggstone', and oolitic limestone looks just like fine fish roe, being composed of very small spherical grains.

It is worth examining some of these sedimentary terms again. As oceanic water moves on to The Bahama Banks it is warmed and precipitates a sediment called *oolite*, which appears as a fine white *sand*. The chemical composition of the oolite is *calcium carbonate* ($CaCO_3$), and it is in its *aragonite* crystal form. It is, therefore, true, although a bit confusing, to say that oolite, calcium carbonate, and aragonite are being deposited.

The process that takes place in the production of oolite is not very different from the formation of salt in a salt pan by the

Table 2.6 Salts produced by the evaporation of sea water.

Compound	Name	Salinity at which mineral is precipitated (Parts per thousand)	% of sea water evaporated
$CaCO_3$	Aragonite	39	0.5
$CaSO_4.2H_2O$	Gypsum	100	80
NaCl	Common salt	350	90
$CaSO_4$	Anhydrite	350	90
KCl	Potash	2 100	Virtually all
Mg salts	Various	2 100	Virtually all

evaporation of sea water. In this case the 'salt pans' are the banks themselves. With each incoming tide, oceanic water sweeps across the edge of the banks to be immediately warmed, usually by about 3°C (6°F), and have its salinity increased from the normal 35 parts per thousand to as much as 40 parts per thousand (i.e. from 3.5% to 4.0%). This is not enough to produce common salt, but it is enough to cause calcium carbonate, another constituent of sea water, to be deposited wherever the right conditions exist (Figure 2.5).

From these elements various chemical compounds are formed as sea water is evaporated.

Sea water is, in fact, almost saturated with $CaCO_3$, so only a small increase in temperature is enough to precipitate it out.

Figure 2.5 *Banks of oolite in the Bimini chain. The Gulf Stream is at the top right of the picture. Dredging takes place around Ocean Cay, and the sand is exported to the USA. (See also Chapter 8)*

Table 2.7 *The main constituents of sea water*

Element	Symbol	Parts per thousand
Sodium	Na	10.0
Chlorine	Cl	19.2
Oxygen	O_2	1.9
Magnesium	Mg	1.3
Potassium	K	0.4
Calcium	Ca	0.4
Sulphur	S	0.9
Carbon	C	0.03

Oolite can only be formed as the fresh oceanic water penetrates the shallow banks. In a normal six-hour tide, this means that it can only be deposited in an area about six miles from the edge of the banks. Before the water can travel any farther, the tide changes and the currents flow off the banks. The photographs show this distribution clearly, as does the map (Figures 2.5, 2.6 and 2.9). At first sight it might seem that the sandbanks are merely sediments from the coral reef zone washed on to the banks, but if this were so there would also be sands on the outside of the cays and reefs, taken there by the outgoing tide. It is clear that this sediment is the product of the incoming tide only (Figure 2.6).

This conclusion is further proven by a microscopic examination of the individual oolitic grains. This shows a *spherical layering* of pure aragonite around a minute *nucleus* - any fragment in the sea upon which the aragonite can be deposited (Figure 2.7g). Once a deposit is started, each grain (called an *'ooid'*) is added to, and it grows, like a hailstone, until it is too heavy to be suspended in the water. It then sinks to the seafloor and is eventually covered by other ooids, at which point growth finally stops. It should be noted that it is necessary for the water to be *turbulent* so that both nuclei and ooids be kept suspended and are therefore available for collecting new deposits of aragonite on their surfaces. This accounts for the fact that some areas on the edges of the banks do not collect aragonite sand. In such areas tidal currents will be too gentle to create the necessary turbulence (Figure 2.8).

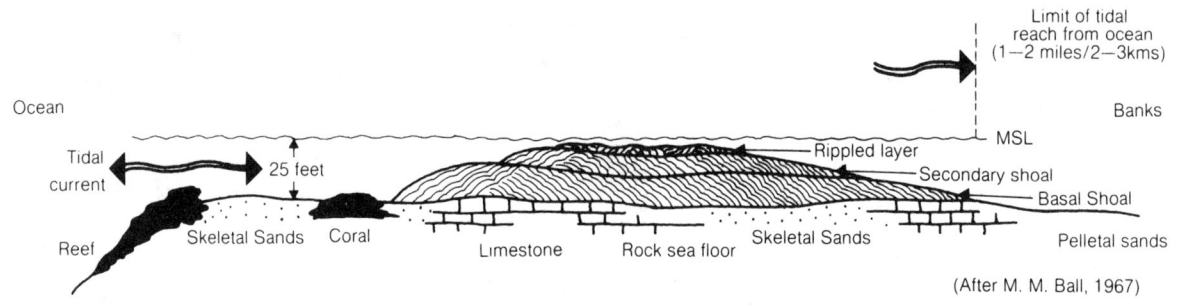

Figure 2.6 Profile of an oolite shoal. Deposition of oolitic grains occurs soon after the tidal waters enter the shallow water and are warmed up. Once the basal shoal has formed, the water becomes shallower and a secondary shoal is built right up to the surface. The top of this is rippled by waves and may dry at low tide.

PELLETS; LUMPS; GRAPESTONE AND AGGREGATES; MUDS

As the map (Figure 2.9) shows, there are large areas of the banks that have sediments that are neither skeletal nor oolitic. The main ingredient in these areas is the *faecal pellet* (Figure 2.7f). This is an ovoid grain about twice as long as it is thick, and it is largely responsible for what are often called *blanket* deposits. Quite simply this means that the interiors of the banks are *blanketed* with a sediment. Such blankets, as their name implies, are usually continuous and featureless, with little life. Oolitic deposits are also blankets.

The pellets are excreted from the digestive tract of some worm or other minute marine organism, hence the name *faecal*. At first they are soft and easily broken up. They are covered with a *mucus* which under a microscope can be seen to be present within the pellet itself, which is, in fact, composed of fine silt particles held together by the mucus. These are extremely small, i.e. about 0.5 mm (0.025 ins) long. It is what subsequently happens to the pellets that determines the nature of the sediment.

In some areas the pellet may be produced where other grains are present, perhaps skeletal or oolitic, and these stick to the pellets' surface. This type of sediment is known as an *aggregate*, that is, a collection of particles.

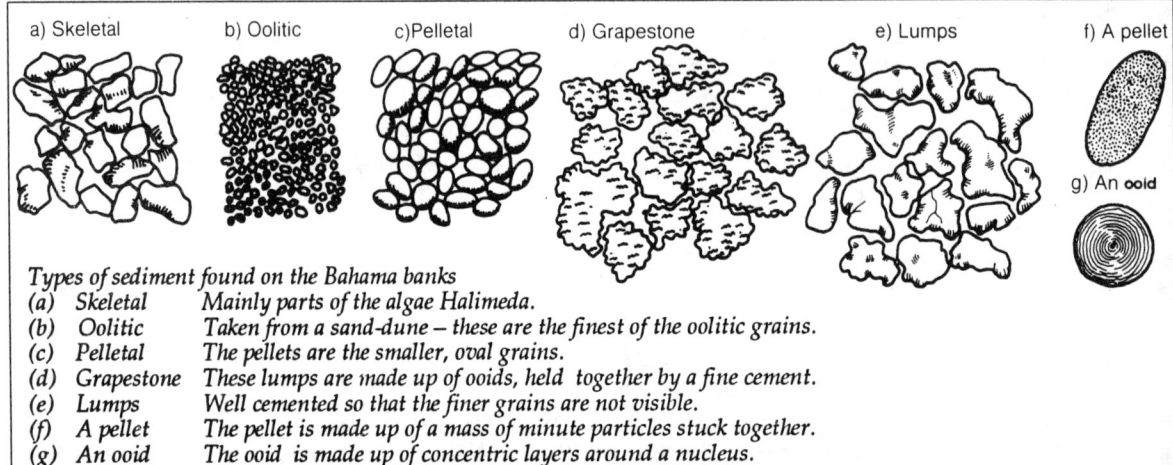

Types of sediment found on the Bahama banks
(a) Skeletal — Mainly parts of the algae Halimeda.
(b) Oolitic — Taken from a sand-dune – these are the finest of the oolitic grains.
(c) Pelletal — The pellets are the smaller, oval grains.
(d) Grapestone — These lumps are made up of ooids, held together by a fine cement.
(e) Lumps — Well cemented so that the finer grains are not visible.
(f) A pellet — The pellet is made up of a mass of minute particles stuck together.
(g) An ooid — The ooid is made up of concentric layers around a nucleus.

Figure 2.7 These illustrations were all redrawn from the original photographs used in the classic paper by W. V. Illing in 1954. They are enlargements, (a) to (e) being magnified 10X, and (f) and (g) 40X. This was the first article to fully describe Bahamian sediments.

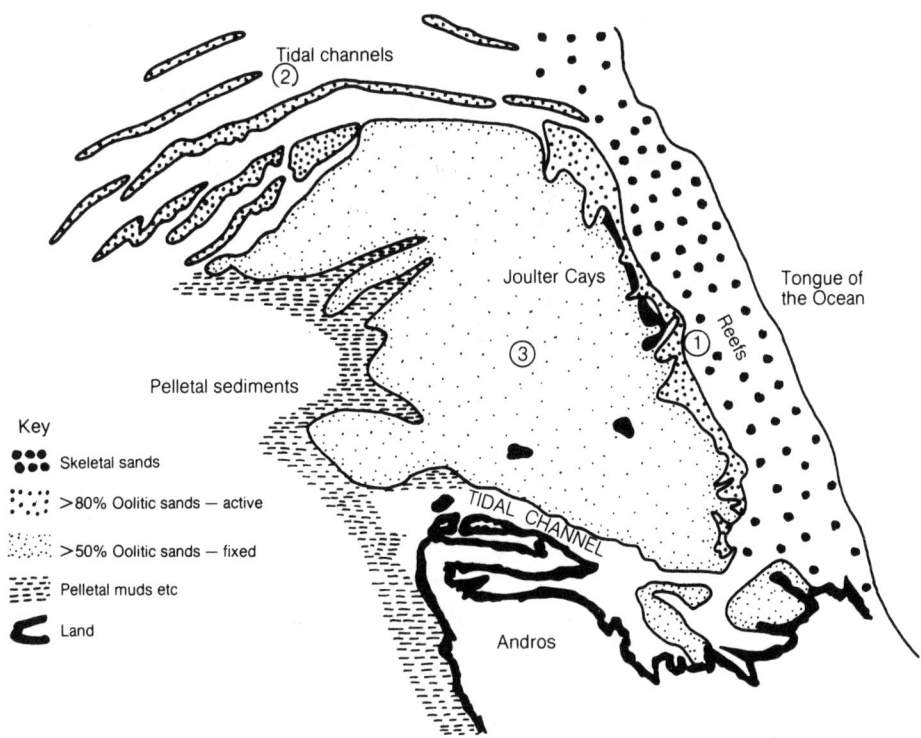

Figure 2.8 Oolitic sands are present in three areas: (1) at the inner edge of the coral reef. These are like the deposits in Figure 2.5 and have been blown into dunes to form the Joulter Cays. (2) Tidal sand bars – the oolite has travelled much farther than normal along tidal channels. (3) Older deposits spread out behind the active zone, and are mixed with pelletal sediments. This zone would form typical marine oolitic limestone rockland if the sea-level dropped. (P. M. Harris, 1976)

Another collection of particles is grapestone which occurs when ooids become cemented together (Figure 2.7d).

Both grapestones and aggregates are sometimes called *lumps*, a general term for these and any other grains comprised of smaller particles cemented together (Figure 2.7e).

So far, we have only considered pellets in combination. The pellets on their own are very small, and only when combined do they reach sand grain size. If found alone they are described as a *pellet mud*. Often the pellet itself is broken up, and an even finer *mud* is produced. 'Mud' is a general term used for particles which are less than 0.125 mm (0.005 ins) in diameter, whatever their origin. The origin may be broken-up pellets, algal aragonite needles, or fine chemical precipitates, and these are usually indistinguishable

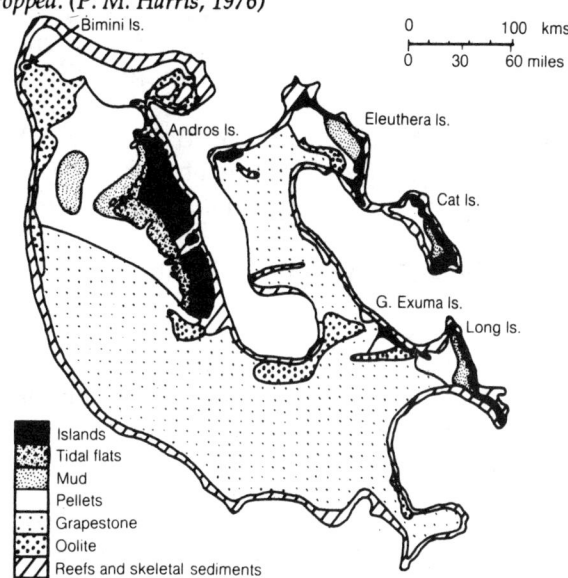

Figure 2.9 Distribution of the main types of sediments on the Great Bahama Bank (from W. Schlager and R. Ginsburg, 1981). It should be noted that the tidal flats, mud and pellets only settle in the sheltered areas behind the larger islands

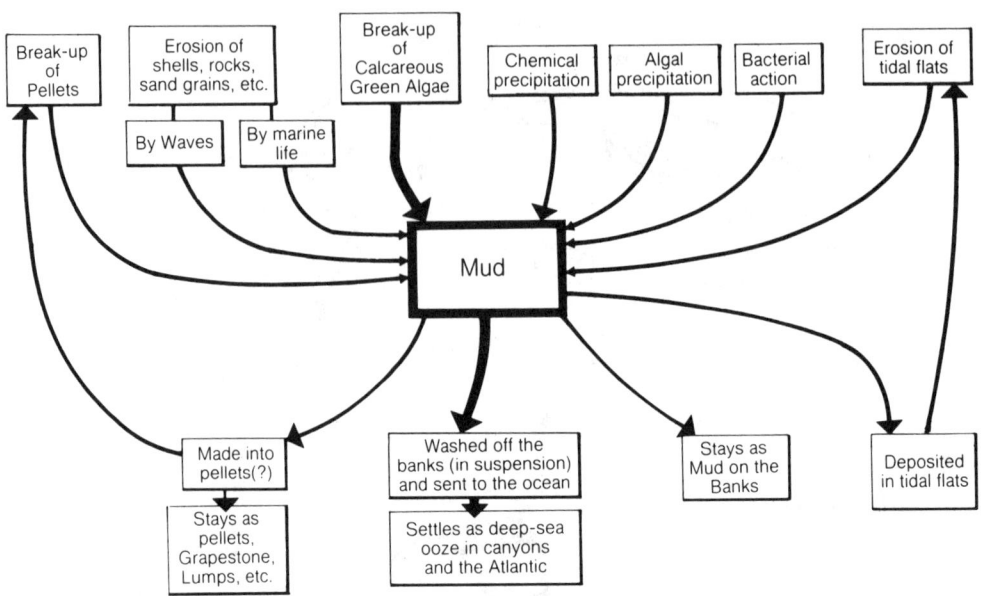

Figure 2.10 Each type of sediment has a 'budget', with a list of inputs and another of outputs. By setting all the possibilities out in a diagram like this, a quite complex story is easily told. Similar diagrams could be drawn for the other sediments.

from each other. The diagram (Figure 2.10) indicates the complexity of one carefully analysed mud, taken from the Bight of Abaco. It has also been suggested that the formation of *pellets* may be the result of marine creatures sifting *mud* out of the sea and then cementing it together to form a faecal pellet. This would explain why the pellets mainly occur in muddy areas, and why they break up into mud. It might also explain why the waters of The Bahamas are so clear - the pellet producers filter it out!

THE SEDIMENTS IN GENERAL

Although a great variety of sediment types have been mentioned, and many more exist, it is nevertheless sufficient to deal only with the main groups in order to have a sound understanding of sedimentation in The Bahamas. The *major* groups are:

- coralgal sediments, also known as skeletal;
- oolitic sediments;
- grapestone, including all lumps;
- pellet mud;
- mud, clay or silt.

This leaves out cryptocrystalline grains and cay rock. However, as long as we realise that in any given place there will be a dominant type of sediment, and this will be one of the five listed above, then we need not worry too much about the nature and origin of the minority components.

CONCLUSION

The Bahamas has been described as a vast carbonate factory, a bucket in which the level is always rising and overflowing into the canyons and oceans around it.

We know that this has gone on for millions of years and at varying rates, but that in the recent Ice Ages it stopped. During this period all the loose sediments were cemented and none of the sediment we see today has been dated at more than 5 000 years old.

For example:

- *Grapestone* has been dated in an Andros mangrove swamp as being 2 500 +/- 150 years old.

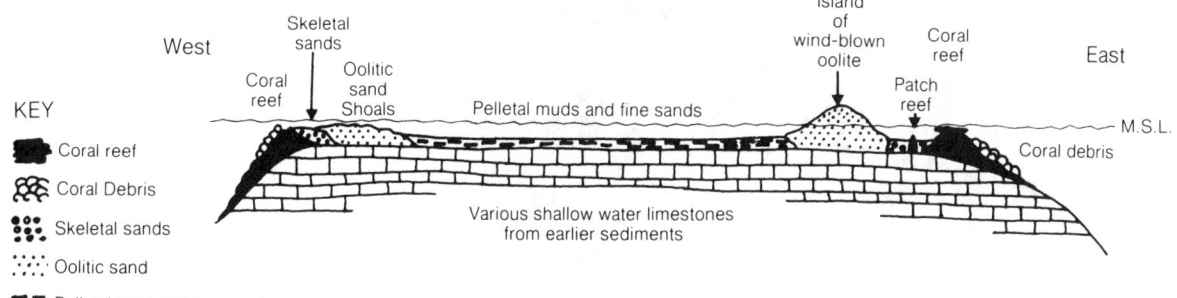

Figure 2.11 *The types of sediment are matched on each side of the bank, but the windward side will have more vigorous coral growth, and the oolite will be formed into sand-dunes.*

KEY
- Coral reef
- Coral Debris
- Skeletal sands
- Oolitic sand
- Pelletal mud and fine sand

- *Oolite* samples taken near Brown's Cay in the Biminis have been dated as old as 2 500 +/-150 years old, and as recent as 225 +/- 100 years old.

- *Peat* (buried swamp vegetation) under modern sediments near Bimini was 4 - 5 000 years old. This probably marks the flooding of a swamp at the end of the Ice Ages, and dates the beginning of the current cycle of sedimentation.

Of these sediments, far more are produced within the bucket, or atoll, (about 100 times more) than at the rim, or coral reef zone. In quantity, then, the interior sediments are far more important.

Finally, we can see that there is a progression from the outer edges, towards the interior (or 'lagoonal') areas (Figure 2.11). On the outside is the most active area, producing coarse grains in great variety, followed by the active tidal zone, generating and enlarging oolitic sediment. In the quiet areas of the inner banks we have the finest sediment in the greatest quantities, and also the greatest mysteries still to be solved. However, this is not a static situation, and wind-driven currents and the tides, helped by occasional storms and hurricanes, carry each type to each of the other areas, so that even in the most remote places traces of every kind of sediment will be found.

STROMATOLYTES

In 1986 Robert Dill of the Caribbean Marine Research Center revealed the presence of giant *stromatolytes* in the waters of the Exuma Cays[3]. This was a striking discovery, as large modern stromatolytes were believed to to exist only in an exclusive and very salty environment in Shark Bay, Australia.

Stromatolytes are partly rock and partly organic. They consist of fine layers of sediment trapped by and within thin films of organic matter. In the Bahamian stromatolytes (Figure 2.12) these very fine organic layers include blue-green algae and

Figure 2.12 *Giant stromatolytes in the Exuma Cays. Those shown vary from one to two metres in height. Photograph courtesy Robert N Ginsburg.*

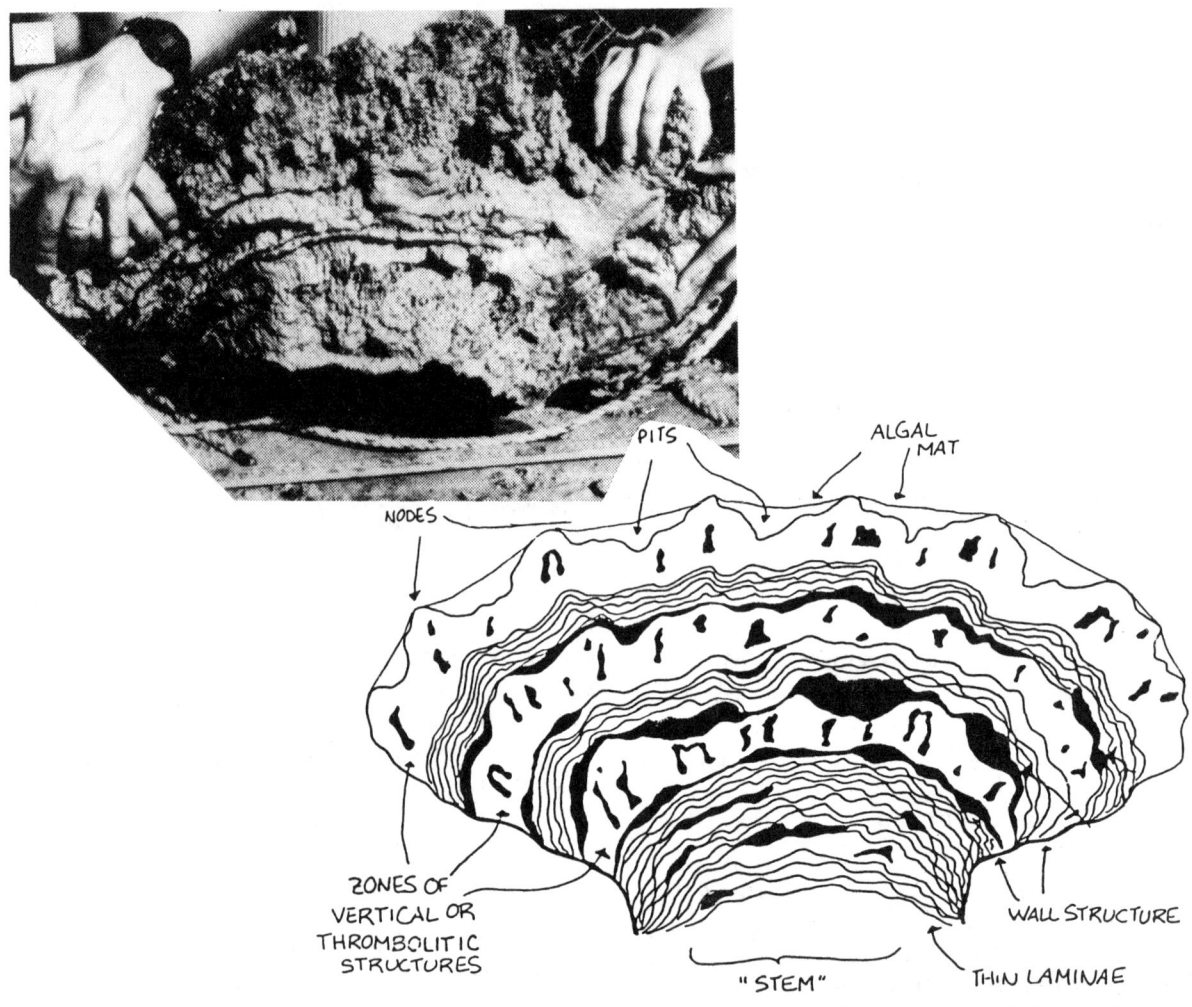

Figure 2.13 Photograph and annotated cross-section of a mushroom-shaped stromatolyte from Storr's Lake, San Salvador. Photograph courtesy of Conrad Neumann, drawing by Linda Mc Neese. (From: Neumann et al, 1989[4])

diatoms which trap and bind oolitic sediment, and build it up into columns 1-2 metres high.

Stromatolytes in general include a large variety of features ranging from small mushroom-like masses in lakes (some are known from San Salvador) to the giant structures of Exuma. All straddle the boundary between a simple sedimentary deposit and a composite organism such as an algal mat. Historically they were widespread in the world's oldest sedimentary rocks, and are sometimes described as the oldest fossils. Subsequently they became rare, and the discovery of the Bahamian examples is of great importance to their further understanding.

1 If the composition of a sandstone is more than 50% calcium carbonate, then the 'sandstone' is called a limestone.

2 Strictly speaking, it is the point at which *zooxanthellae* can no longer photosynthesise food for the coral to feed on. *Zooxanthellae* are tiny unicellular algae that live in the coral tissue.

3 Dill, Robert F, Shinn E A, et al: Giant subtidal stromatolyte forming in normal salinity waters. *Nature*, 1986, 324, pp 55-8

4 Neumann, Conrad, et al: Modern stromatolytes and associated mats, San Salvador. *Proceedings of 4th Symposium on the Geology of The Bahamas*, Ed. John Mylroie. Bahamian Field Station, 1989, pp 235-265.

3 THE CANYONS

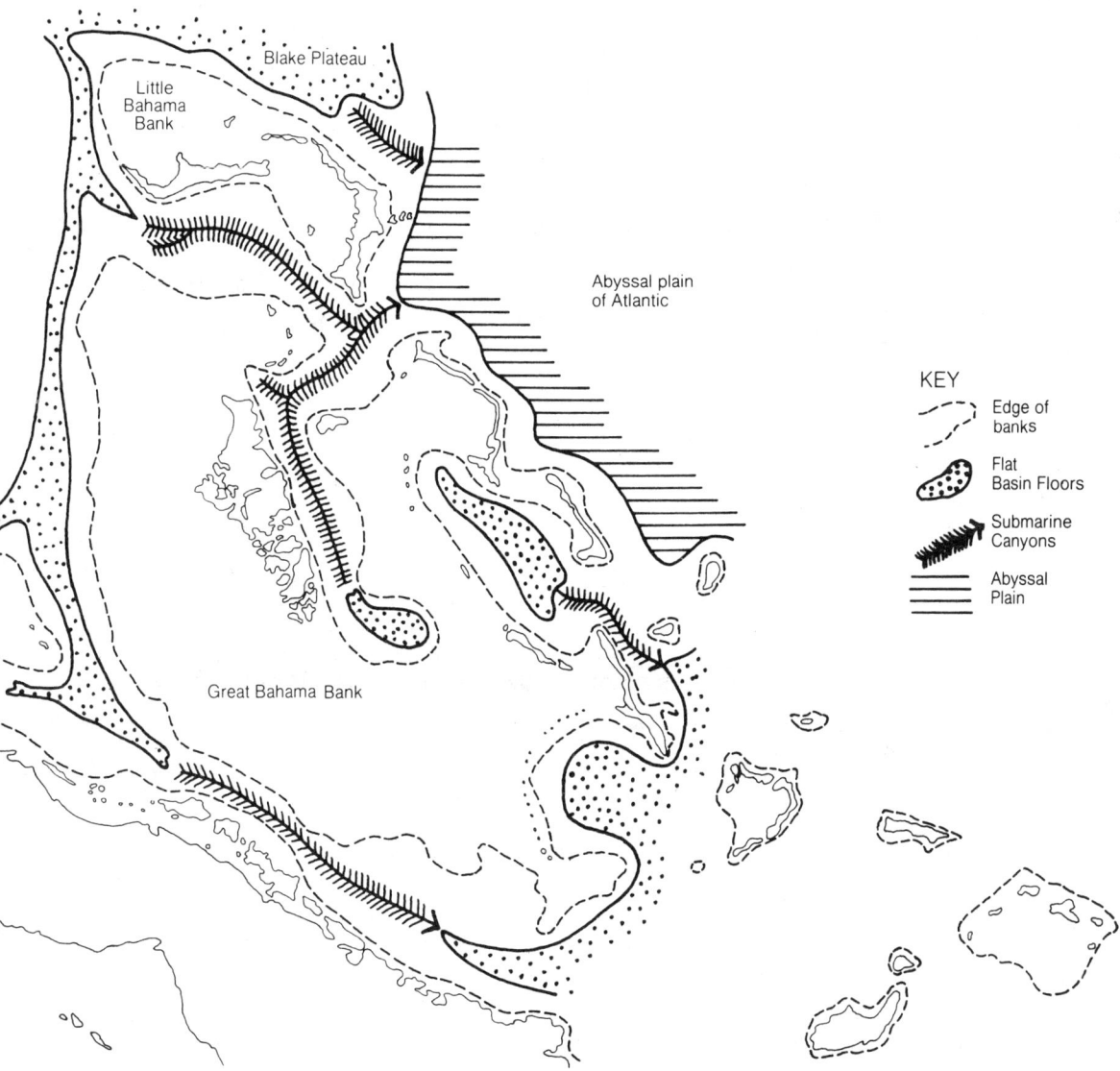

Figure 3.1 *The canyons are cut into the floors of the basins and troughs, and allow drainage of the higher-level basins into lower-level basins and the Atlantic. In this way the banks dispose of their surplus sediment.*

Huge and mysterious, the great canyons that cross and penetrate the Bahamas Platform easily live up to their reputation in the cold light of geological investigation (Figure 3.1).

One geological paper described the Providence Channel between Eleuthera and Abaco as 'having the highest canyon walls of any in the world', and 'the total length of the . . . is 150 miles, which is exceeded only by two canyons in the Bering Sea'[1]. Not only are these the highest submarine canyons, but at 5 kilometres (3 miles) high they are higher than any on land as well. The Grand Canyon is only 1.5 kilometres (1 mile) deep for instance. They also have the world's steepest slopes over such a depth. This is all the more striking because of their proximity to the banks, which are so uniformly shallow. How is it that some of the deepest and longest submarine troughs are found within and around such a vast area of shallow carbonate platforms?

The answers we have show that the banks and the troughs are directly related in some ways, the same processes being responsible for both. However, not all the answers are known, and the ultimate origin of these remarkable features has yet to be decided.

The map (Figure 3.1) shows many channels, troughs, tongues, sounds, basins and straits. The most noted are those that penetrate and surround the Great Bahama Bank, and these are the ones that have been most studied. Although there is doubt as to the origin of the troughs the following facts are generally accepted:

- The channels are a composite feature, consisting of a major U-shaped *trough*, the floor of which is cut by a V-shaped *Canyon* (Figure 3.2).

- The great steep-sided walls are *constructional* rather than erosional, and the agent of construction was the coral reef.

- The V-shaped canyons are *erosional* features, the agent of which is the occasional turbidity current. Not all parts of the troughs are affected.

One of the earliest discussions about the troughs and canyons (they have various names, but only these two have a precise meaning) took place in 1933 when the distinguished geologist H. H. Hess correctly identified the first two features noted above.[2] He pointed out that:

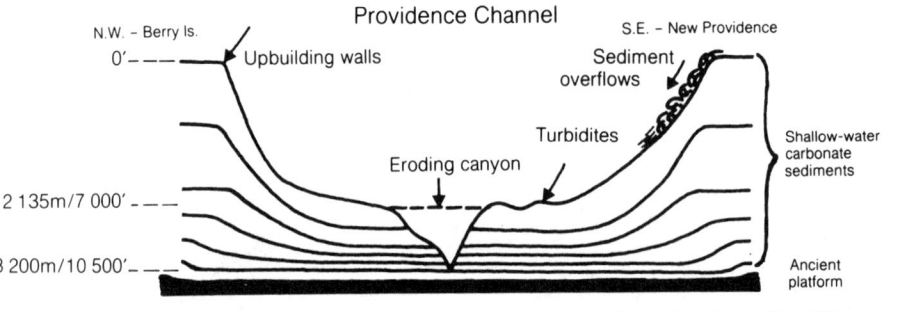

Figure 3.2 This section helps us to understand the development of the channel. About 100 million years ago after the original platform had been formed, deposition in the channel areas stopped. On either side the modern bank platform grew up, occasionally overflowing into the new troughs. Eventually turbidity currents cut submarine canyons down the centre of the troughs, to carry this sediment away.

The explanation of the steep walls must undoubtedly lie in some process which caused their upbuilding after the erosional valleys had already been formed. They are thus depositional rather than erosional features.

Later he introduced the coral reef as an agent:

. . . as submergence proceeded, the calcareous reef material of the platform built up as fast as relative sea-level rose.

... if upward building of the reef material was responsible for this structure, it seems logical to believe it was also the most important factor in the formation of other parts of the platform.

Hess clearly anticipated the later ideas of a coral wall (he called it a 'reef-cliff') containing the bank sediments.

On the other hand, his belief that the floors of the troughs were cut by rivers is not now accepted. Hess wrote:

... the floors of the valleys have been graded (eroded) by the action of running water under sub-aerial (terrestrial) conditions ... (this) is substantiated by such strong evidence that it seems beyond question.

In other words, Hess considered rivers responsible for the 'valleys' at the bottom of the troughs. Given the shape of the channels, this was not surprising, although his explanation for them being so far below the surface was less attractive. If the V-shaped canyons were cut by rivers, then they were cut at the surface and then submerged when the trough as a whole submerged. It would be remarkable to find them so well preserved millions of years later.

THE ORIGIN OF THE TROUGHS

Four possible origins have been widely suggested:

- That these are *rift valleys* - suggested by the long straight parallel sides. However, there is no sign of the volcanism

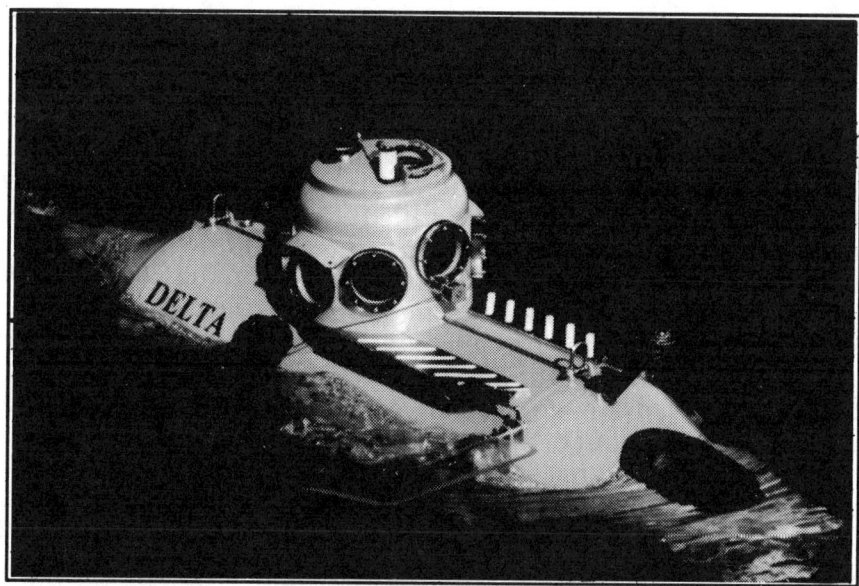

Figure 3.3 The miniature research submarine DELTA, prior to a dive.. DELTA is capable of diving to 3 660 metres (12 000 feet) which takes about two hours. While on the bottom or against a canyon wall, it can take colour photographs and sample the rock with the aid of a mechanical claw which loads specimens into special bins. Photograph courtesy of Delta Oceanographics, California.

that usually accompanies such features, nor of any earthquakes usually associated with faulting.

- They are related to weaknesses caused by earlier *faulting*, which may have started at the same time that the Atlantic was created. The rectilinear pattern supports this view as *step-faults* often develop in this fashion. The parallel alignment of the Florida Straits, the Tongue of the Ocean, Exuma Sound and the Atlantic margin supports this. The recent discovery of more buried N-S troughs supports this, as does the seismic evidence. (See p 13 and below)

- They were cut by *rivers* and submerged, as discussed above.

- They were cut by *submarine currents*. This is the likely explanation for the channels within the troughs, but does not account for the troughs themselves.

Another consideration is that the onset of major ocean currents, such as the Gulf Stream which, of course, runs through the Florida Straits, prevented the bank and coral deposits from accumulating along their paths. By scouring their channels these currents could have prevented algal growth and stifled coral reef activity. Similarly the dead-end troughs such as the Tongue of the Ocean and Exuma Sound could be due to the large amounts of sediment being swept off the banks. It has been said that the troughs and canyons are the platform's drainage system, carrying surplus sediments out to the Atlantic Ocean.

Whatever it was that started the troughs off, there is no doubt that the vertical upbuilding of the coral reef margin has been responsible for adding to their height, perhaps for as long as the last 100 million years. It is worth noting that the Florida Peninsula and its associated banks have no troughs at all.

The hidden troughs

It has already been shown how seismology can give us a kind 'ultrasound' view of the internal structure of the banks (p.13) In 1987 Eberli and Ginsburg[3] suggested that the the Great Bahama Bank had been rifted twice since the mid-Cretaceous period. West of Andros they identified two faults (Figure 3.4) with a downthrow of 500 metres (1 640 feet), which had created a trough they named the *Straits of Andros*. A bit further west they identified a shallower and more recent trough they called the *Bimini Embayment*. Both of these were substantial depressions, the Straits of Andros being comparable to the Tongue of the Ocean. Despite this they are today filled in.

It has already been noted that the banks produce more sediment than actually accumulates on top of them. The surplus sediment is washed over the bank edges on a regular basis, and accumulates at the foot of the bank margins. In some instances, as in the Tongue of the Ocean, and the Providence Channels, turbidity currents travelling through submarine canyons (Figure 3.1) carry this away so that the troughs do not fill up. This did not happen in the fossil Straits of Andros and the Bimini Embayment, which filled up (or more correctly, filled *across* - lateral accretion from the east was ten times as fast as vertical infilling) by the end of the Tertiary era.

This area of the Great Bahama Bank was thus once four separate banks (Figure 3.4), and about 40% of what we know as bank-top today was deep water.

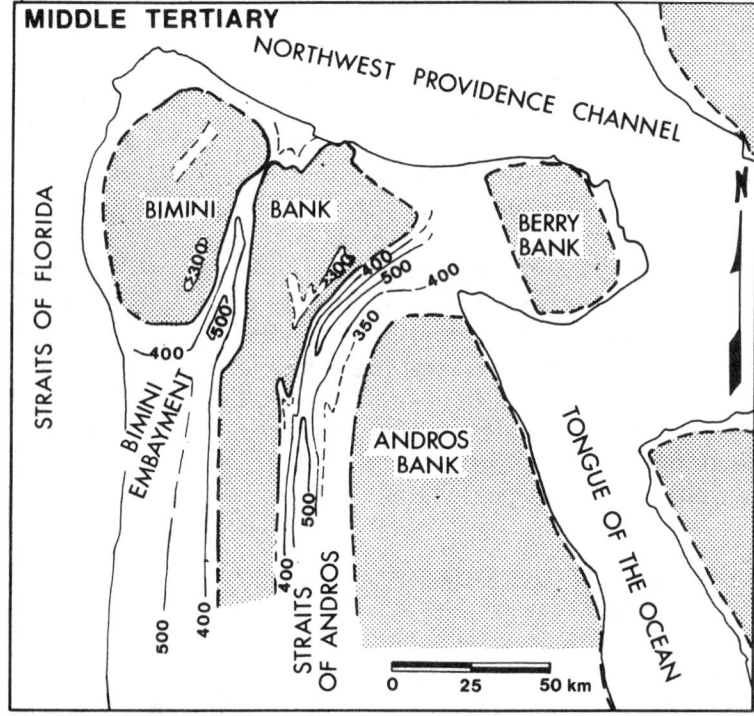

Figure 3.4. Reconstruction of the northeastern part of the Great Bahama Bank, showing the Straits of Andros and the Bimini Embayment. Both of these have now been filled in. This view should be compared the cross-section on page 13. (From Eberli and Ginsburg, 1987)

It should not be thought that this process is inactive today. Eberli and Ginsburg also showed that outbuilding continues along the western margin of the Great Bahama Bank out into the Straights of Florida. In fact since the late Cretaceous (the last 65 million years) this margin has grown westwards by some 25 kilometres (15 miles) compared with its vertical growth of 1.5 kilometres (0.9 miles or about 1 000 feet).

THE NATURE OF THE TROUGHS

Fortunately, we know quite a lot about what the troughs look like, for the 1970's saw the advent of the miniature research submarine. These tiny vehicles operating from a mother ship have investigated the walls and floors of many troughs (Figure 3.3).

Examples are the Deep Sea Research Vehicles (DSRV) *Alvin* and *Aluminaut*, which made dives in the Tongue of the Ocean as early as 1967 and 1968 respectively. *Alvin* also made 16 dives between 1975 and 1978, and *Nekton* made 34 dives in 1976.

In addition, there have been many surveys to take soundings (depths) and photographs, and to dredge samples. From the surface there have been seismic surveys and piston coring, both intended to give fuller details of the various types and thicknesses of sediments in the troughs.

Of the various features observed the most notable have been the *eroded cliffs* with slopes varying from 35° to vertical, and often including sections of sheer-faced reef wall over 30 metres (100 feet) high. This was most common during the first 380 metres (1 250 feet), after which the walls could be better described as *gullied slopes*, having a much gentler gradient of 5°-25°. This extended down to the trough floor, at about 1 500 metres (5 000 feet) or more, and was basically a slope cut by many deep gullies about 200 to 400 metres (600 to 1 200 feet) apart.

The floor itself has a *flat bottom*, except where the *canyons* have been incised in it. The canyons rarely start at the heads of the troughs, but once established they make a deep V-shaped nick at the floor and then spread out so as to eventually occupy all of it (Figure 3.6).

THE V-SHAPED CANYONS AND TURBIDITY CURRENTS

These are erosional features cut into the sediments laid down on the trough floors. The agent of erosion is almost certainly the *turbidity current*. These can be described as a submarine current of sediment-laden water. The presence of the sediment makes the water heavier than normal, and it flows along the sea-floor at speeds of up to 70 kilometres/hour (45 mph). As the appearance will be that of a cloud of muddy water rolling downhill, the term 'turbidity current' has been adopted by geologists (Figure 3.5).

Turbidity currents in The Bahamas seem to be initiated in two ways. The first is as an avalanche of debris off the bank margins. This cascades down the trough walls, stripping everything in its path and exposing the bare limestone rock. As it gets deeper, the flow tends to split up and channel itself into separate flows which cut the numerous gullies mentioned above. The sediment eventually slows down and spreads over the floor of the trough.

The second stage occurs when the accumulated sediment on the trough floor moves off down the trough itself, cutting a V-shaped channel which deepens and widens as the current progresses. This current will, in most cases, be a

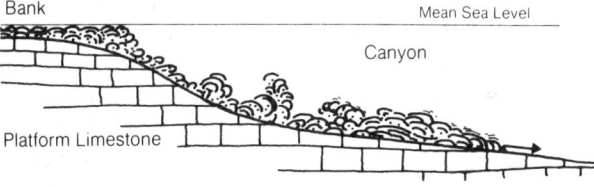

Figure 3 5 The turbidity current starts on the banks when an accumulation of sediment is disturbed, such as during a storm. The turbid, sediment-laden current then flows down the drop-off and will continue along the centre of the canyon, eroding the sea-floor on its way.

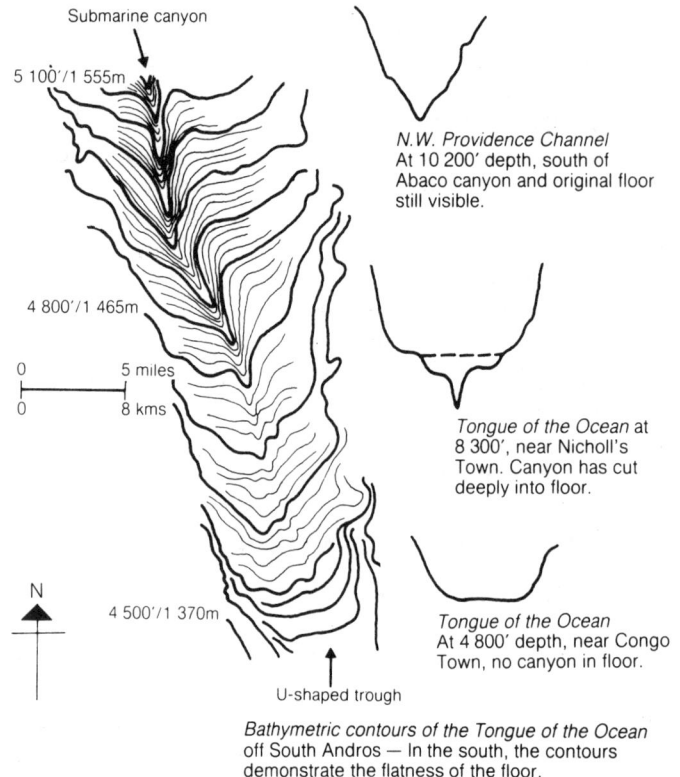

Figure 3.6 Plan and profiles of the trough and canyon in the Tongue of the Ocean

continuation of the first type, but is much less common. The sediments laid down by turbidity currents are identifiable, and are known as *turbidites*. Some of these have been dated and indicate that at the southern end of the Tongue of the Ocean a turbidity current occurs about once every 500 years, but at the northern end, farther away from the largest source of sediments, one every 2 000 years is more likely. In the Providence Channel, the frequency varies from one every 500 years to one every 10 000 years, depending on the location. In this channel, the speed of a turbidity current is estimated to be about 25 kilometres/hour (15 mph). It probably needs a severe disturbance, such as a hurricane, to trigger a turbidity current.

In Exuma Sound one major turbidity current was identified from its turbidites and mapped. It took place about 100 000 years ago and was 20-25 kilometres (12-15 miles) wide. After travelling for 100 kilometres (60 miles) as a broad sheet it was channelled into the central, or axial, valley, and continued on into the Atlantic Ocean. Smaller flows occur here at a rate of about one every 10 000 years.

The strength of these currents and their ability to erode is seen in the presence of coral boulders, up to 3 metres (10 feet) across, far from their point of origin. In some cases, large pieces of rock debris have been found well over 16 kilometres (10 miles) from the coral wall, despite the nearly flat floor of the trough. Similarly a shallow water oolitic sediment has been found over 50 kilometres (30 miles) from its source, in beds of up to 15 cms (6 inches) thick.

As time has passed, the troughs have become deeper and the turbidity currents stronger. The V-shaped submarine canyons that they cut have been deepened and gradually extended backwards towards the heads of the troughs. A rate of **headward erosion**, as it is called, of 1.5-3 kilometres (1-2 miles) every million years has been going on for about the last 70 million years, and, as the map shows, the canyon in the Tongue of the Ocean (Figure 3.6) has been cut back by about 220 kilometres (135 miles), or about half-way towards the head of the trough.

THE SEDIMENTS OF THE TROUGHS

Measurements have been taken with seismic surveys and piston cores. (A *piston core* is obtained by simply dropping a special tube vertically into the bottom sediments, which are then trapped inside and can be brought to the surface. This is much quicker and cheaper than a drilled core, but it can only penetrate about 6-10 m (20-35 ft).) It seems that about 1 525 m (5 000 ft) of sediments have been deposited in the troughs, some of it coming from the banks and the rest produced within the troughs themselves.

From the banks, a continuous rain of fine sediment spreads out over the floors and blankets the underlying surface. This accounts for about half of the total, and accumulates at about 2.5 cm (1 inch) per 1 000 years unless it is carried away by turbidity currents. Eventually much of this material will end up on the abyssal plains of the Atlantic Ocean via the submarine canyons.

The other half of the sediment is derived from turbidity currents, although in the lower parts of some canyons these may account for as much as 70% of the total (Figure 3.7). The content of these sediments, often known as *debris sheets*, varies from well-sorted sand to a muddy mixture of pebbles and rubble. Much of the latter material will be eroded particles from the walls of the troughs and the heads of the canyons. Usually individual sheets are about 1 metre (3 feet) thick or less, but they are thicker close to the walls. However, not all of the sediment originated in shallow water, some of it was actually formed on the floors at depths of over 1 220-1 525 metres (4 000-5 000 feet). Dredged samples of rock have shown the occasional presence of deep-water life and deep-water limestone, which clearly demonstrates that deep-water sedimentation takes place quite separately from the accumulation of imported shallow-water material. One sample of deep-water limestone was taken from the wall of the submarine canyon in the Tongue of the Ocean, and dated at about 12 million years old, showing that the Tongue was a deep-water trough at least that long ago.

1   J. E. Andrews et al, in 'Great Bahama Canyon' *Geological Society of America Bulletin*, 81, April 1970.

2   H. H. Hess, 'Submerged River Valleys of The Bahamas', *Transactions of the American Geophysical Union*, 1933.

3   Eberli, Gregor P and Ginsburg, Robert N, Segmentation and coalescence of Cenozoic carbonate platforms, north-western Great Bahama Bank. *Geology*, 15, 1987, pp 75-9.

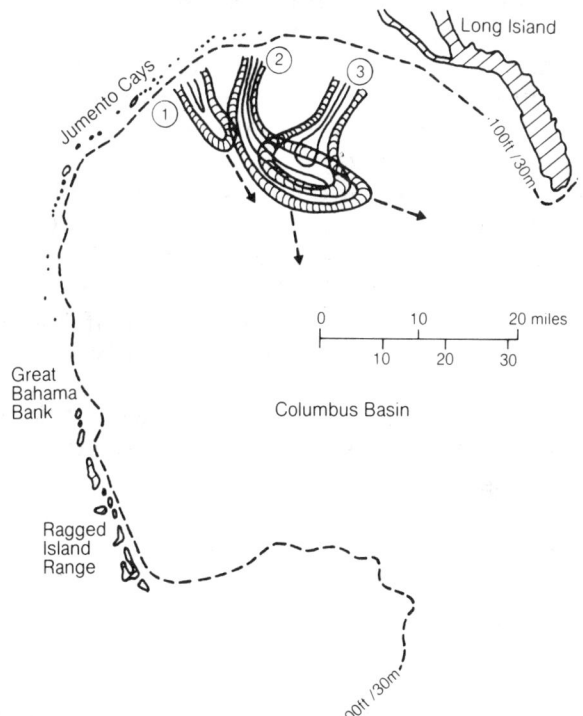

Figure 3.7 The outlines of three turbidity currents are shown by the map of their deposits, known as Turbidites. Only the coarser deposits could be mapped, and the currents and fine sediment would have continued far out into the basin. (From the study by B. D. Bornhold and O. H. Pilkey, 1971)

4 THE ISLANDS AND THEIR RECENT GEOLOGICAL HISTORY

So far we have looked at The Bahamas as a geographical and geological whole, a unit that interests us and is the foundation of this study. However, the land is our actual living environment and it is necessary that we take a particular look at that, at the many varied islands and cays that make up the landscape of The Bahamas.

To explain the presence of the islands we must examine developments among the upper sediments on the surface of the platform. Under normal conditions we can picture the platform as a super-atoll, bounded by coral reefs inside of which lie extensive plains of oolitic sands. Within this outer boundary are the banks proper, vast blankets of organic sediments covered by 6-10 metres (20-30 feet) of sea. The shallowest parts of the surface are the coral reefs and oolitic sands, which reach to within a metre of the surface. All is relatively smooth, the greatest relief away from the coral rim being the sandbanks of oolite, which will themselves be cut by tidal channels in a variety of places. These channels would rarely be more than 3-6 metres (10-20 feet) deep, certainly not enough to explain the relief of 30-60 metres (100-200 feet) found in nearly all the larger islands.

To account for this we need to go back in time just a little way, to the most recent of all geological events, the last Ice Ages.

THE ICE AGES - FALL IN SEA-LEVEL

The Pleistocene Ice Ages began approximately two million years ago, and may not have ended yet. As Table 4.1 shows, there were four periods of *glaciation* separated by three *interglacials*, and these interglacials were periods when the climate was probably

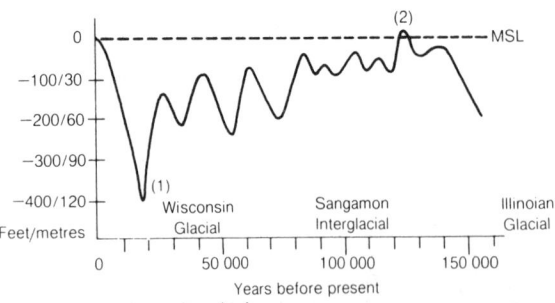

Figure 4.1 Glaciation was not a simple process and the effect on sea-level was quite varied. Note (1) the minimum of about -120 metres (-400 ft) and (2) the maximum of about +6 metres (+20 feet).

Table 4.1 The Pleistocene Period

Approximate years before present	Glacial event	Probable extreme sea-levels (metres)	(feet)
0-5 000	Present (Holocene)	0 +/-6	0 +/-20
10 000-75 000	Wisconsin glacial	-120	-400
100 000-125 000	Sangamon interglacial	+6	+20
150 000-200 000	Illinoian glacial	-145	-475
250 000-375 000	Yarmouth (Great) interglacial	?	?
400 000	Kansan glacial	?	?
500 000	Aftonian interglacial	?	?
600 000	Nebraskan	?	?

very much like it is at the present time. Figure 4.1 shows the last 150 000 years of this period and from the time-scale on the diagram we can see that it is not possible to tell whether we are at the end of the Ice Ages or simply in another interglacial.

During the *glacials*, as the periods of glaciation are called, the situation in the northern latitudes was very much like a bad winter that never ended. The effect of this on The Bahamas was not so much one of climate (although colder conditions may have affected the growth of coral and other organisms), but more one of a *change in sea-level*.

When snow fell in the higher latitudes, it did not melt in summer and return to the oceans. Instead, it accumulated in great ice caps and glaciers, and as more and more of the world's water was transferred to the land, so the level of the oceans dropped. The best evidence suggests that, in the third glacial, sea-level in The Bahamas fell by well over 120 metres (400 feet), and, in the last one, by just under 120 metres.

With falls of such magnitude we can now imagine the Bahamian platform as a series of plateaux, separated by the deep channels we know today. All of the various bank sediments would have been exposed to the atmosphere, and modified in some way. Most affected of all was the *oolite*, for several very good reasons.

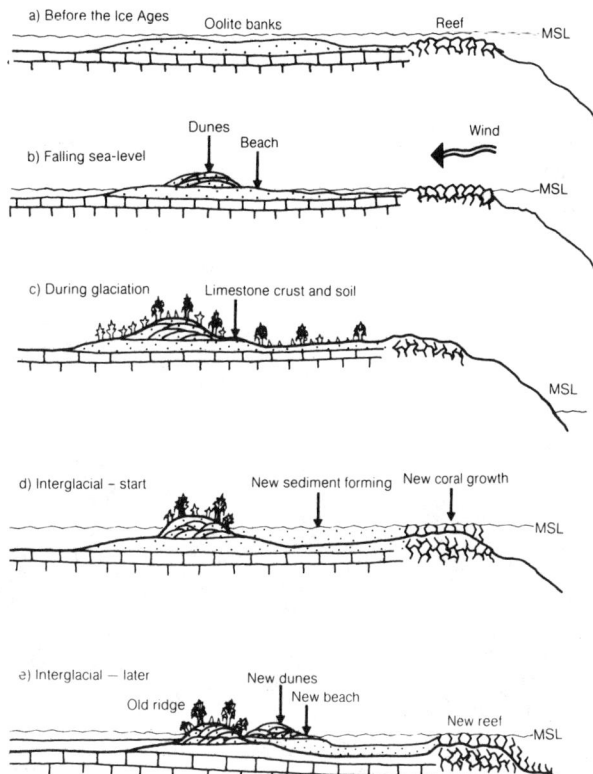

Figure 4.2 As sea-level falls (b) the oolite is blown up from the beach to form dunes. When sea-level falls farther no more oolite is formed (c) and the land is covered with vegetation. When sea-level rises enough to flood the banks (d), new sediment is formed and is washed up on new beaches. Eventually (e) a new line of dunes is formed. There may also be some erosion of the older dunes in stage (d). In the next glacial period sea-level will fall again and the cycle will be repeated.

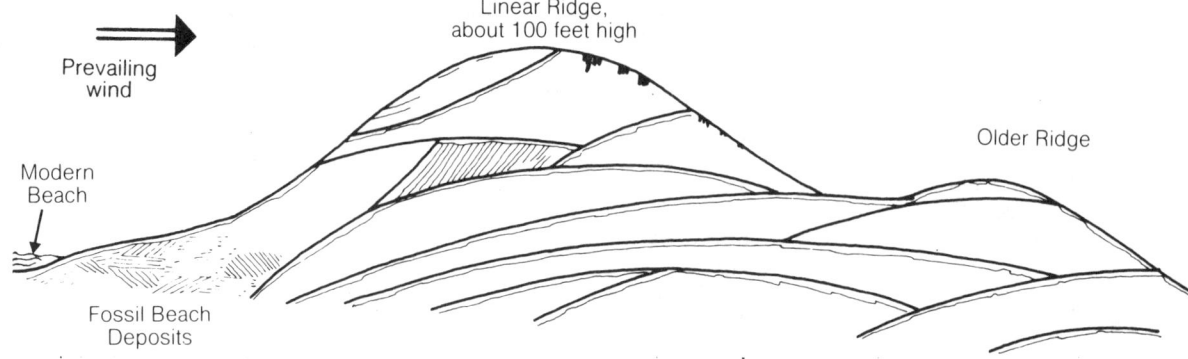

Figure 4.3 This cross-section is typical of what may be seen within the ridgeland system. The double ridge in this case is built up of many overlapping sand dunes, now lithified. The dunes are usually marked by layers of fossil soil and roots, and in many cases they have been partly eroded.

THE OOLITIC RIDGES

With The Bahamas now dry land, several things happened that could not have happened before. First of all, we can assume that the prevailing winds were still the north-easterly trade winds. These are what are known as planetary winds, and they are basically the result of equatorial heating and the shape of the Earth, both of which are constant factors. Blowing from a variety of easterly directions, these winds moved any loose material in their path, very much as they do on modern beaches or in desert regions today. The most prominent sediment on the exposed bank was the oolite. It stood near the edge of the banks and was higher than its surroundings (Figure 4.2).

There were other reasons why the oolite was vulnerable to the wind. It was the finest and lightest of the fringing sediments. The grains were rounded and rolled over each other easily. There was little if any marine vegetation to trap it, as it was produced chemically and not organically, and was continually being created while sea-level was normal. This made it too sterile for most plants.

Figure 4.4 Bedding planes in the Gambier Ridge. Weathering in this exposed face reveals the cross-bedding (Figure 4.5) which is typical of wind-laid sands. The boundary between the two main sets of strata is an unconformity, which indicates that the lower section was subject to erosion until deposition resumed (upper set) from a different direction.

As the winds blew across the new land, the oolitic sand was piled into great sand-dunes at right angles to the wind. Examination of Bahamian ridges today shows that they are, in fact, quite complex, being comprised of many dunes, some of which were eroded, and all of which were superimposed on others, and in turn often buried (Figures 4.3 and 4.4).

It was not, of course, necessary for the sea to drop hundreds of metres for the sand to be piled into dunes - it only needed to be left a few metres above sea-level. It is, therefore, a bit difficult to say exactly when the ridges were formed, as even small changes of sea level during an *interglacial* would have led to alternate flooding and drying of the land.

What seems to be most likely is that as sea-level fell, the shallowest parts of the banks - the oolitic deposits - became exposed, and the Bahamas had its first beaches. The first ridges at least (the Blue Hill/ Gladstone Ridge in New Providence) (Figure 4.6) must have formed at this time. Once sea-level fell a lot, the supply of sand ended, and no more ridges formed. But, each time sea-level rose in the interglacial periods, new sediment would be formed offshore

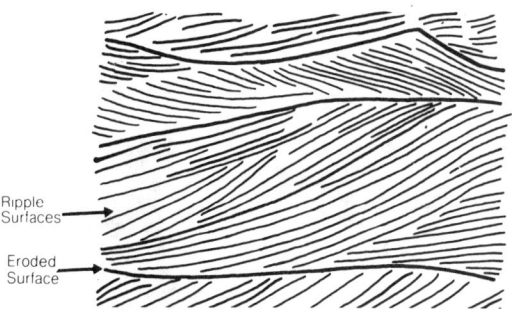

Figure 4.5 A pattern often seen in exposed ridgeland and known as cross-bedding. The fine layers are produced when the wind creates surface ripples. Soil formation and erosion is marked by coarser bands.

and washed on to the shore. *Beaches* would now form in front of the new ridges, and so conditions were right for more sand-dunes to form. So, although the initial fall in sea-level was necessary to get things started, the actual building of many lines of dunes would have been most likely during and at the end of interglacial periods. (see Figure 4.2).

In some cases, the wind came from the north and the north-west, associated with cold air masses (see Chapter 9) from North America, and, as in New Providence, the ridges ran east-west (see Figure 4.6). Generally the winds did not blow from the west,

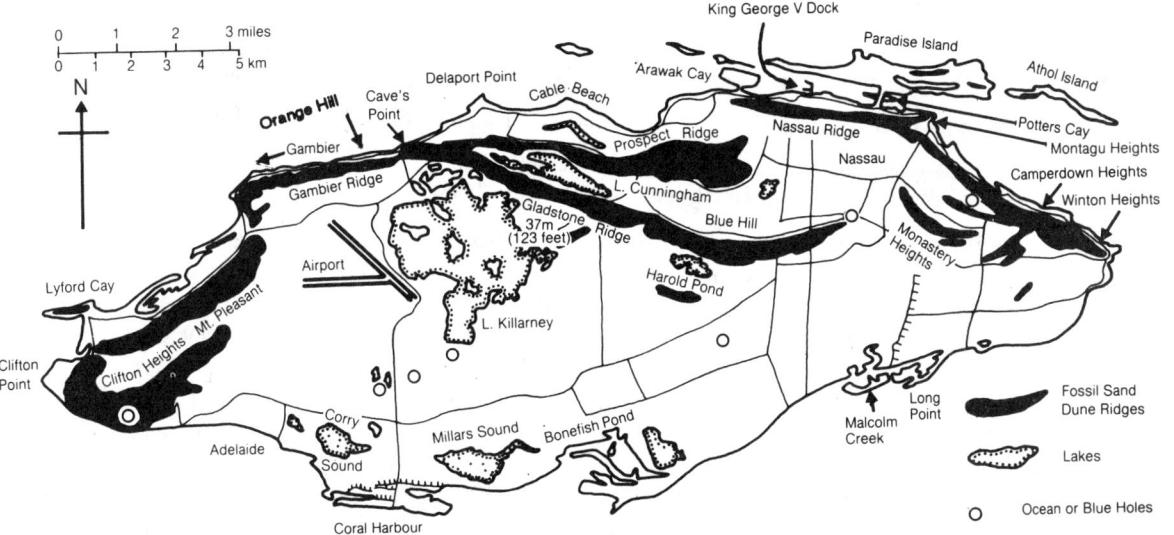

Figure 4.6 The Ridges of New Providence

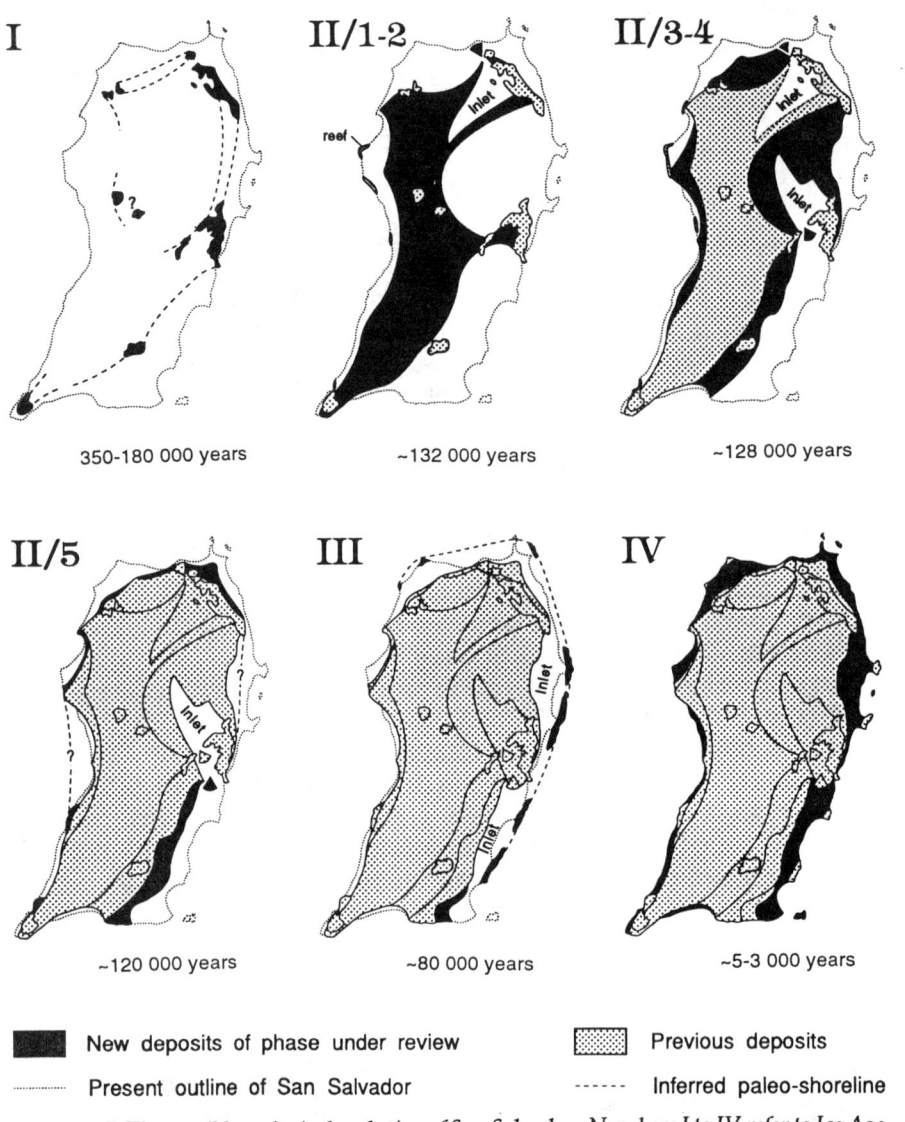

Figure 4.7 *The possible geological evolution of San Salvador. Numbers I to IV refer to Ice Age phases, and ages are before present. (Paul Hearty and Pascal Kindler, 1993)*

and very few islands were created along the western edges of the banks. Only in the areas nearest to Florida did this happen giving us the Bimini chain and the low-lying strip of Grand Bahama running from Freeport to West End. The great majority of the islands are at the eastern edges, and, in fact, there are virtually no eastern margins without islands or cays. In the southeast Bahamas the much smaller and fragmented banks were affected by more southerly winds, and often these banks were so small that the whole of the surface was eventually built-up by drifting sand, as was the case in San Salvador, for instance (see Figures 4.7, 5.1).

Over the whole period of the Ice Ages, sea-level fell sufficiently to expose the banks at least four times. Periods of drowning in-between created fresh oolite, and so a fresh line of dunes, later to become ridges, could be formed.

Dating the ridges directly is very difficult as the sands were formed before the ridges were built, and dating the sediment would not give us the date when a ridge was built. The ridges contain few fossils, mainly *cerion* snails and *tree roots*, and the various dating methods are not precise enough to distinguish between tens of thousands of years (Figures 4.7 and 4.8). Unfortunately, although geological dating is now very good at giving dates in millions of years back to well over 3 000 million years ago, such small periods of geological time as the Bahamian Islands were built in, probably less than 200 000 years, are not easily subdivided. If the deposits were of marine origin, then more fossils, especially coral, would be found, and, if swampy conditions had existed, the peat formed in them could also be dated by radio-carbon methods. Nevertheless, one area that has been successfully dated is the half-mile wide ridge nearest to the sea at North Palmetto Point in Eleuthera. The ridge is 10-12 metres (35-40 feet) high and is composed of sand and young rock between 2 500 and 5 000 years old. We know that 5 000 years ago sea-level was about 3 metres (10 feet) lower than today (p. 39), so we can assume that conditions were right for dune building when sea-level was 2-3 metres (5-10 feet) lower than it is now. It can also be noted that, once sea-level reached its present level, sand dunes do not seem to have developed to any great extent - no part of the Eleuthera ridge is younger than 2 500 years old. Only sand actually on the beaches (modern beach sand at N Palmetto Point is 900+/-70 years old), and in areas of oolitic deposition, such as the Schooner Cays (600+/-50 years old) at the head of Exuma Sound, has been found to be less than 1 000 years old.

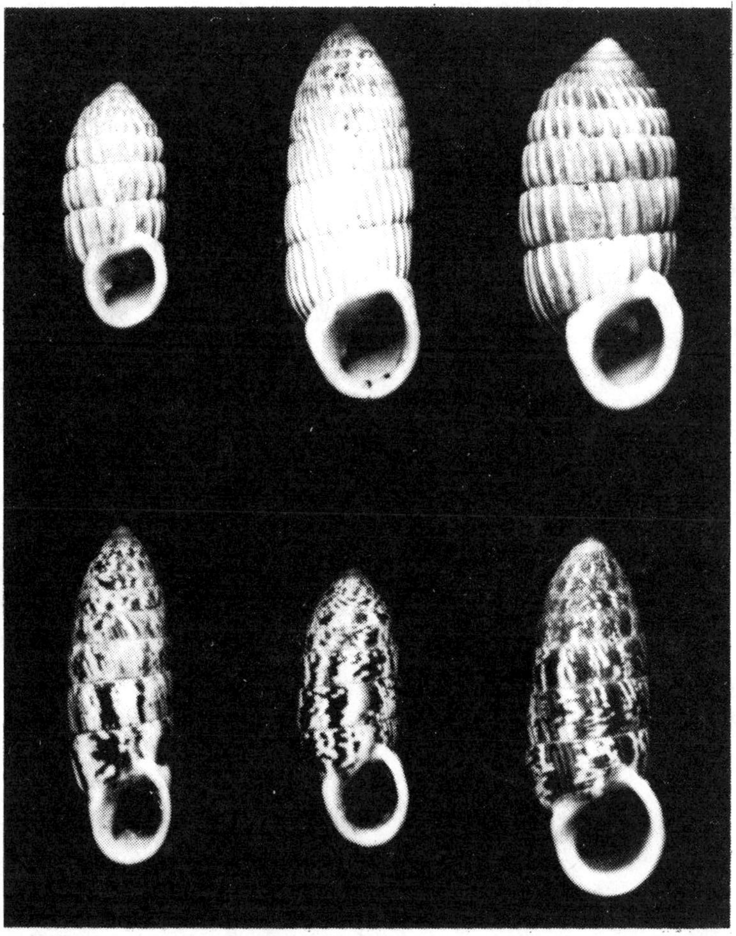

Figure 4.8 Cerion from the Little Bahama Bank. The "Ribby" variety inhabit the bank edge coasts, while the "Mottled" variety (bottom row) live inland. Photograph courtesy Stephen J Gould.

Although the ridges are present in every major island, large areas are not, in fact, hilly at all. Particularly in New Providence and the larger islands we find extensive areas of flat *rockland*.

■ *Amino acid racimization* (AAR) is a relative dating technique that has been largely developed in Bermuda and The Bahamas. The amino acids in dead animals, and hence in fossils, change from one form to another, and by measuring the ratio between these two forms a relative age can be obtained - the older the rock the higher the ratio. The ratio itself does not give an age, but if an

Figure 4.9 Fossil cerions in the Gambier Ridge—further proof that these ridges originated as sand dunes. These land snails found embedded in the oolite (marine) sand of the ridge clearly indicate that the ridge was constructed of marine sediments later redeposited by the wind on land.

AAR ratio is obtained from a limestone whose age is already known, then that AAR ratio will be indicative of the same age for similar deposits. This technique has been used widely by Hearty and others[1] to help determine the geological history of The Bahamas (Figure 4.7).

■ *Cerion morphology* is another relative dating technique developed by Stephen Jay Gould in the 1970's[2]. It is based on the realisation that *Cerion* snails have evolved remarkably rapidly in relation to the local environment. In any environment the presence of a particular *Cerion* morphology (ie a *Cerion* snail with a specific kind of shell) will give the relative age of that rock. Once again absolute dates are not possible, although the snail shell could also be subjected to radiocarbon dating techniques. Once an age has been determined by other means that *Cerion* will be indicative of a particular stratum in that environment. (Figure 4.8)

Figure 4.10 A fossilised tree root in the Gambier Ridge – further proof that these ridges originated as sand dunes. Note that the root and stem run vertically through the sloping beds, suggesting that the beds were laid sloping and not later folded.

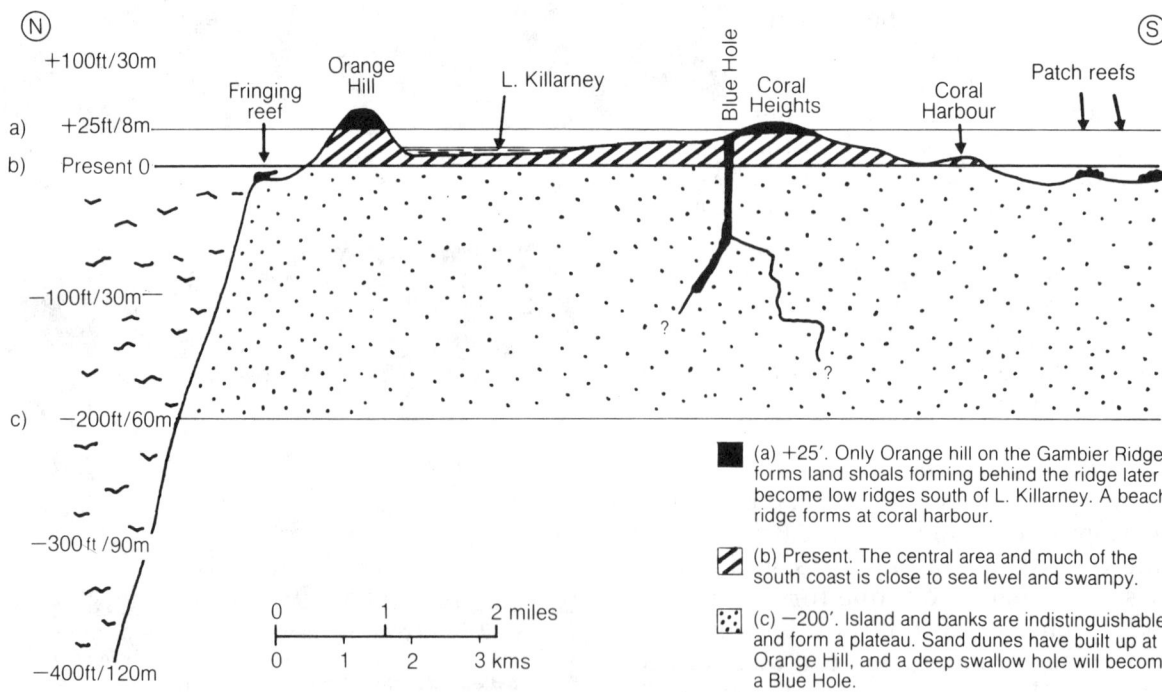

■ (a) +25'. Only Orange hill on the Gambier Ridge forms land shoals forming behind the ridge later become low ridges south of L. Killarney. A beach ridge forms at coral harbour.

▨ (b) Present. The central area and much of the south coast is close to sea level and swampy.

⋮⋮ (c) −200'. Island and banks are indistinguishable and form a plateau. Sand dunes have built up at Orange Hill, and a deep swallow hole will become a Blue Hole.

Figure 4.11 Effect of changing sea level on New Providence.

The Rockland

To create a marine limestone which is now dry land we have to accept that sea-level was once *higher* than it is now - the opposite situation to that which created the ridges. As it happens, the Ice Ages are again the cause, this time in the *interglacial* periods. As the diagram (see Figure 4.1) shows, during the last interglacial sea-level did rise higher than at present, probably about 5-6 metres (15-20 feet).

Around the islands, in the quieter water, sediments accumulated rapidly from the action of marine life (skeletal), and from chemical precipitation (oolitic). When sea-level fell again, these very gently sloping deposits became land adjacent to the ridges, and progressed from dry rockland to wetland (marshes and lagoons) to tidal flats, and eventually to the very shallow offshore banks we know today. A north-south section through New Providence illustrates this well, but cross-sections of Abaco and Andros are also typical (Figure 4.11).

In some areas *coral reefs* formed and these were then left high and dry. This was not very common in the northern Bahamas, although one patch reef can be seen off West Bay Street (New Providence) at about the present high tide level. This must have originally been at least 5-6 metres (15-20 feet) below that level. In the south-east Bahamas, and especially in Mayaguana, exposed fringing coral reef structures are much more common.

Evidence for Changing Sea-Levels

So far we have discussed changes in sea-level by simply assuming that we know they occurred. It is true that a lot of evidence exists around the world for the changes caused by the Ice Ages, and obviously as the seas and oceans are all interconnected these changes must have affected The Bahamas as well.

However, we cannot simply say that a fall in one place had the same effect as a fall somewhere else, because as well as sea-level changes, there is the possibility of the land moving. Although we know that sea-level fell about 120 metres (400 feet) at one time, it does not automatically mean that the Bahamian platform was 120 metres above sea-level. In the coral-capped island of Barbados there are sea-cut cliffs and terraces as high as 300 metres (1 000 feet), but this does not mean that the sea was once 300 metres higher than it is today. What happened there was that uplift of the sea-floor, and the land, pushed both the coral and the cliffs well above their original levels.

As we have already seen, The Bahamas is regarded as tectonically stable - there have been no earthquakes or volcanic activity in the recent past. Nevertheless, we should examine the evidence for higher and lower sea-levels:

Higher Sea-Level

■ *Fossil corals.* We have already mentioned that today coral can be found at or above the present high-tide level. A small

Figure 4.12 Brain coral exposed at low tide in New Providence. This former patch reef was once covered by water about 5 m (15 ft) deep, perhaps 150 000 years ago in the last interglacial. During the following glacial period the sea floor was land and soil and a limestone crust formed on top of the coral. This crust, which is now being eroded, can be clearly seen covering some of the coral.

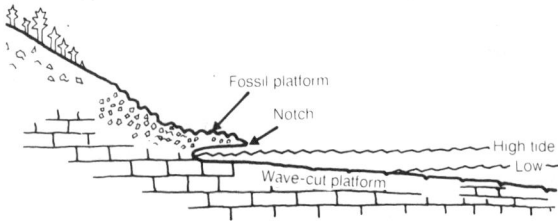

Figure 4.13 Wherever the sea is eroding, a gently sloping shelf will be cut as the shoreline is pushed back. With changing sea-levels, fossil platforms will also be found both above and below present sea-level.

patch reef in New Providence, at about one metre above present sea-level, contains star, starlet and brain corals, all fairly large species usually found at depths of 5-6 metres (15-20 feet) or deeper. From this we can estimate a sea-level at least 6 metres (20 feet) higher than at present. This particular exposure of coral has been dated at about 125 000 years old, which coincides with the time of the last interglacial (Figure 4.12).

Another example is found in San Salvador where there is an extensive coral reef well preserved at Cockburn Town. Studies suggest that sea-level here was 5-6 metres higher in the past.

Before we can say that sea-level was definitely 6 metres or more higher we must be sure about the stability of the earth's crust, especially with regard to *subsidence*. We may accept that there has been no uplift, as there is no evidence of faulting, folding or tilting of the strata, but we have already discovered that subsidence is a continuing part of the geological history. The rate of subsidence at the present time is difficult to calculate, but could be about 1 cm (0.5 inches) per 1 000 years. In the case of coral 125 000 years old, the amount of subsidence would be 1 x 125 = 125 cms. Therefore, if sea-level *appears* to have been 6 metres higher, it was probably 6 + 1.25 = 7.25 metres higher, in fact.

■ *Coastal erosion features.* If we look at the coast in areas where it is being eroded, we can see a number of very distinct features. Rocky coasts have *cliffs*, and these are *notched* by the sea undercutting them to form *knicks* (Figure 4.13). If there is a weakness in the rock, *sea caves* may develop. Consequently, if we find these features on land above sea-level we can deduce that sea-level was once higher (Figure 4.14). The well-known caves at Caves' Point in New Providence are examples of this. However, caves alone could be produced in a number of ways, so we should look around to see if there is any other evidence. At Caves' Point there are several knicks at the entrance to the caves, identical to ones being cut today.

Figure 4.14 The sea erodes by undercutting. As the notch deepens, portions of rock break off (foreground) and create a cliff. The process continues, leaving a wave-cut platform extending out to sea.

Going west from these caves the seaward face of the ridge in which they are cut is notable for not having a rounded slope, but, in fact, has a nearly vertical bare rock face. At the foot of it are huge boulders and further knicks. No land process in The Bahamas could have caused such erosion, but very similar features are seen at Clifton cliffs at the western end of the island. All along the north side of this hill, which stretches from Caves' Point to Oakes Field, and which we can call Prospect Ridge (see Figure 4.6), there is clear evidence of sea erosion. It seems that this was once the northern shore of New Providence, probably 125 000 years ago when the coral already mentioned was growing offshore. The caves are about 3 metres (10 feet) above present sea-level.

Figure 4.15 *The well-known cliffs at Clifton, New Providence. The narrow layers of cross-bedding suggest sediments laid in the sea under the influence of strong currents. Since deposition, the beds have been faulted and eroded.*

beach rock has been fossilised and left high above the present beach. Similar deposits can be seen on Salt Cay north of New Providence. In these areas, sea-level was once about 2-2.5 metres (6-8 feet) higher.

Another piece of evidence would be the presence of *beach rock* above sea-level. This

■ **Raised beaches** Beaches can be considered as the opposite of cliffs, and represent deposition rather than erosion. Whenever we find such features above sea-level we know that sea-level was once higher. Some of the features that we find are whole sections of beach showing the *cuspate* (rise and fall) relief of a broad sandy beach. If we walk along a broad beach on which waves regularly break, such as Cabbage Beach on Paradise Island, we will see this feature. It is rather like the scalloped edge of a steak knife. Raised beaches showing this feature can be seen at Grotto Beach on San Salvador, where cuspate

Figure 4.16 *Further evidence of a higher sea-level is demonstrated by these sea-floor ripples, now well above sea-level at Clifton*

is a type of rock which forms from beach sand (see p. 82) and is, in fact, the same kind of rock found in the beach cusps of San Salvador. (See also Bimini p. 83)

Many creatures live in the area between high and low tides - the *intertidal zone*. If the rock has fossils of these creatures in it, or any other evidence of their presence such as worm burrows, air-holes, etc., we can recognize it as belonging to a past beach. Such features have been found in sand-dune ridges at Lyford Cay, New Providence, about 8-8.5 metres (26-28 feet) above sea-level, the highest level known for sea-level to have risen in The Bahamas.

■ *Marine limestone and current bedding* Obviously there are many other indications of a higher sea-level. Two that can be easily understood and seen by the reader are:

- The flat rockland which consists of hardened *marine sediments* that were once laid down on the sea-floor - obviously the sea once covered this land. Long narrow ridges up to 6 metres (20 feet) high in such areas are usually old beaches that once marked the shore-line. The Seven Hills area of south Beach is named after a succession of fossil beach ridges.
- The action of tidal currents pushes sea-floor sediments backwards and forwards, so that one layer slopes one way, but is then covered by another layer sloping differently. Such beds can be seen clearly in the cliffs at Clifton, now well above present tidal action. The typical criss-cross or herring-bone pattern is known as *current bedding* (Figure 4.15 and 4.16).

LOWER SEA-LEVELS

■ *Wave-cut platforms and marine terracing* Just as cliffs and knicks above sea-level indicate a fall in sea-level, so will any coastal feature that is now found submerged. One of the most common offshore features is the *terrace*.

When the sea cuts a cliff, the flat area in front of the cliff is known as a *wave-cut platform* (see Figure 4.13). Should the sea-level subsequently rise, this platform will appear as a shelf or *terrace* on the sloping sea-floor, most notably where it slopes towards the drop-off and is less likely to get buried by later sedimentation. These terraces are found all around the edges of the Bahamian banks. A profile (Figure 4.17) of the drop-off at Fernandez Bay, San Salvador, shows terracing at regular intervals, with a particularly well-developed one at 45 metres (150 feet). It is generally believed that when sea-level changed it did so rather erratically, and the times of rise or fall were separated by long periods when sea-level stayed constant. It was during these *'still stands'* that the terraces were cut.

■ *Drowned parts of the landscape - limestone crusts and peat* A limestone crust is a hard cap which forms on the surface of limestone rock (see p. 68). It can only form on land and so if found at or below sea-level it indicates that sea-level was once lower. In many islands, bared and eroded crusts are to be seen in the intertidal zone, and indicate a rise of about five feet or more in sea-level.

Just off the coast of Bimini, *peat* has been dredged up from 3 metres (10 feet) of sea-water. This is clear evidence of a marsh now drowned. Borings on Andros have also found peat below the surface, at 4 metres (13 feet) and 3 metres (9 feet) below sea-level. All these discoveries have fortunately been dated by radio-carbon methods, and they allow us to make certain conclusions about the recent past (Figure 4.18):

- The Bimini peat is about 4 370 years old.

- The Andros peat was dated 6 500 years old at 4 metres (13 feet) and 4 000 years old at 3 metres (9 feet) years old.

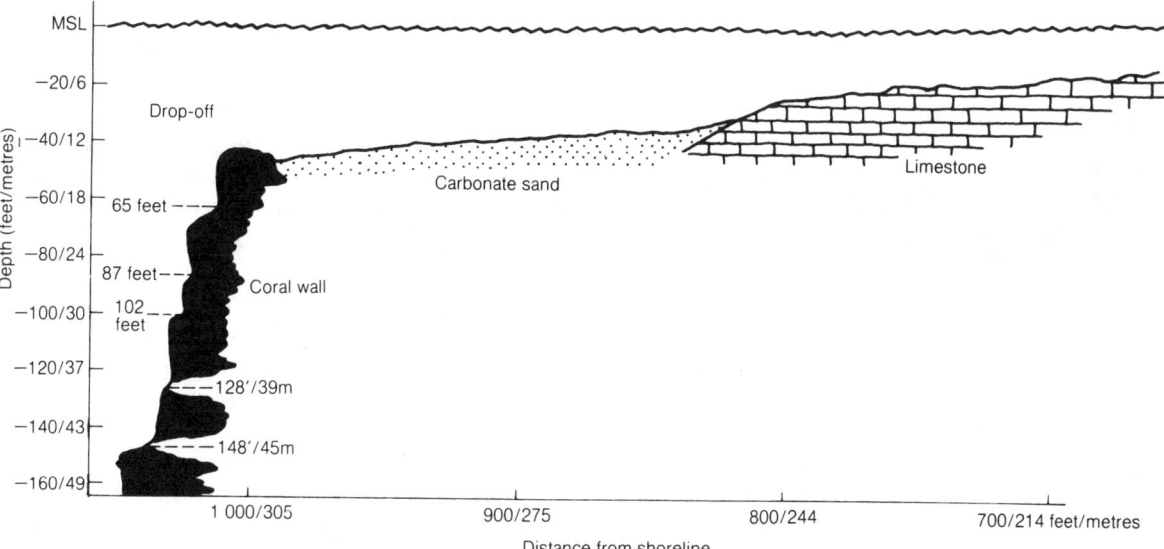

Figure 4.17 Profile of San Salvador Banks and drop-off, at Fernandez Bay (taken from: Field Guide to the Geology of San Salvador. Ed. D. George, 1981). The depths against the coral face indicate the presence of distinct shelves or knicks, believed to represent erosion at past sea-levels. The geology also supports the 'bucket' theory of atoll formation.

- 13 500 years ago a swamp existed while sea-level was 4 metres lower than at present. Allowing for subsidence at 1 cm/1000 years, we must deduct 13.5 x 1.25 = 17 cms (6.75 inches) from this figure. (In practice this figure is so small it is usually ignored.)

- 4 370 years ago the sea-level was 3 metres lower, and by 4 000 years ago it was 2.75 metres (9 feet) below the present level. At these times there was a still-stand that lasted long enough for peat to be laid down in swampy conditions at sea-level.

- It seems reasonable to assume from this information that the peat provides a record of the final rise of sea-level following the end of the last glaciation. At this time the average rate of sea-level rise was about 7.5 cm (3 inches) per 100 years.

Many other features formed on land or at the shore-line can now be found offshore, including gullies and solution holes ('banana' holes). An interesting example is the fictitious *'pavements of Atlantis'*, seen off Bimini. These are, in fact, deposits of beach rock formed along straight beaches and later

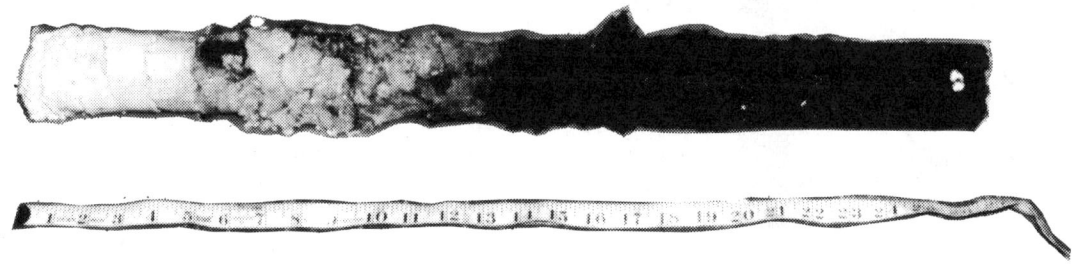

Figure 4.18 A piston core from Graham's Harbour, San Salvador. The top is to the left and shows about 30 cm (12 ins) of clay on top of peat (black). This would suggest the bay was once a swamp which was later submerged.

Figure 4.19 Cargill's Creek blue hole in North Andros has an irregular opening with evidence of local faulting.

drowned by a 4.5 metres (15 feet) rise in sea-level.

■ *Blue holes and underground caves* These are features which can only be formed above sea-level (see p. 64). In addition, some of the features connected with them, such as stalactites, are further evidence of an atmospheric origin. Consequently any depth recorded for a blue hole will also be an indication of how low sea-level was at that time. Several blue holes reach 130 metres (400 feet) or more, so it can be said sea-level was about this low at some time in the past, probably during the last glaciation.

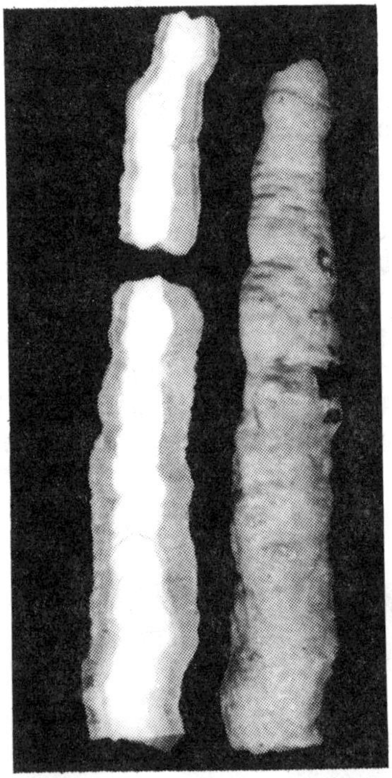

In recent years attempts have been made to date the blue holes from the ages of the stalagmites and stalactites in them. This is very complicated, because these features will obviously only form when the blue hole is dry. If the blue hole has been flooded more than once, there will be more than one layer of calcite encrusting it. While it was flooded marine or fresh water life may have bored into it, providing further information about the blue hole's history. One study dated a stalagmite as 150 000 years old. This would suggest that it formed at the end of the third (Illinoian) glacial advance, and that the blue hole, in South Bight, Andros, was formed earlier in that glaciation, or in an earlier glacial episode.

FROM SEDIMENTS TO ROCKS

There is one last question to answer before we can finally say that we know how the Bahamian islands were formed. We have learned about the sediments laid down in the sea, and also about those blown up by the wind. We also know that The Bahamas is made of limestone rock. But *how* do we get from the sediments to the rocks? In geology, the process is known as *diagenesis*. Basically, the process is one in which the grains of sand in the sediment become *cemented* together. Exactly how this occurs is often a mystery, and it can happen in many ways. A few examples will show us the processes most common in The Bahamas, and at the same time demonstrate to us yet another way in which The Bahamas is remarkable in the geological world. In this case, it is the speed at which diagenesis occurs which is so unusual, and there are few parts of the world where sediments are converted to rocks more quickly. In some countries sediments have remained unconsolidated (i.e. loose) for over 100 million years. In The Bahamas a rock could be formed in less than

Figure 4.20 A sectioned Stalagmite from a blue hole on Sweetings Cay, Grand Bahama. Photograph Courtesy of Rob Palmer

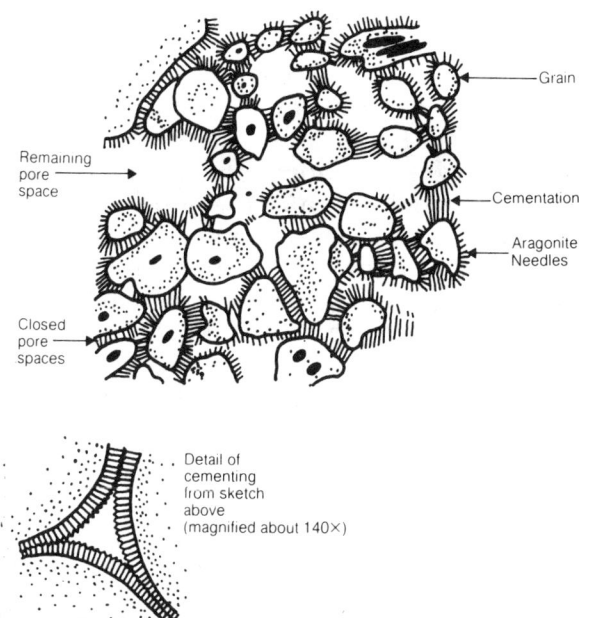

Figure 4.21 Cementation and crystal growth. Around most of the grains, needles of aragonite have grown outward. In many cases these have reached other grains and cemented them together. In some cases the pore space has been completely filled, but often a pore space of smaller size remains. (Magnified about 40x)

a 100 years, and some beach rock is so recent that it includes fossils of glass from cola bottles!

There are two ways in which sands are likely to be consolidated in The Bahamas:
- Cementation
- Recrystallisation

CEMENTATION

Although the exact way in which this occurs varies a lot, and is very technical as it deals with the formation and growth of crystals, it is relatively simple to describe.

Marine cementation is caused by each grain of sediment collecting around it a sort of skin of fine crystals. Wherever two grains are touching each other these thin coatings of crystals interlock and join the grains together, like a glue or cement. Even if they are not touching, the crystals may grow out until the gap between the grains is crossed and then they interlock. The fine crystals, which are usually of *aragonite* (but sometimes a magnesium-rich calcite known as *dolomite*), are attracted from the sea water to the grains, which acts as a sort of nucleus around which they grow (Figure 4.21).

The production of *beach rock* is a bit different and much more rapid. Cementing takes place just below the surface, where groundwater from the land reaches the sea. The beach is rapidly heated by the sun as the tide falls. The water evaporates and deposits calcium carbonate (again aragonite) around the grains of sand, cementing them together very quickly. On sunny days the beach surface temperatures may be well over 38 °C (100 °F), and this is part of the reason for the speed of cementation.

Cementation of the *sand-dunes* is due to rainwater dissolving some of the calcium carbonate in the upper layers and carrying it below the surface. When the rain stops, the surface water dries off and the calcium carbonate is redeposited, both around and between the sand grains. This can also be very rapid, and probably accounts for the height of the complex dune ridges that we have today. The sand dunes were *lithified* (made into rock) too quickly for the winds to move or destroy them later, and once formed they acted as a trap for new dunes to build upon.

RECRYSTALLISATION

In this case the grains of sediment change their crystal type, the most common changes being from *aragonite* to *calcite*, and from either of these to *dolomite*.

Aragonite ($CaCO_3$) is a dense crystal form of calcium carbonate which most of the Bahamian sediments start out as. It can be seen as a white pearly crystal if the shell of a conch is broken the whole shell is made up of *aragonite*, as are lobster shells, crab shells, and so on. However, aragonite changes into *calcite* in time, and, although it looks just the same to the naked eye, it is less dense and so occupies more space. Therefore, if a mass of aragonite sand grains changes to calcite, the grains will all be larger (8% bigger) and so will grow into each other and close up most of the pore spaces. This is why some limestones in The Bahamas, such as beach rock, look coarse like 'sandstone', while others are massive and solid, like concrete. A good comparison can be made at Caves' Point in New Providence by inspecting the flat rocks on the beach and the hard rocks of the caves themselves.

Dolomite ($CaCO_3.MgCO_3$) is less common, and only forms today in a few areas, such as on tidal flats. If *aragonite* is converted to dolomite, a small expansion of 3% will take place. However, it is more usual for dolomite to form from *calcite* deep underground - at a depth of at least 30-150 metres (100-500 feet) - and this is where it is found in The Bahamas. It is probably the pressure at this depth which causes the change in the crystal form.

When grains, or even fossils, re-crystallise, another point to note is that the new crystals will fill up any spaces between the old ones, which before might have been only loosely touching. Thus the process of re-crystallisation is always a solidifying one. However, although this will make the rock much less porous, it will compensate by developing a more organised and efficient *cave* system so that movement of the ground water can still take place. Old re-crystallised limestone is often very cavernous as a result.

[1] Hearty, Paul J, & Kindler, P - New Perspectives on Bahamian Geology: San Salvador, Bahamas. *Journal of Coastal Research*, **9**, (2), 1993, Pp 572-594.
Hearty, P J et al - Aminostratigraphy and age of Pleistocene limestones of Bermuda. *Geological Soc of America Bull.* **104**, 4, 1992, p 471-480.

[2] Gould, Stephen Jay - Cerion - the evolving snail *Bahamas Journal of Science*, **1**, 1, 1993, p 10-15.

5 THE RIDGELAND LANDSCAPES AND LANDFORMS

All the main processes which go to make up the major *landscapes* of The Bahamas have now been identified and described. They can be considered to be of four main types:

- the ridgeland;
- the rockland;
- the wetland;
- the coastland.

The ridgeland and the rockland are the primary landscapes. The wetlands and the coastlands can be considered as secondary types, because they are, in fact, formed where the primary types are either flooded or reach the sea. Within each of these landscapes we will also find distinctive features, usually unique to that landscape. These are the *landforms*, which will also be described and discussed.

THE RIDGELAND LANDSCAPE

The dimensions of the ridges are well known visually as they occur so frequently. The higher ridges nearly always exceed 30 metres (100 feet), but only on Cat Island is 60 metres (200 feet) exceeded. Of the 23 largest islands, cays or groups of cays:

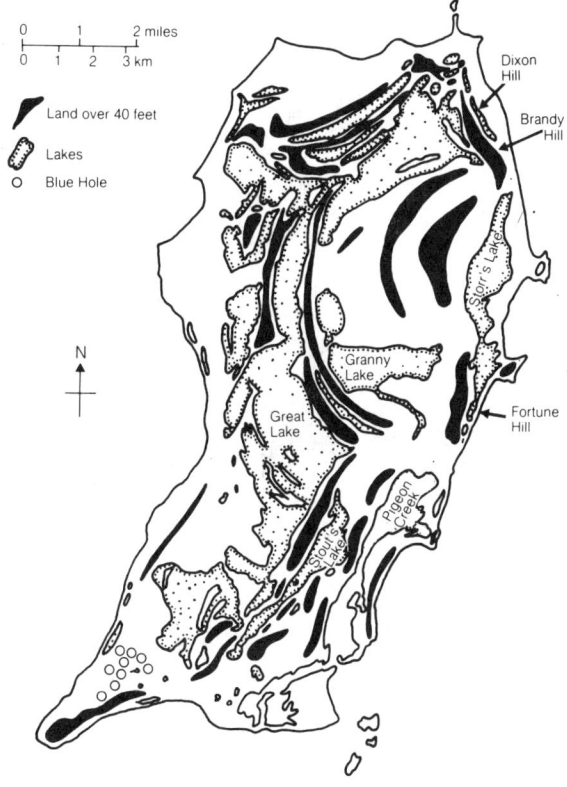

Figure 5.1 The Ridges of San Salvador

- One has a ridge over 60 metres (200 feet) in height
- Three have ridges over 45 metres (150 feet) in height
- Thirteen have ridges over 30 metres (100 feet) in height
- Five have ridges over 15 metres (50 feet) in height

and only one has no ridge over 15 metres in height (Biminis).

So, generally speaking, most islands have ridges reaching between 30 and 45 metres (100 and 150 feet), and in New Providence and San Salvador the maximum heights are identical at 37 metres (123 feet). A closer look at New Providence shows that there are nine distinct ridges, averaging 5.3 kilometres (3.3 miles) in length, while San Salvador, an island of similar size (161 square kilometres (63 square miles) compared with 204 square kilometres (80 square miles) on New Providence) has 13 ridges averaging 4 kilometres (2.5 miles) in length (Figure 5.1). Thus San Salvador has a total of 51 kilometres (32 miles) of ridges while New Providence has 48 kilometres - not a great difference.

It can be seen, therefore, that the ridges are not an exceptional or an occasional feature, but common enough to provide heights of over 15 metres in all the major islands except Bimini. Even Andros exceeds 30 metres near Congo Town, despite its reputation for being flat and swampy, while the well known Morgan's Bluff reaches 20 metres (65 feet) in the north.

Not all ridges run in a straight line. Due to the way many dunes form behind a bay

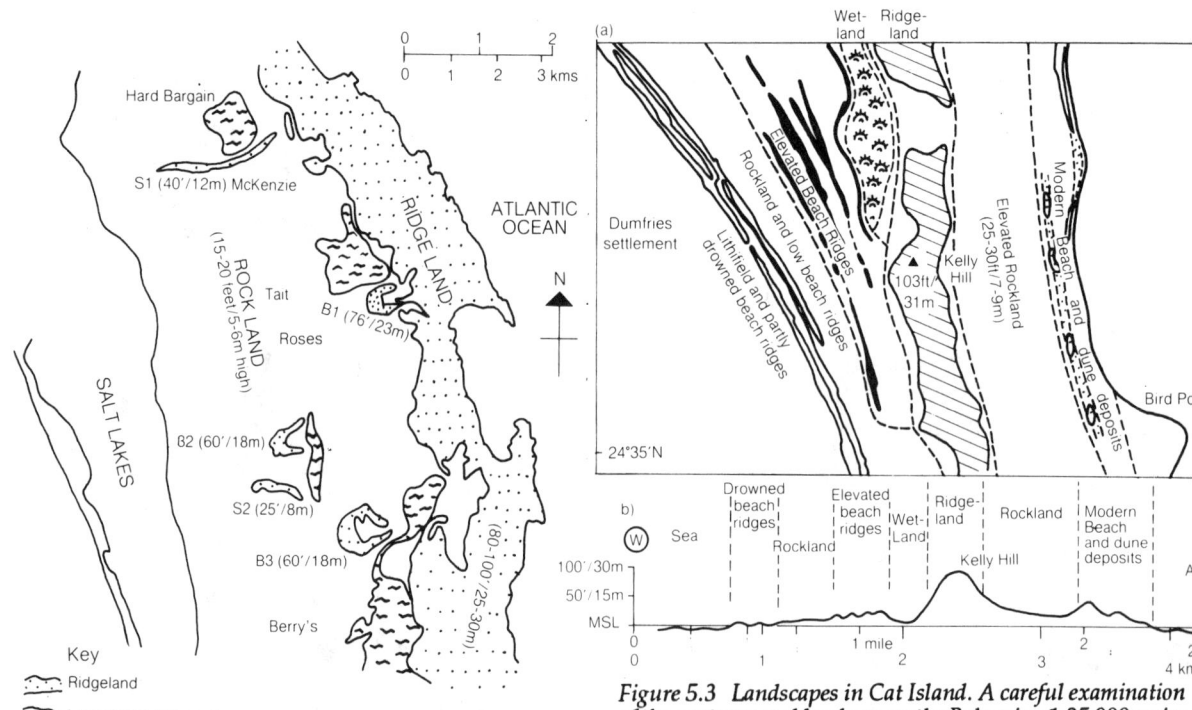

Figure 5.2 *'Desert dunes'* on Long Island. Altogether five longitudinal (seif) and crescentic (barchan) dunes can be found on the rockland of this part of Long Island. They have since been cemented into rock, probably in the last 5 000 years.

Figure 5.3 *Landscapes in Cat Island.* A careful examination of the contours and land use on the Bahamian 1:25 000 series maps will usually reveal the various landscape types without difficulty. Here the ridgeland, rockland and wetland are easily recognized. Narrow strips of high ground (25 feet contour) usually indicate beach ridges from higher sea levels, while ridges at 25 feet and 50 feet on windward coasts will usually mean modern deposition. The unusual western coast appears to consist of a partly drowned series of beach ridges.

Figure 5.4 A typical ridgeland landscape near Gregory Town, Eleuthera. Pineapples grow in pockets of lateritic soil in the foreground while slash-and-burn clearance of the coppice vegetation goes on in the background.

they are often curved in shape (technically they form a *catenary* between two headlands), as on San Salvador. It should be noted that these ridges are the present day representation of a past geography that created the dunes in the first place.

A striking example of the way in which ridges developed from sand-dunes is to be seen on Long Island south of Hard Bargain. Two of the typical dunes that form under *desert* conditions are longitudinal dunes (known as *seifs)* and crescentic dunes (known as *barchans).* As the map shows (Figure 5.2), unmistakable fossil examples of these are present on the rockland well inland of the main ridges, suggesting that they have 'migrated' across the rockland from the east.

The map also shows the extent of the more recent Ridgeland in Long Island, a belt about one mile wide occupying the eastern side of the island. Cat Island and Eleuthera are similar (Figure 5.3).

The impact of the ridges on the landscape depends very much on the way in which they are related to each other. On San Salvador, a lot of ridges roughly parallel to each other have created many lakes in-between, and have generally made the use of the interior impossible (see Figure 5.1). On New Providence this has only occurred once resulting in the formation of Lake Cunningham. Mainly the ridges are in line with each other and set well apart (see Figure 4.6). The smaller cays and chains of cays, such as the Ragged Island range, the Exuma Cays, and the Cays to Eleuthera (including the well-known Rose Island) are generally a single or double line of ridges which have been breached at intervals, probably by storms at times of higher sea-level in the past. Where there is a double ridge, a lake or swamp may

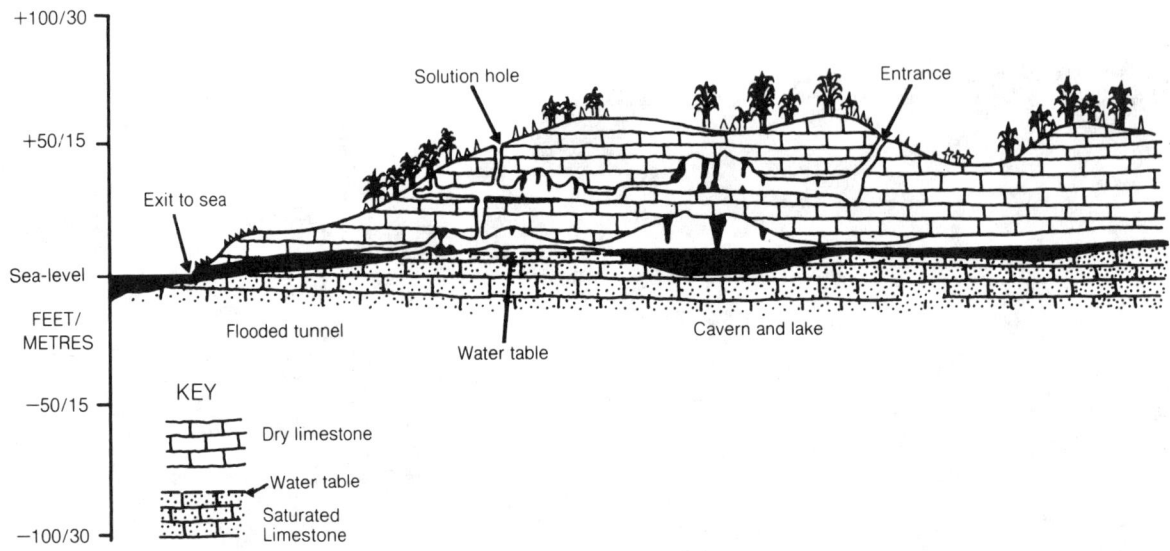

Figure 5.5 *The drawing shows the typical layout of a dry and wet cave system at two levels. The upper level would have been formed when sea-level was about 6 metres (20 feet) higher than today. The lower level drains towards present sea-level. Below these, many other flooded systems may exist.*

be trapped between, as on Paradise Island and Rose Island, or a harbour formed, as at Hope Town, Abaco, and Norman's Cay and Staniel Cay in the Exumas.

In a few cases, ridges have been formed hard up against each other to provide an elevated surface which is composed of the tops of many dunes built in succession. This is the case in central Eleuthera, where a gently hilly plateau, 30 metres high near Gregory Town and usually over 15 metres high elsewhere, has been formed. Similar conditions exist in Long Island and Cat Island, but usually on a smaller scale (Figure 5.2, 5.3).

THE LANDFORMS OF THE RIDGES

The ridges, in fact, are relatively uniform in character and have few distinguishing features, or individual *landforms* as we shall call them. Ridges start out life as *coastal sand-dunes*, but these are more properly described under the heading of the coastal landscape (p. 69). Of great importance to the later development of the ridge is the *cave* and its related features. Caves occur in all the other landscapes as well, but usually these are so low-lying that the caves are flooded. Those associated with the blue holes are good examples of this. It is only when a cave is found on relatively high ground, well above the water table, that it is dry and accessible. Hunt's Cave in New Providence, and Hamilton's Cave on Long Island, are good examples.

Limestone is a rock which dissolves easily in rainwater, which is why there are no rivers. Instead, the water finds its way underground, eventually to the water table. Caves are the result of this downward movement, and usually a cave consists of two sets of characteristics as a result. It will have *vertical* sections, where the water is falling downwards, and *horizontal* sections where the water, now an underground stream, is flowing, probably towards the sea. Caves of any size will have a combination of vertical and horizontal sections, such as Hatchet Bay cave north of Alice Town in Eleuthera, and Lighthouse and other caves on San Salvador. Even the well-known larger cave at Caves

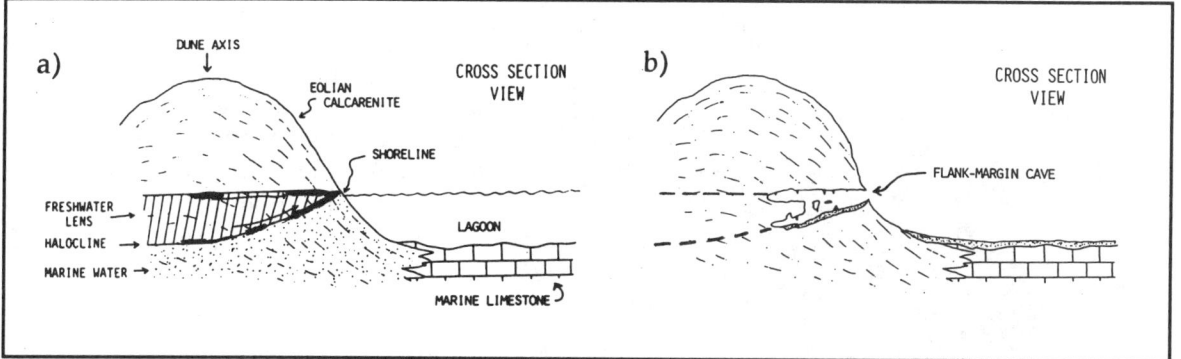

Figure 5.6 a) Dissolution takes place at the top and bottom of the water lens, and especially where these meet near the coast. b) A flank-margin cave is the result. (From J Mylroie and J Carew, 1990)

Point on New Providence has two distinct levels. The reason for having several levels may be explained, by each one representing a different water table level. Water-table levels are related to sea-level, and as the sea-level changed so did the water-table, with the underground streams moving to different depths or levels. The actual relationship between the cave and the fresh-water lens is somewhat complex.(See also p. 94) Recent studies of the base of the fresh-water lens, where fresh water meets salt water in the *mixing zone,* has shown that chemical conditions exist there which cause increased rock dissolution. As a result it is now realised that both the top and the bottom of the fresh water lens are the zones for cave formation. Where these layers meet, at the edge of the lens, is likely to be most favourable for dissolution and cave formation. Mylroie and Carew have proposed the name *flank margin cave* (Figure 5.6) for this type of cave, and suggest that most Bahamian caves were at least initiated this way.

Within the caves we find several other features (Figure 5.5):

- *Shafts* - the vertical sections, one of which often forms the entrance (Figure 5.7).

- *Tunnels* - horizontal or gently sloping passages. *Rounded* tunnels were filled with water right up to their roof, which will also show evidence of erosion similar to that of the floor and walls. *Triangular* or *rectangular* tunnels are formed by streams running across the floor and undercutting the walls. Sediments and stones will

Figure 5.7 The entrance to Hatchet Bay Cave, Eleuthera

Figure 5.8 This tunnel was once part of the underground drainage system. Now dry, the peaked roof suggests that it developed along a line of weakness such as a minor fracture

be found on the floor and dripstone features may be present. Often a flooded tunnel will convert to one with a stream and then dry up altogether, so compound shapes can be seen (Figure 5.8).

- *Caverns* - are large openings where several tunnels meet. They may have a lot of collapsed rock from the roof lying on the floor, and the roof may be very high. They may also extend to lower levels and contain lakes (Figure 5.10).

- *Stalactites, stalagmites, rock curtains and other dripstone features* - technically known as speleothems, these features are common in the bigger Bahamian caves. They are due to water rich in calcium carbonate dripping through the roof or down the wall of a tunnel or a cavern. In the air of the cave some of the carbon dioxide in the solution is lost and the calcium carbonate is deposited, on the roof (stalactite), the floor (stalagmite) or the wall (curtain). A *column* will form when stalactite and stalagmite join. The redeposited calcium carbonate is given the name *travertine*. It may be stained various shades of yellow or red due to the presence of iron oxides derived from the rock or soil above. All these features can be collectively called *dripstones*, as they start out life from dripping water (Figure 5.10).

A point to note is that the presence of dripstones in any cave, whether flooded or not at the present time, indicates that it was once dry after its formation. These features can only form in air.

- *Lakes* - The presence of a subterranean lake means that the water table has been reached. It may be in the lower part of the floor of a cavern, or occupy a whole network of tunnels and caverns at a lower level, and merely be visible from a shaft at a higher level.

Throughout the entire history of The Bahamas, caves have been formed, and they exist at all depths down as far as has ever been drilled. Some caverns are hundreds of feet deep and, in 1947, 2 440 metres (8 000 feet) of drilling pipe was lost in a huge cavern over 4 420 metres (14 500 feet) down in Andros. The Lucayan Cavern on Grand Bahama is over 8 540 metres (28 000 feet) long (8.5 kilometres /5.3 miles) and constitutes one of the world's longest underwater caves. Caves far below the water table can be useful in allowing the water to move freely through the otherwise impervious crystalline limestone that may exist below many islands. This fact is taken advantage of in the *deep-well disposal* projects common in southern Florida, and more recently (1991) being used in the Bahamas for sewage disposal. In the Yellow Elder subdivision effluent is injected hundreds of metres below the surface into the salt water zone, where it apparently remains stable and harmless. In such cases, cavernous zones well below the fresh water lens (if there is one) are used, such as the deep disposal unit drilled to 195 m (640 feet) under Potter's Cay, New Providence, in 1971.

Figure 5.9 Salt Pond Cave on Long Island is one of the largest caves in the Bahamas and is unique for its remarkable dead end. The distinct line about half way up the walls is the level to which this cave was originally filled with bat guano.

Figure 5.10 A cavern in Hatchet Bay Cave, Eleuthera. The column has been formed by the joining of a stalactite and a stalagmite.

6 THE ROCKLAND LANDSCAPE AND LANDFORMS

This is flat and rocky land, and without vegetation it would undoubtedly be a stony desert. It occurs in all the larger islands, and extensively on the bankward sides of the Pine Islands (i.e. Andros, Abaco, Grand Bahama and New Providence). Even the narrow islands of the eastern margin have important strips, sometimes the site of settlements, such as Deadman's Cay on Long Island and Port Howe on Cat Island.

As a landscape, these areas are more notable for their vegetation than their relief. In the Pine Islands, as might be expected, the rockland is covered with thousands of acres of pine trees (Figure 6.1) Where the water table reaches the surface the pine trees give way increasingly to palmettos and eventually to a marsh-type vegetation. Rockland also includes the areas that have most successfully been farmed, such as the San Andros area of Andros and the old BAIL sugar estate on Abaco. Most of the Freeport/Lucaya residential development is on this type of land. Much rockland started out as shallow water banks of oolite when sea-level was higher than at present. In some cases, however, such as most of Abaco north of Marsh Harbour, it consists of many parallel lines of *beach deposits*. The result is that the surface is less flat than the oolitic areas, and the skeletal sediments of the beaches have created a softer limestone more suitable for farming (Figure 6.2). This is very much the case near Treasure Cay, where the Bahamas Star farm covers several thousand acres.

Although the rockland may appear uninteresting at first sight, when looked at closely, its surface is quite varied. Being limestone the surface is subject to *solution weathering*, that is, dissolving by rainwater (which becomes slightly acidic as it passes through the atmosphere and the soil). Landscapes which are of this type are usually referred to as *Karst Landscapes*, after the area of limestone first studied in Yugoslavia.

Unfortunately, it is misleading to describe the limestone features of the Bahamas as karst, because the majority of karst landforms are not present at all. In addition, The Bahamas has many features which would not be found in a normal account of limestone landscapes and are not usually discussed in the traditional textbooks. There seem to be two good reasons for this. Limestone was first studied in the countries of Europe and North America which have temperate climates, and most of the books were

Figure 6.1 A road through the pine barrens. The picture clearly shows the thinness of the soil cover even in a forested area. Only a few inches have been shaved from the surface, yet pure limestone has been exposed.

written for students in these countries. The type of 'karst' found in The Bahamas, and the West Indies in general, has to be considered as a separate class usually referred to as *Tropical Karst*. Also The Bahamas is somewhat unique in the purity of its limestone; its mode of formation from shallow water marine sediments; its youthfulness; and the relatively high water table. Taken together, these have prevented the formation of the most typical features, whether of the temperate or the tropical type. There is, indeed, a case for considering 'Bahamian Karst' as a separate type altogether.

THE LANDFORMS OF THE ROCKLAND

Within this rather specialised landscape the surface is fretted with numerous *sinkholes* such as the well-known *banana holes*, but also locally called *pineapple holes* (small ones), *solution holes* and *potholes*. These vary enormously in size from the width of a finger to several feet across. *Blue holes* are special cases. Between the holes are sharp ridges of solid rock, loose boulders, and projecting *castles*. In some areas *plates*, or flat rocks, lie loosely on the more solid rock below. The accompanying sketches (Figure 6.4) show a variety of surfaces, each one different in detail, but generally being a mixture of holes and rocks which could be called 'clints and grikes' in a traditional karst area. Clints and grikes are, in fact, much more regular and linear in plan and do not show the platey forms.

The other feature of note on the rockland surface is a hard crust which is simply referred to as a *limestone crust*, but which can also be called *caliche* (any concretion made out of limestone), *calcrete* (the technical name), and *'flint rock'* which is the local name, as the crust is usually very hard (see p. 67).

SINKHOLES

Bahamian limestone, which is relatively young, is often very *porous*, that is it has *pore spaces* between the individual grains, which in a young rock are not fully cemented together. As cementation continues *porosity* will decrease, to almost nothing. Porosity can be measured as a percentage, where the figure quoted will be the amount of space as a percentage of the total rock. Typical figures are shown in Table 6.1.

Table 6.1 Porosity percentages for some typical Bahamian limestones.

Sand on the beach	55%
Newly formed beach rock	35%
Well-cemented sediments	15%
Recrystallised limestone	5%

Figure 6.2 A mechanised farm at Rock Sound, Eleuthera. The disc plough is used to crush and till the soil/rock surface, which with careful fertilising and irrigation can still be very productive. The crop is pawpaws for export to Florida.

Only the older limestones would have reached the crystalline stage. Therefore, we can see that water will have little difficulty in penetrating the more recent marine limestones of the rockland, and as we know, it will immediately start to dissolve them. As the rainwater works its way downwards through the rock, some of the pore spaces will be enlarged faster than others, and these will attract more water, which will again increase erosion. Very soon pores will become enlarged and joined up by channels which at the surface will appear as holes - sinkholes - through which the rainwater is sinking. Each little patch of limestone surface will have its preferred hole, and very soon the whole surface will have a drilled-out appearance (Figure 6.3). The holes keep widening, the rock between them becomes jagged and sharp, and often breaks off to form loose fragments or boulders. Secure pieces of limestone stand up as 'castles', and the whole bed of limestone is gradually *honeycombed*, and keeps collapsing inwards (Figure 6.6).

Large sinkholes appear as time goes on whenever smaller ones join up, and the enlarging process can go on indefinitely. As a general rule, however, the holes will only get very wide if the water table is very deep below the surface. Solution channels also form below the water table, but at a slower rate. The water in a fresh water lens is always on the move, and not being saturated it can continue to dissolve the limestone. At the mixing zone it is again at its most aggressive (See p. 57).

So, for the rockland, we have a pitted and rocky surface because the water table is always near the surface. But, as the diagrams show (Figure 6.6), when the water table was lower it was possible for much larger holes to form and the largest of these were the blue holes. Today we find them flooded and

Figure 6.3 A typical rockland surface, littered with pine needles. Exposures of rock, known as 'castles', have been pitted by solution weathering. Between the castles larger holes have developed and become filled with an organic soil derived from the pine forest.

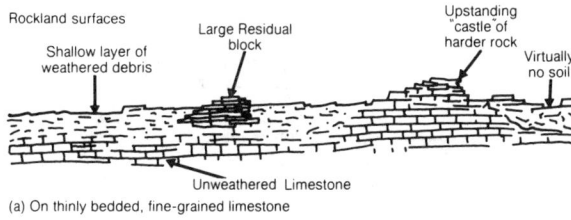
(a) On thinly bedded, fine-grained limestone

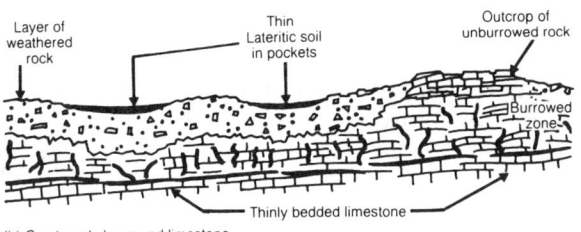
(b) On strongly burrowed limestone

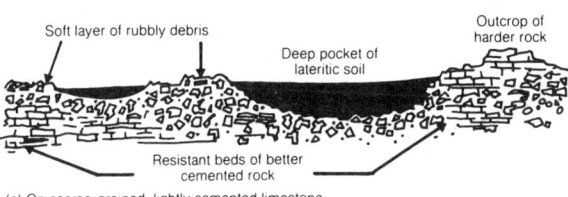
(c) On coarse-grained, lightly cemented limestone

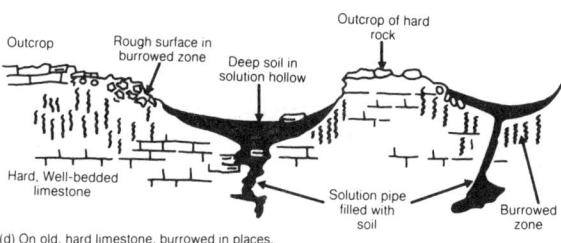
(d) On old, hard limestone, burrowed in places.

[Diagrams based on land resource study, **27**, Fig. 3]

Figure 6.4 Although all rockland is basically a rocky plain, a great variety of land surfaces can be seen. These sketches show four varieties, and it can be seen that the differences are mainly due to the type of limestone underneath. In general there will be a greater amount of surface debris when:
(a) the limestone is young, lightly cemented, and porous;
(b) the limestone is layered in thin beds, usually disturbed and broken;
(c) the limestone has been burrowed in the sea by marine creatures, such as worms, crabs, molluscs, etc. These burrows allow easy penetration by rainwater, roots, etc..

inactive, but still the most striking of all the Bahamian landforms.

BLUE HOLES

All the main islands of The Bahamas have blue holes, but those of Andros are best known. Andros has 178 on land with at least 50 in the sea. Blue holes may also be called *ocean holes* if they appear tidal or otherwise connected with the sea.

For a long time, ideas about the origin of the blue holes were confused, with superstition and myth more acceptable than geological theory to the average islander.[1] Geologists who visited the islands concluded that they could only be very large sinkholes, probably created in the Ice Ages. Similar features were well known in Europe and North America as 'potholes' by cavers, only in this case they were dry, or had streams running into them. Proof that they were indeed created during the Pleistocene Ice Ages lies in the following facts:

■ As sea-level did not drop much more that 122 metres (400 feet) in the Ice Ages we would not expect to find any blue holes much deeper than that. The deepest known is Dean's Blue Hole near

Figure 6.5 The exit from an underground cave system (such as in Figure 5.8). Both figures show caves formed when sea level was higher. Undoubtedly an active system is in operation in the limestone some distance below this abandoned one.

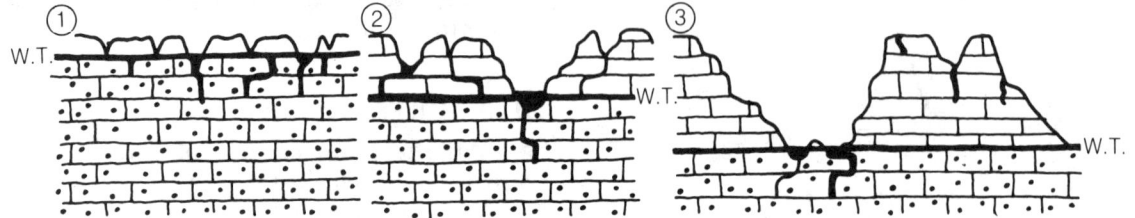

Figure 6.6 The formation of sink holes. As a rule, solution of the limestone will create sink-holes down to the level of the water table (W.T.) Each diagram 1, 2, and 3 shows the effect of the depth of the water table on the size of the sink holes. Solution will continue below the water table but at a slower rate.

Clarence Town, Long Island, measured at 201 metres (663 feet) as recently as 1992 by a dive team led by Jim King. (Figure 6.7) Before this the deepest blue holes were all thought to be in Andros which has one near Twin Lakes that is 110 metres (363 feet) deep, and three others nearby over 107 metres (350 feet).

■ If they were sinkholes they should have connecting tunnels and caverns, with dripstone features in them. Several blue holes have now been discovered with stalagmites, proving without doubt that at one time the hole or cave was empty and penetrated by dripping water. Quite extensive cave systems have been explored in both Andros and Grand Bahama.

■ Wherever dating has been possible the dates have fitted in well with known dates for sea-levels in the Ice Age period (See p. 38).

The extreme depth of Dean's blue hole requires some explanation, as it is deeper than the fall of sea-level in the ice age. One must suppose that in this unique case the blue hole, or underground cavern, developed as an upper extension of a pre-existing cavern. As Dean's blue hole developed it must have broken through the roof of an older and very large

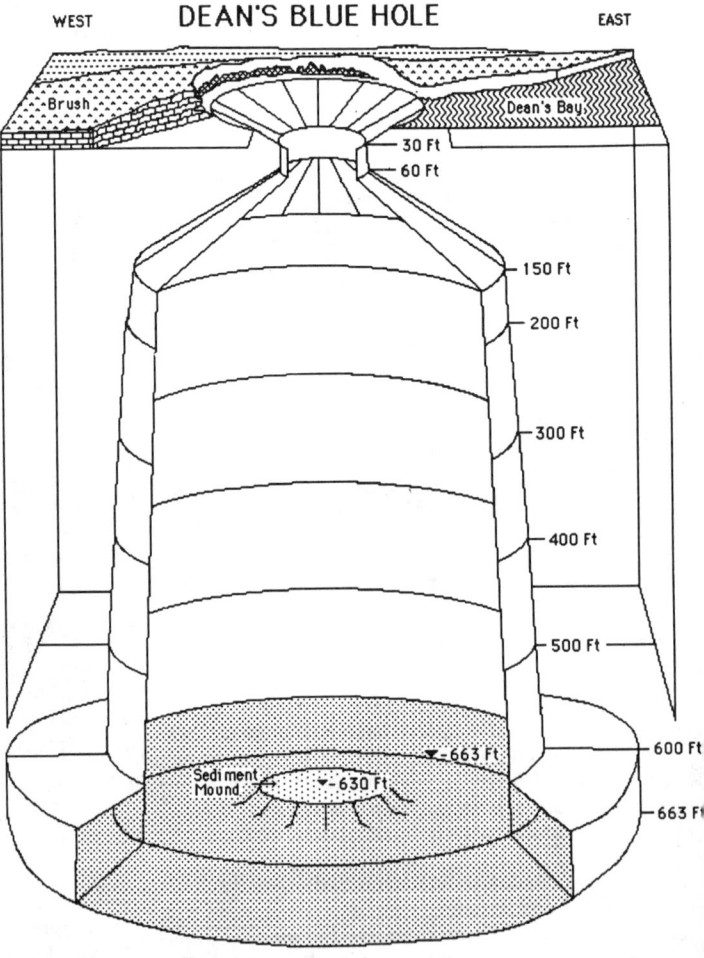

Figure 6.7 Generalized view of Dean's Blue Hole, Long Island (From William L Wilson, 1992)

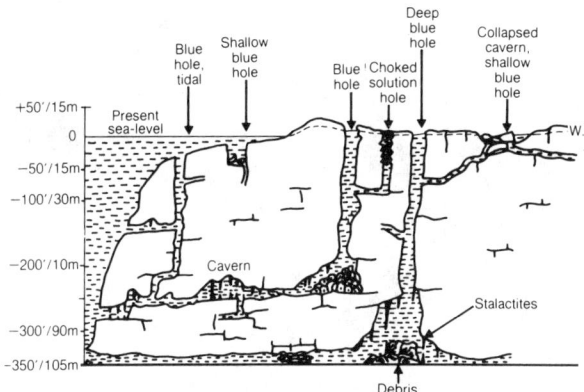

Figure 6.8 An impression of how blue holes might look below ground, and below the sea. Most of the possibilities are illustrated (W.T. = water table). All blue holes connected to the sea will be affected by the tides.

cavern. As Figure 6.7 shows, the submerged portion is enormous, one of the largest underground chambers known anywhere in the world. Mars Bay blue hole (below) has a similar shape and sand cone at the bottom.

This knowledge also tells us why we find some blue holes in the sea. During the periods of glaciation, the entire Little, Great and south-eastern Bahamas Banks were dry land, and would have been subject to erosion and solution just like the rockland is today. Blue holes would have formed in many areas, but most of them would have been filled in by marine sediments once the rising sea covered them up. In some areas they have stayed open, most notably off the east coast of Andros. This could well be due to the passage of water through them as the tides rise and fall, particularly if there is an outlet into deep water (the Tongue of the Ocean in the case of Andros) (see Figure 6.8). Whirlpool conditions have often been seen at the surface of blue holes. This is, in fact, a unique feature of Bahamian blue holes. They do exist in other parts of the world, notably in Belize and off the coast of Yucatan in Mexico, in the Gulf of Campeche, where they are known as *cenote*, but none of these places have *tidal* blue holes.

The *shape* and *size* of blue holes is also of interest. Normally they are circular, but some are not. They are most likely to be circular when they have been formed from an opening at the surface, as the numerous little streams running into the hole will tend to concentrate their erosion on any projecting 'headlands'. With the high purity of Bahamian limestones there will also be a tendency for the most efficient shape to form, which in this case will be circular as this will have the shortest wetted perimeter for any size of hole. On a smaller scale there will be little channels cut in the edge of the hole giving it a fretted appearance, and at the water's surface the 'lip' will be undercut (Figure 6.9). The level of water in the blue hole is often affected by the tides, and also by water table levels in the rainy and dry seasons, so the undercut section may be as much as 0.5-1 metre (2-3 feet) in depth.

Irregular shapes are mostly associated with faulting. The best example of this is a string of blue holes running approximately north-south in South Andros. The series starts at South Bight and follows a major fault slightly inland but at an angle to the coast. By the time the fault reaches Mars Bay the fault is in the sea, and Mars Bay itself is noted for a very deep blue hole (80 metres/270 feet) just offshore. These blue holes were well-studied in the 1980's by Rob Palmer and and the chasm-like shape of these blue holes (Figure 6.13) is quite different from the circular ones. Apart from these, many of the blue holes found in the sea are irregular in shape, presumably because they have not been subjected to surface erosion like the ones on land. Sea water is saturated with calcium carbonate and cannot do any further dissolving, so the shape of the off-

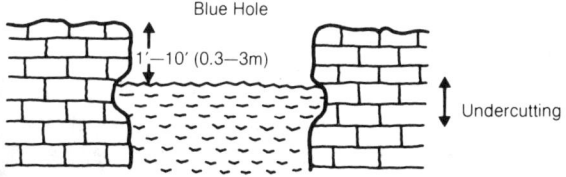

Figure 6.9 Cross-section of the lip of a typical blue hole

Figure 6.10 Church's Blue Hole, near Fresh Creek, Andros. This large blue hole is set in typical pine-covered rockland.

shore blue holes is probably much the same as when the sea rose to its present level. On land, the irregular shapes were rounded off by rainwater acting on the lip of the hole.

Some blue holes are formed by the collapse of a cavern roof, rather than as an enlarged sinkhole at the surface. The opening to the Lucayan Cavern, known as Ben's blue hole is of this type. Below the opening is a large amount of roof debris, including the tops of stalactites which now project up from the floor like giant coffee tables.

Figure 6.11 Three blue holes along the South Andros Fault line, near Congo Town

Most blue holes are quite wide, 15 metres (50 feet) or more across, but some are much bigger such as Church's blue hole near Fresh Creek in Andros which is 134 metres (440 feet) across (Figure 6.10). The Andros holes average about 12 metres (40 feet) deep, but some are less than 6 metres deep while others reach over 90 metres (300 feet). Some well-known blue holes are:

Near Treasure Cay, Abaco	57 m 186 feet
Rock Sound, Eleuthera	43 m 140 feet
Mermaids Pool, New Providence	14 m 45 feet
Church's, N Andros	31 m 102 feet
Stargate, S Andros	97 m 320 feet
Dean's, Long Island	201 m 663 feet

Blue holes such as Dean's and Mars Bay are somewhat different, the small opening giving no clue to the vast chamber lying just below the surface.

Blue holes have some life in them, depending on the food available. Leaves and other vegetable matter collect in them and this supports a few small fish and other creatures. (Readers are referred to the bibli-

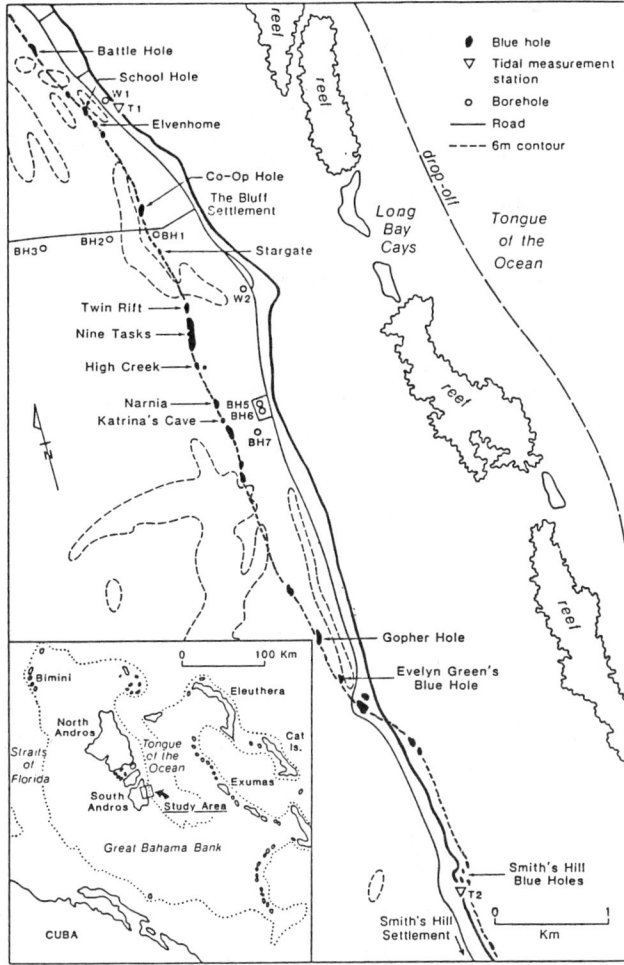

Figure 6.12 Location of fracture-controlled blue holes in South Andros. The fault is shown by the dashed line and the blue holes are solid black. (From P L Smart et al 1988)

ography, and the books and articles by Rob Palmer, for further information on this subject). Offshore, blue holes are equally poor producers of food, but are often well populated by all sorts of marine life because of the shelter they provide.

The water in many blue holes is fresh at the surface, but at a certain depth becomes brackish and then saline. The blue hole can be seen as nature's well, with the deeper ones passing through the fresh-water lens to the salt water below. The blue hole at James Cistern in Eleuthera has been used as a public well for many years, but all of those in Long Island are salty at the surface.

LIMESTONE CRUSTS

These are probably present over all the older rock surfaces in The Bahamas, but are, in fact, only seen when the soil has been stripped away.

The crusts are usually white or reddish in colour, and vary in thickness from about 2.5 mms (0.1 inches) to as much as 50-75 mms (2-3 inches). Areas which have been exposed but not otherwise eroded show the crust to be a continuous feature, resembling a blanket draped over the potholed limestone below, and smoothing off the usually rugged rock surface (Figure 6.14). On close inspection the crust appears to be built up of fine layers, and can be described as *laminated*. Above all it is hard, and quite a bit harder than ordinary limestone, and this accounts for its local name of *'flint rock'*.(Figure 6.15a) Unlike the limestone below, it is not porous, but very dense with interlocked crystals.

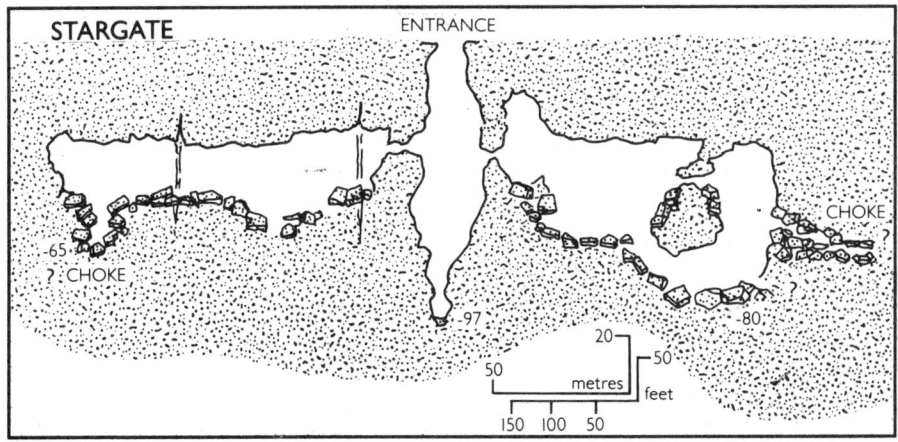

Figure 6.13 A cross-section of Stargate blue hole, South Andros, showing its great length and depth (metres). Despite this it is never more than ten metres wide. (From Rob Palmer, 1990)

The origin of crusts is not entirely clear, but a few of the features that are known can be summarised below:

- Crusts are only found in the tropics, which suggests that they have something to do with the climate. In hot, wet conditions, chemical action is much faster than in the temperate regions. Also evaporation rates are high, which encourages precipitation.
- They are only found on land, and are rapidly eroded when exposed in the intertidal zone. They are, therefore, almost certainly formed on land.
- The red colouring is now known to be derived from the dust blown across the Atlantic Ocean from the Sahara desert, and is most common in soils. It seems that the crusts are most often formed beneath the soil.
- The micro-crystalline nature, and absence of individual grains, suggests that they did not form as sediments but rather as new calcium carbonate layers on top of the original rock.
- The laminations suggest that they have been built up layer by layer.

It appears from all this evidence that crusts form after rain dissolves some of the surface limestone, and then redeposits it in a layer containing various impurities, when the rainwater is evaporated at the surface. This can take place in the open or under a soil, and if the latter is the case there may also be red iron oxide staining.

The crust often forms like a plaster cast over or within other features, such as sinkholes. On the coast both 'mushroom' and 'cup'-like shapes can be formed as a result of the erosion of the softer rock from beneath the crusts (Figure 6.15b).

The presence of a crust is the main reason for the *'ripping'* (or bull-dozing) of land for agricultural purposes. The crust prevents the plant roots from reaching the softer rock below, which may be a source of water.

Figure 6.14 Limestone crust lying like a blanket on exposed rockland near the coast. The crust forms rapidly on both exposed and soil-covered rock, and may be up to an inch thick.

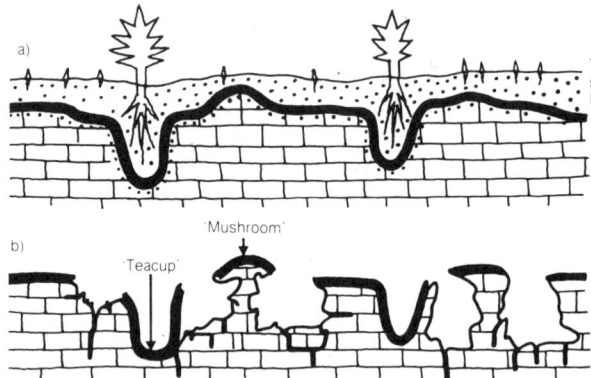

Figure 6.15 The crust probably forms most commonly under a soil surface, and completely covers the eroded limestone below (a). With erosion of the soil, only the crust is left to protect the softer limestone below, and, as this is penetrated, the typical jagged rock surface of the rocky coastlands begins to form (b). 'Mushrooms' and 'teacups' are common minor landforms at this stage.

Once the crust is broken up, and often removed to the side of the field, the plants can reach water in the spongy limestone below. However, it cannot be assumed that the rock below the crust is soft, porous or moist - it must be tested before ripping.

---

[1] Unlike many of the topics discussed in this book, blue holes have been written about quite widely. The authority is Dr George J. Benjamin who wrote 'Diving Into the Blue Holes of Andros', *National Geographic Magazine*, 1970, II, No. 360, pp. 347-63. He also made the film 'The Ocean Holes of Andros', *National Geographic Films*, and contributed to a study of blue holes in *Three Adventures* by Jacques I. Cousteau.

7 THE WETLAND AND COASTAL LANDSCAPE

As much of the wetland is never used, and probably cannot be used, it is not a landscape much visited by the average person. Access is difficult, either from excessive vegetational growth or through being too wet. Nevertheless, many islands have very large areas in this category, not least the most populated islands of New Providence, Grand Bahama, Abaco and Andros.

Most of the wetland areas are covered by shallow water, at least for part of the year, and such areas will change - or *evolve* - gradually into more solid land. Because of this it can be seen that some of the types of wetland are, in fact, simply younger, or older, versions of another type.

THE COASTAL WETLAND

Once part of the offshore area starts to dry out at low tide it can be considered part of the land rather than the sea. Such areas are known as *tidal flats*.

Figure 7.1 In the wettest areas algal mats rather than mangroves help to bind the sediments together. Gradually the floor of the flat will build up and become drier, and a different set of plants will continue the land-forming process.

Figure 7.2 A tidal flat near Stafford Creek, Andros. Black mangroves grow in thick clays which are brown at the surface but black and sulphurous underneath.

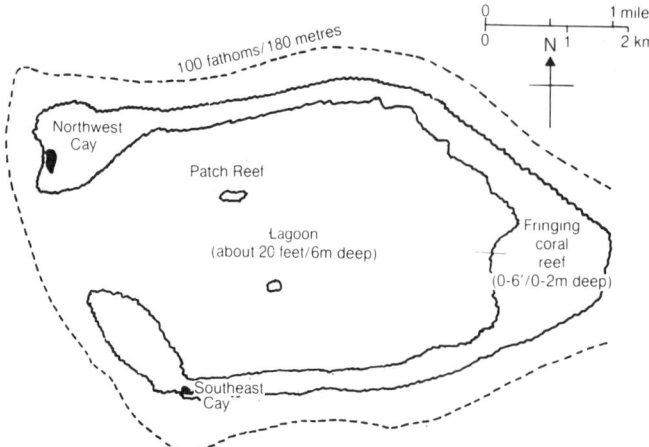

Figure 7.3 Hogsty Reef. The most obvious example of a Pacific-style atoll to be found in The Bahamas. Others may have existed in the past.

■ *Tidal flats* in The Bahamas are sandy in most areas, but on the bankward side of some islands they become more silty or even muddy. If a shallow hole is dug it will be found that within 25 mms (1 inch) of the surface the colour turns to dark grey or black, and *anaerobic* (without oxygen) conditions exist. The water table will be within 30 cms (1 foot) of the surface.

Among the distinguishing features are the plants of the flats. In the wettest areas an *algal mat* (mainly formed from microscopic algae and bacteria), may cover large patches. *Batophora*, which has a club-like shape, can grow on top of the mat (Figure 7.1). Also in the wetter areas will be *red mangroves* and *black mangroves*, the first on their stilt-like roots, the second with radiating pneumatophores all around them (Figure 7.2). The pneumatophores act like snorkels and pass oxygen to the roots below the surface. Towards the edge of the flats the mangroves will increase in number and be joined by the *white mangrove* and *buttonwood* trees. These four species are the main colonisers of the tidal flats and indeed of all the other wetland areas in The Bahamas.

■ *Tidal creeks* Running through a tidal flat there is often a tidal creek. In Andros some of the creeks are extensive and penetrate far inland, such as Fresh Creek and Stafford Creek. At times they may look like rivers on the map, but they are, in fact, marine features. Their current reverses with the tide; they rise and fall with the tide; and they are saline. In some cases, such as Fresh Creek (hence the name), the fresh water lens breaks into the creek at low tide, and the surface layers may be fairly

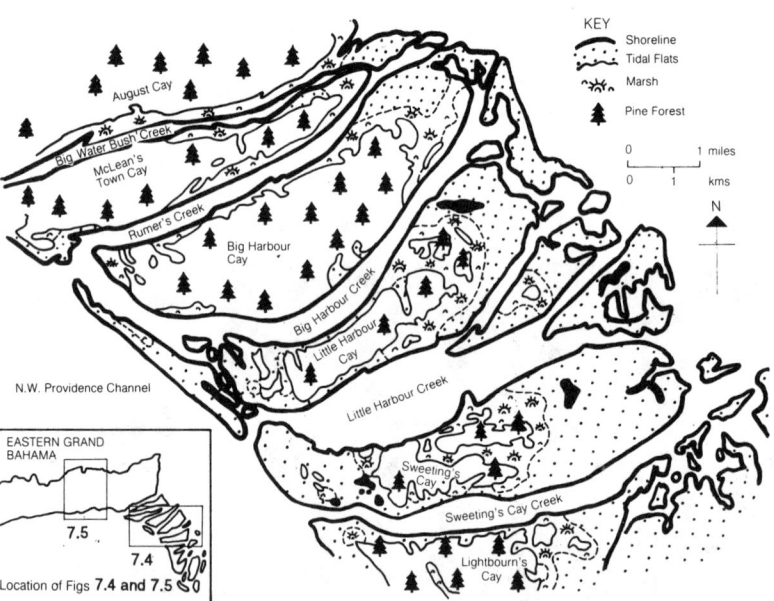

Figure 7.4 Creeks and cays of eastern Grand Bahama. Many tidal passages are to be found in eastern Grand Bahama. The area is a combination of tidal flats, swamps and land. To the north-west the creeks get narrower and the cays bigger. In the south the cays are mainly wetland, such as Sweeting's Cay, with several 'islands' of land being connected by swamp and surrounded by tidal flats. Eventually this area will look like the land in Figure 7.5.

fresh. This does not make them rivers, of course. A good example in New Providence would be Bonefish Pond, as would Pigeon Creek in San Salvador (see figure 5.1).

In Andros and Grand Bahama the name 'creek' is also given to tidal passages between cays, such as Sweeting's Cay Creek and Little Harbour Creek on either side of Sweeting's Cay in eastern Grand Bahama (Figure 7.4, 7.5); and Little Creek and Deep Creek in the Kemp's Bay district of Andros. (The larger channels of this type are known as *bights* in Andros.) Probably the best known channel is Hawksbill Creek, which splits Grand Bahama in two.

Figure 7.5.3 Ancient tidal creeks and channels at Blackwood Point, Grand Bahama. This map shows us the extent to which Grand Bahama was once a cluster of cays cut by numerous channels. Today the creeks have been largely filled in, but the outline of ancient channels can be easily seen by tracing the outline of modern ponds and swamps. The broad tidal flats in the north, and narrow strips in the south, should also be noted. In the past this area would have looked much like the Sweeting's Cay area (Figure 7.2) does today.

■ *Lagoons* This name is applied to a lot of features in the tropics. There are two common definitions, the first being an area of salt water enclosed by a coral reef (Figure 7.3), the second a more specific area of coastal water enclosed by a sand spit (Figure 7.9). When referring to coastal landscapes the second meaning is more useful. If the first were used, *all* of the banks would have to be included and it is better to use this as a geological term rather than a geographical one.[1]

The coral reef or atoll-style lagoon which is most common in the Pacific is rare in the West Indies. In The Bahamas, Hogsty Reef is the only living example which comes close to having the classic set of features. At present, the lagoon is enclosed by a horseshoe-shaped, but submerged coral reef. Only at the two ends is there any land in the form of two small cays (Figure 7.3). Nevertheless, it is typical of the smaller atoll-lagoon type of formation, and with a fall in sea-level could become a horseshoe island enclosing a shallow lagoon. Conception Island is the best example today. More coral atolls have existed in the past, and the shape of Crooked Island/Acklins Island, and the Caicos Bank, suggests that these may once have been lagoons surrounded by coral reefs. Recent drilling on Crooked and Acklins Islands has found much coral below present sea-level to support this idea.

■ *Coastal ponds* The coastal pond is a later stage of the lagoon. The lagoon is a piece of sea enclosed by outbuilding land or a reef, but still open to the sea. In the *pond* stage it is totally enclosed, and eventually it will fill up and become a *swamp*. An example of this is Malcolm Creek in New Providence. This appears as an open lagoon on the map of New Providence for 1963 (surveyed 1958-61), but as a closed pond on the current 1975 edition (surveyed 1974). (see Figure 4.6) Ponds, whatever they are called on the map, are a common feature of the south coast of New Providence, and the bankward coasts of the larger islands. Many of the original salt ponds of the south-eastern islands are of this origin, although some may have been deliberately closed off by man. Lagoons and ponds occupy almost all of the southern half of Long Island's west coast.

The natural *salt pond* is a special case and can occur wherever evaporation is greater than rainfall, a condition found throughout the central and southern Bahamas. In extreme cases, the ponds will dry out altogether in the dry season to create *salt flats,* a relative of the tidal flat. This is only significant in Inagua, however.

A feature of some salt ponds, is their unusual colouring due to the presence of algae or bacteria in them. Algae are encouraged if the pond becomes saline, and it then takes on the colour of the algae, green, brown or red, and sometimes yellow or purple. The algae form an impervious mat several inches thick on the bed of the pond and prevent leakage of the water downwards. When the pond gets extremely salty the algae will die and be decomposed by bacteria, giving off a strong smell. It is at this point that the darker colours are usually created, and this will make the pond hotter, increase evaporation, and lead to the deposition of salt crystals (and perhaps other evaporites such as gypsum). A pond whose salt content is greater

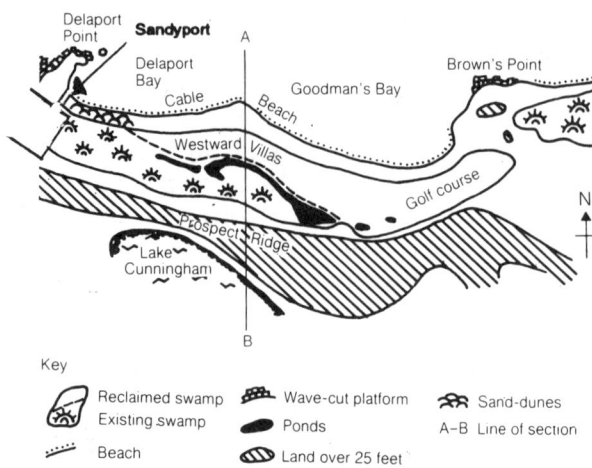

Figure 7.7 *The Cable Beach area is in fact a narrow strip of beach and sand dunes stretching from one headland to another. It is bounded by the sea in the north and swamp to the south. About half of the swamp has been reclaimed.*

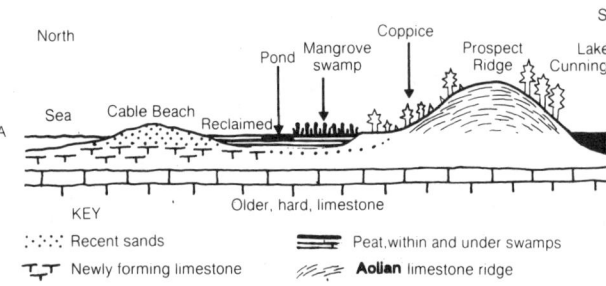

Figure 7.8 *This sketch section shows how the ridge of sand that is Cable Beach trapped the swamp on its inland side. Even without human help it would eventually dry up.*

than sea water (35 parts per thousand) is said to be *hypersaline.* Salinity values as high as 89 parts per thousand in winter, and 123 parts per thousand in summer, have been measured for Granny Lake on San Salvador. Several of the south-eastern islands, including Inagua, have examples of this type.

■ Coastal marshes and swamps

These can either be:

● a development of the *tidal flat* which has become colonised by marsh plants and is no longer below high-tide level, although it still becomes flooded. Much of the marshland of western Andros,

Figure 7.6 *The permanently flooded marshland of West Andros is dominated by red mangroves growing in a white calcareous mud.*

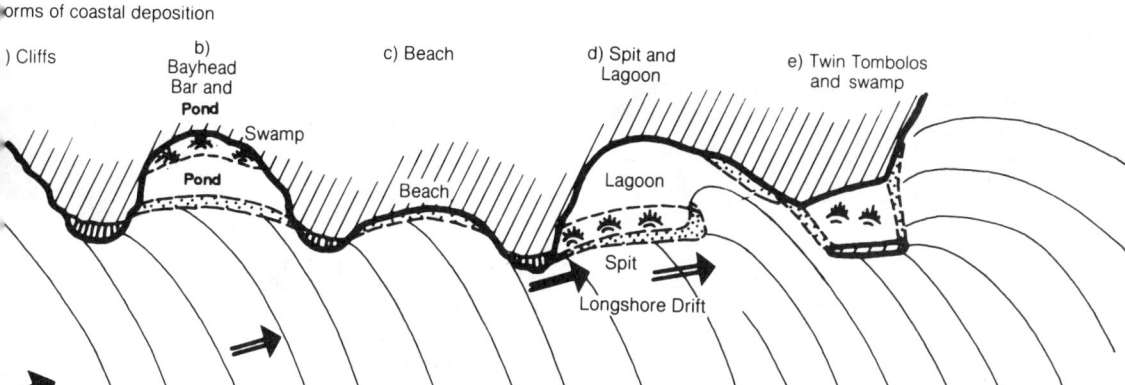

Figure 7.9 Notice that it is the wind that is the driving force. The waves created by the wind cause erosion of the headlands, and transports the sand by longshore drift. The form of deposition depends on the shape of the coast and the depth of the water. Shallow water destroys the waves and leads to deposition.

western Abaco, and northern Grand Bahama is in this category;

● a *pond* which has become filled in, possibly by man, and colonised. Much of the area behind Cable Beach and Delaport in New Providence is of this category, including the sites of Sandyport and Westward Villas and the golf course. South of Westward Villas there are still large areas of ponds, while on the golf course some ponds have been preserved as part of the landscaping. From Brown's Point to Delaport Point sand accumulated in Goodman's Bay and Delaport Bay to such an extent that it sealed off the southern parts, which became ponds and marshes. The northern face of the extensive sand barrier then became the well-known Cable Beach (Figures 7.7, 7.8)

Similar coastal wetland features can also be seen along the coast of nearby Southern Florida. The resort area of Miami Beach is really a large-scale version of Cable Beach. It is separated from Miami by the *lagoon* called Biscayne Bay, and northwards there are a whole series of *ponds* and reclaimed *swamps*.

THE INLAND WETLAND

■ *The lakes* Most of the Bahamian lakes are linear or crescentic in shape, and this easily identifies their origin in depressions between ridges. *Ridgeland lakes* will form wherever the land between two ridges falls below the level of the water table. Usually they are small, but there are many large examples as well (Figure 7.11).

The other type of lake is a shallow, saucer-like depression in the rockland. Presumably this formed while the rockland was still below sea-level, and in some cases tidal currents may have been responsible. In general, *rockland lakes* are less common than ridgeland lakes.

■ *Swamps* All of the lakes mentioned above are shallow, usually only a few feet deep, and rarely more than 3-4 metres (10-12 feet) deep. They often have swampy islands of red mangroves within them and swamps around their edges. Gradually the swamps expand and the lakes shrink, so that all the lakes eventually become swamps.

Both the airfield areas of New Providence occupy land within or next to swamps, as at

Figure 7.10 A lakeshore beach, Little Lake, San Salvador. The beach is made entirely of tiny shells.

Figure 7.11 One of the many ridgeland lakes that occupy the interior of San Salvador

Table 7.1 Typical Bahamian lakes.

Ridgeland lakes	Rockland lakes
Lake Cunningham, New Providence	Lake Killarney, New Providence
Great Lake, San Salvador	Lake Rosa, Inagua
Carmichael Pond, Long Island	Great Lake, Cat Island
Flamingo Pond, Mayaguana	Harold Pond, New Providence

Windsor Field by Lake Killarney, and Oakes Field by Big Pond (see Figure 4.6). All the major Bahamian islands have such marshy areas which were once lakes, and which usually flood when the water table rises in the rainy season.

THE COASTAL LANDSCAPE

Like the wetland, the coastland is a special case of the two dominant landscapes. The features produced where these two meet the coast are quite different, the ridgeland being noted for its sequence of headlands and bays, with occasional stretches of cliffs, while the rockland either contributes to much of the coastal wetland discussed, or produces fairly uninterrupted stretches of low cliff or narrow beach.

THE LANDFORMS OF THE COAST

These fall naturally into two types;

- Landforms due to *erosion:* cliffs and headlands; wave-cut platforms.

- Landforms due to *deposition:* sand-dunes; beaches; spits, bars and tombolos; storm beaches; beach rock.

Landforms due to erosion

■ *Cliffs and headlands* We can consider any area of exposed rock which is being eroded by the sea to be a cliff, even if it is only a few feet high. The *height* of a cliff is determined by the height of the land that the sea is attacking, and not the sea itself. If the landscape at the coast is ridgeland, as at Clifton in New Providence, then continued erosion will create a cliff as high as the ridge. At Clifton Point the cliffs are vertical and reach about 10 metres (30 feet) (Figure 4.15). Other notable cliffs include Hole in the

Wall, Abaco; Morgan's Bluff, Andros; Gordon's Bluff, Crooked Island; The Glass Window, Eleuthera; and Martin Bluff, Cat Island.

The word *'bluff'* is often used to name cliffs. It should be noted that most of the cliffs above are close to the ocean or deepwater channels, and so get little or no protection from shallow water or coral reefs. This allows the waves to strike the coast with their full force (Figure 7.12).

If it is a rockland landscape that forms the coast, and the land is only a few feet above sea level, then the cliff that forms will also be only a few feet high.

Within the cliff face are several well-known geographical features that can be studied in most physical geography textbooks. Examples of all of these can be found in The Bahamas and readers should spend some time looking for them along their nearest rocky shores. Some of the more common features are:

■ *Caves* In order to avoid confusion with the caves already described (p. 56), and which were formed entirely by solution, we should properly term these *sea caves*. Sea caves may be formed entirely by marine forces such as excessive undercutting, or may be the enlargement of a breached solution cave. The Exuma Cays have superb examples, as at Warderick Wells and Rocky Dundas, which was used for several scenes in James Bond films.

Figure 7.12 Eleuthera is noted for its spectacular cliffs, which are found on both sides of the island. These are on the exposed Atlantic shore near the Glass Window.

Caves, like lakes, have a temporary existence, and will eventually collapse. One of the early indications of this collapse is the

Figure 7.13 Cliffs at Cut Cay, San Salvador. A relatively soft limestone is being rapidly eroded to form a varied and attractive coastline containing coves, caves, beaches and headland.

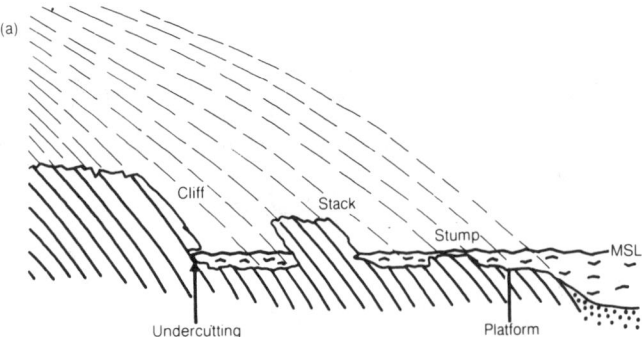

Figure 7.14A Erosion of coastal ridgeland, e.g. Marsh Harbour, Abaco. The lines show the layers making up the ridge, with dashed lines showing how much has already been eroded.

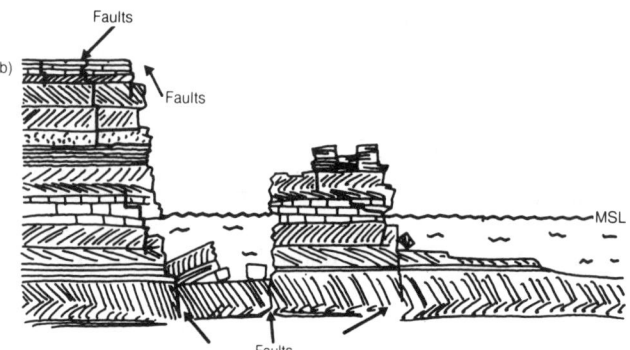

Figure 7.14B Erosion of horizontally bedded limestone, e.g. Clifton, New Providence. The high land here (8-10 metres /25-30 feet high) was built up in level beds. The photographs below and on page 47 show sloping deposition on horizontally eroded bedding planes. The result is a pattern of rectangular faults, and blocks breaking off, producing a vertical cliff face.

during a severe hurricane. Well known by name is Hole in the Wall, Abaco, but few get a chance to see it. Undoubtedly there are many others, but they are even more fragile than caves and often quite small (Figure 7.16), so they have to be looked for.

■ *Stacks and stumps*   When part of a headland becomes detached, such as by the collapse of an arch or the erosion of a channel, the detached part is known as a *stack*. If this is in turn eroded so that it is awash at high tide it is known as a *stump*. Many headlands show a progression of these features, as at Delaport Point in New Providence, but unless the headland itself has high cliffs the stack will not be very spectacular (see Figure 7.17).

■ *Honeycomb weathering*   This is a general term given to the jagged surface of bare rock along the shore. It is most common in the dune rock (Figure 7.19). The vertical edges may be pieces of *limestone crust*, but if spiky they are more likely to be *fossilised plant roots* (called *rhizomorphs* - from 'rhizo' = root, and 'morph' = shape). The sand-dunes which eventually formed the ridges had various plants growing in them, and their roots secreted substances that hardened the soil or sediments around them.

blow hole, a hole in the roof caused by the pressure of waves breaking into the cave. The well-known Preacher's Cave in North Eleuthera is a good example showing many features including blow holes.

■ *Arches*   When a cave erodes right through a headland or any narrow piece of land, an arch is said to be formed. The Glass Window of Eleuthera was the most famous example, but its arch was destroyed in 1926

Figure 7.15 A sea cave enlarged by wave action in the cliffs at Clifton, New Providence

Figure 7.16 A small arch on the south coast of Long Island

When erosion takes place in the spray zone of the shore the hardened rock of the rhizomorph stands out as a spiky projection. If it is broken off and inspected a small hole will be found running through the centre. This is where the actual root was, although traces of black carbon are usually all that remain of it.

In addition to these resistant features we must also consider the action of various boring *blue-green algae,* and *molluscs* which live off the algae and bore little hollows into the rock. The minute algae penetrate the pore spaces of the rock in such large numbers that the area they colonise is discoloured and known as the *black zone.* Due to their action, small flakes of rock are continually breaking off to leave behind small white depressions which add to the honeycomb effect. Even more noticeable is the action of the snails (snails are molluscs and the most common are the limpets, top shells, and bleeding tooth) which in some cases can be found several inches deep inside the rock, having burrowed a hole the diameter of their shell to do so. With large numbers of snails all doing the same thing the rock soon becomes pitted and honeycombed, with razor-sharp edges between the holes. The general term for this action is *bio-erosion.*

■ *Wave-cut platforms* This is a very common landform which develops in front of cliffs. It is simply the uneroded base of the cliff after the shoreline has been cut back. It is usually visible as a rocky platform extending out from the shore, but wherever there have been falls in sea-level it will appear as a rocky (and honeycombed) shelf a few feet above sea-level. As Bahamian rocks are soft and erode easily, these are common features in all the cliffed areas.

Landforms due to deposition

■ *Sand-dunes* These are fairly common in The Bahamas, and are prominent on the north side of Paradise Island, behind Harbour Island's Pink Sand beach, along much of the east coast of Eleuthera, Cat Island and Long Island, and on the Atlantic shores of San Salvador, for instance.

Figure 7.17 A stack being undercut by wave action and bio-erosion, south coast of Long Island

Figure 7.18 Rhizomorphs exposed in the face of an eroding dune ridge on Long Island's east coast

The beach area collects sand as a result of wave action, and at low tide this is dried and exposed to the wind. The wind blows the finest sand up the beach, above the high-tide level. Seaweed at this point may help to trap it, but more important will be salt-tolerant plants (known as *'halophytic'* vegetation) that can live just above the high-tide level. These plants include the railroad vine, sea purslane and saltwort, all of which creep along the sand putting down roots at intervals. They soon cover a wide area and trap more sand, which they grow above as fast as it accumulates. The built-up sand at this point is known as the *fore dune,* and paves the way for another range of plants to establish themselves on the face of what will be the main dune.

Some sand is blown through the first line of plants and the dune spreads inland. Here there is more protection from the salt and spray, and a different range of plants is found. These are more varied and include grasses like sand-spur (or 'burr') grass, sea oats, and succulent plants like the spider lily and bay geranium.

The sand-dune may reach as high as 12-15 metres (40-50 feet) in this stage in The Bahamas. Behind the crest, which is providing protection from the wind to an increasing degree, a much bigger range of plants will develop, including the sea grape, geiger tree, the grey nicker or nicker vine, and the silver top palmetto. Quite often the Australian Pine (Casuarina) originally introduced by man will be found in this zone.

Figure 7.19 Jagged coastal rock at Gambier on New Providence. The honeycomb effect is caused by differential erosion of the limestone rock and the numerous rhizomorphs it contains. This type of 'ironbound' shoreline is most common where the ridgeland meets the coast.

Once formed, the sand-dune is a natural barrier against wind and wave action and so protects the land behind it. We know that the cementing of the dune sands into dune rock, and the repeated building up of sand-dunes against each other, give rise to the long ridges common in The Bahamas, but we must also realise that the modern dune is a landform in its own right. Where it is wide enough, tourist and other accommodation may be built on top of it, as on Harbour Island, and especially on Paradise Island. It also provides a popular environment for golf courses, and open woodland for recreational use. Being highly porous it will hold rainwater and is used as an *aquifer* by many houses and small hotels along the coast, a practice quite common in Eleuthera. Along the shore sand-dunes provide protection for coastal roads, and also create a screen between beach users and the traffic. Unfortunately, dunes are easily eroded if their vegetation is damaged, and many of those which once existed along West Bay Street in New Providence have now been lost. Remnants can still be seen at Orange Hill, and by Delaport Point. Heavy use of the beach and the practice of parking cars on and in the dunes has uncovered the sand and allowed it to be blown away. Even on the more secluded Paradise Island misuse is causing erosion, but elsewhere in The Bahamas good examples still exist, as on Long Island and Cat Island.

It is fair to ask why even the biggest dunes today are nowhere near the size of the ridges of solid limestone. It seems that the conditions that created the multiple dune ridges do not exist in The Bahamas today, and that, when they were being built, sea-level was rising and a greater supply of sand was available. In fact, even the dunes which we have today seem to be relics of the recent past, and this is one of the reasons for their relatively easy destruction.

■ *Beaches* These are well known and require little additional description. In general the more sheltered bank-side coasts will have fewer and narrower beaches than the exposed windward coasts. Eleuthera provides good examples, and the contrast found in New Providence between say Cable Beach and Adelaide Beach is also typical. The larger beaches are much more varied, often being backed by sand-dunes and having their own minor landforms such as increasingly steep *ridges* higher up the beach. These are due to different high tide levels and wave sizes. Another feature is the alternating sequence of rises and falls known as **beach cusps**, formed by the swirling action of large waves as they strike the beach. Generally speaking, the larger the waves, the wider the beach, because the waves can carry the sediment that much further up it (Figure 7.20).

Why we have a beach in one place but not in another is an interesting question. We know that beaches can form on both windy and sheltered coasts, and so can cliffs, so clearly that is not the answer. There are really three things we have to consider:

- a supply of sediment;
- a means of transport;
- a trap for the sediment.

- *Sediment* is generated in shallow water, particularly on and behind the reefs. Beaches are not likely to form where there is deep water right offshore, and, in fact, we have already seen that cliffs are common in most of these locations. The beach must be close to a good supply of sediment.

- *Transport* is needed to ensure that the sediment reaches the beach. Wave action is the most important means of transport, and tidal and wind-blown currents are only likely to be significant where they are exceptionally strong, or the sediment is very fine. Bahamian beaches have sand-sized grains almost everywhere, but there are two areas noted for their muddy deposits - the Mud to the west of Andros, and the Marls of the Bight of Abaco. The shores near these deposits are mainly tidal flats with low muddy cliffs, but some shelly beaches have also formed.

Large waves are very efficient at moving sand and large particles, and storm waves (see p. 81) are noted for their exceptional destructive power as well as their ability to build up large beaches. Waves both carry the material to the shore, and then along it, a movement known as *longshore drift.*

Finally, the sediment has to be *trapped* or it will be swept away by the longshore drift and eventually lost in deep water. Probably

Figure 7.20 A narrow beach along the west coast of Long Island. Beach rock from a previous beach at a higher sea level is eroding immediately behind it to produce the typical beach rock slabs.

two-thirds of all the sediment produced on the Bahamian banks is swept off into the deep water channels and ultimately into the Atlantic, where it settles out in great fans (like deltas), or plains of abyssal ooze. Only a small part of the rest ever gets to the beaches. A typical beach trap will be between two headlands which will prevent the sand from escaping.

If we study the north shore of New Providence we can illustrate some of these points (see Figure 7.9). Brown's Point marks the beginning of Goodman's Bay and Cable Beach, which extends with a few rocky interruptions as far as Delaport Point. This is a typical **bay-head beach**, and smaller examples are found between Delaport Point and Rock Point, and Rock Point as far as Caves' Point. West of Caves' Point is the Gambier Beach which ends at the rocky outcrop at Gambier Village. Love Beach marks the end of this sequence and leads us to some rather different types of deposition, including spits and tombolos . Beach erosion is extensive along this coast and many of the rocky areas were once sandy beaches.

■ *Spits, bars and tombolos* These are distinguished from beaches by having water on both sides. The seaward side usually has a beach, and indeed many beaches are simply parts of these rather larger systems of coastal deposition.

● *A bar* usually develops in a bay instead of a beach if the waves lose their energy before reaching the shore. The sediment is then deposited in shallow water and eventually builds up to trap a lagoon behind it. Cable Beach was probably a bar before it took on its present form. Nearly all the features enclosing the ponds and lagoons mentioned earlier (p. 72) are bars or spits (Figures 7.21 to 7.25).

● *A spit* is distinguished from a bar by being attached to the land at one end. The spit at Xanadu in New Providence is a good example. It extends from Old Fort to Creek Point, where Lightbourne Creek enters into a small lagoon, the rest of which has become a quite large swamp (Figure 7.22, 7.25).

● *A tombolo* is similar to a bar, but one end is joined to an offshore island or cay, and the other to the shore. As a result it forms a natural causeway. Until the 1830's, Lyford Cay really was a cay and boats could pass inside it at high water. Now the land is 3 metres above sea-level, and only the name remains. This is, in fact, an example of a *double tombolo*, because sand built up on the west side in West Bay and on the north side as well (Figure 7.25).

These features depend very much on the action of *longshore drift* for their creation, especially the spit. In New Providence the prevailing easterly winds cause sediment to be swept westwards along the northern and the southern shores. As the sediment rounds each headland some is trapped to form bay-head beaches and bars, or if there is no other headland it simply builds a long tongue of sand out parallel to the shore and forms a spit. Eventually the remaining sediment reaches Simms' Point or Clifton Point and it is then swept on into deeper water and lost. Spits and bars can be seen at Long Point, Cay Point and Malcolm Creek along the south coast (see Figure 4.6).

■ *Storm beaches* (Storm berms) The lasting effects of storms and hurricanes are not always realised, nor is the frequency with which they occur. Generally speaking storms are the most important builders and destroyers of the coast, and much of what we see today is the result of their work in the past.

We should first of all consider their *frequency*. In an 87 year period, meteorological records showed that hurricane conditions existed at Nassau on ten occasions (and we can assume the same frequently for the rest of The Bahamas). This is equivalent to 115/1000 years, or in the geological period from the Pleistocene to the present, a total of 115 000 hurricanes in any part of the country! In geological terms, it is fair to say that hurricanes are regular and frequent visitors.

We must now consider the effect of these forces. Essentially they have enormous lifting and transporting power, and on the coast will operate at a significantly higher level than normal sea-level. This is because:

- Under storm conditions sea-level will rise, a condition known as a *storm surge*. Typically, in a severe hurricane, normal tides will be suspended and a new level about 3 metres higher will be established. This is due to the low atmospheric pressure common to hurricane activity, and to the wind piling water up in enclosed areas. (Should the wind reverse, and blow offshore, tide levels may drop enough to completely expose the floor of shallow bays, etc.)

- *Waves* will be very high, 3-4 metres (10-14 feet) at least in exposed areas. Due to the higher tide levels, they will pass over protecting reefs and banks with ease and bring the most severe conditions to previously protected land.

It is therefore common to find that a completely new shore-line has been created.

There will be severe damage as much as 6 metres above normal sea-level, and for the same reasons sediment can be deposited up to this level. Under hurricane conditions, a lot of fine sediment will be stirred up from the sea-floor, and flooded buildings have often been found to be full of mud and sand when the waters have receded. In natural landscapes this material can add signifi-

Figure 7.21 Narrow beach backed by beach ridges which have formed a spit on the south coast of Samana Cay. A secondary spit is forming in the foreground. Based on corings and the current rate of deposition the main spit formed in 200-250 years.

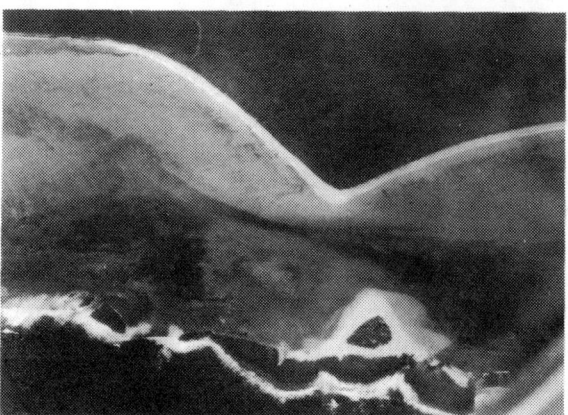

Figure 7.22 Bird Point, near Dumfries Settlement, Cat Island. This point is a cuspate foreland built out from the coast by successive beaches. Eventually it will create a tombolo joining it to the offshore cay, where the sand is also accumulating.

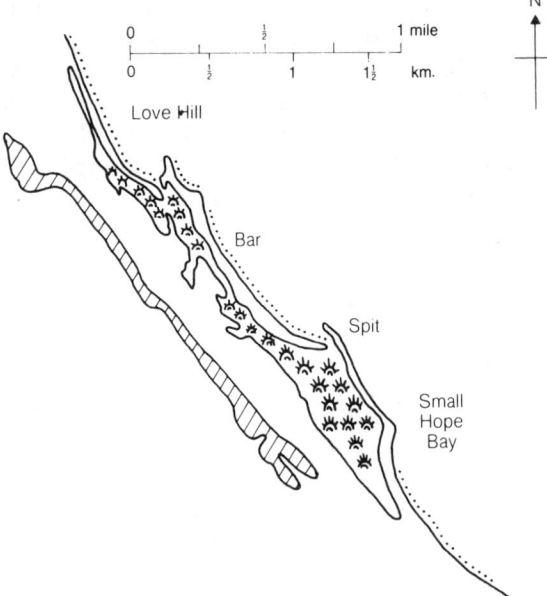

Figure 7.23 An offshore bar, about a kilometre long north of Fresh Creek. On the seaboard side are beaches and on the landward side swamp and mangroves now fill the lagoon This must be very much like the Cable Beach area in New Providence before the beaches joined up.

cantly to the land surface. Studies on the western side of Andros have shown that for a hundred miles along the coast there is a wedge of soft sediments up to 4 metres (13 feet) thick that is almost entirely due to storm waves during the last 15 years.

Much more striking is the boulder-sized material, anything in size from a conch shell to 20 kilogram (44 lbs) pieces of brain coral, that is swept up in great banks behind the regular beaches or even on top of low cliffed and rocky coasts - this is what forms the *storm beach* or *berm* (Figure 7.26). All the material that has collected offshore over the years is added to all the additional material broken up by the storm, and the whole mass is thrown high onto the shore. Once there, the debris will remain in place almost permanently, for there are no other forces strong enough to dislodge it. So impressive do these ridges of boulders seem that they are easily mistaken for man-made embankments or walls. Another name for these ridges is *boulder ramparts*.

■ *Beach rock* This was first discussed when dealing with diagenesis (p. 50). Beach rock is a common feature of Bahamian beaches. It is easily broken and will often crumble between the fingers. It is very porous and the pores can be seen with the naked eye, as can the cement holding the grains together. Unlike dune rock, it weathers to form a smooth surface and has a sandy colour, although it is often stained black on the surface by blue-green encrusting algae. It is developed from beach sand under the surface of the beach, but it is often exposed during periods of beach erosion (Figure

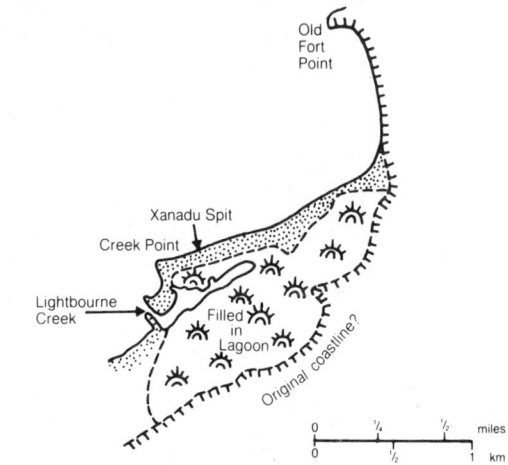

Figure 7.24 The spit at Xanadu reaches 10 metres (30 feet) in height. It originally enclosed a lagoon, but swamp development has reduced the penetration of the sea to the small tidal creek.

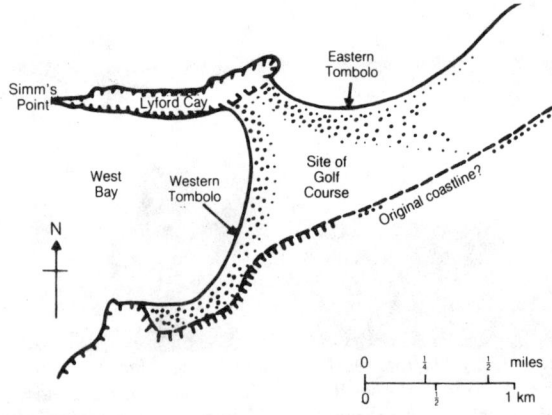

Figure 7.25 A possible reconstruction of the connection of Lyford Cay to New Providence.

Figure 7.26 (a) An impressive storm beach built up by Hurricane David on Pigeon Cay, off the Andros Coast.

Figure 7.26 (b) shows a close up of the debris making up the beach, mainly conch shells and coral pieces.

7.27). If this happens, it erodes quickly to form large regularly sized rectangular blocks (Figure 7.28). It is this uniformity that has led people to believe that long stretches of fossil beach rock are, in fact, man-made roads, and those seen underwater off Bimini have been erroneously described as the *'pavements of Atlantis'!* [2] However, in a country naturally short of building stone, these sturdy slabs do serve a useful purpose for building garden walls, parapets and even buildings, although their softness and porosity do make them of limited value for this purpose (Figure 7.29).

Another of the striking things about this rock is the speed at which it forms, and it is possible to find quite modern rubbish such as bottles and cans in some deposits.

In some islands, such as San Salvador, beach rock from higher sea-levels has been preserved in low cliffs now exposed above the modern beaches. By looking at this rock, end on, it is possible to see a cross-section of the ancient beaches, showing beach cusps, worm-casts and tunnels, various grades of sand, and, in fact, a complete profile of the prehistoric shore-line (see Figure 7.20).

Figure 7.27 Undisturbed beach rock on Saunder's Beach, New Providence. The regular jointing has deceived many people into believing theat these rocks were cut and made by man.

Figure 7.28 Beach rock on San Salvador. Note the smooth surface, slabby form, and ease of erosion.

Figure 7.29 Beach rock in use in San Salvador. Natural slabs of beach rock have been trimmed to form the walls of this attractive house and garden. The rock was taken from the beach just a few metres away.

1   Map names can be confusing when they do not agree with geographical descriptions. It should be remembered that the given name may refer to the state at the time the feature was named. Hence a creek may now be a pond. Also local usage of the names may have been different, such as a creek being used for anything with a tidal flow, or a pond for any form of still water.

2   For a study showing the natural formation of these 'roads', and a general discussion on the Atlantis issue, see Shinn, E A, 1978.

8 THE NATURAL RESOURCES

A natural resource is something provided by nature, but which usually needs some sort of development before it can be used. *Soil* and *water* exist everywhere – they are *ubiquitous* and they are only special in the extent to which they are particularly better or worse than might be expected. There is another group of resources which are not so common, however, and these include the many kinds of *mineral resources* which a country may or may not have, depending on its geology and climate. These are described as *sporadic*. The Bahamas is not well endowed with these, for it has no metallic ores, nor have any economic amounts of fossil fuels been discovered. However, there are indications that *petroleum* may be present, and there are two non-metallic minerals which are exploited on a large scale, namely *salt* and *aragonite*.

Bahamian soils

A soil is usually considered as a structured or layered medium with a distinctive mineral and organic content. If we briefly consider some of the more important soil properties we can see the way in which Bahamian soils relate to world soils in general.

- Soils may be *acid* or *alkaline*. As calcium carbonate is an alkaline compound, Bahamian soils are invariably alkaline, and may be excessively so.
- The *texture* of soils ranges from clayey to sandy to stony. Clay is rare, and sandy and stony soils are common in The Bahamas. A *loam* is a mixture of sand and clay and is an excellent soil texture. Despite the common use of this term for some Bahamian soils, there are no true loams in The Bahamas.
- The layers in a soil are known as its *horizons*, and fully developed, *mature*, soils usually have four or five that are readily identifiable (Figure 8.1a). Thin limestone soils may be restricted to only one or two horizons above the bedrock, and as a result Bahamian soils are invariably classed as *immature* by world standards, and may also be called *protosols* (ie a *'pre-soil'*). For this reason they are often very thin or discontinuous.
- There are two major groups of soils, the *pedalfers* common to wetter areas, relatively rich in iron and aluminium, and subject to *leaching* (the washing out of minerals by percolating rainwater); and the *pedocals* which are common in drier

areas and have a high calcium content. All the Bahamian soils except the laterites are pedocals.

- *Fertility* in a soil is measured in terms of its content of the chemical bases such as calcium (Ca), potassium (K), and magnesium (Mg). Also required is nitrogen (N) derived from the atmosphere by certain plants. Bahamian soils are invariably deficient in potassium and nitrogen.

To sum up, most Bahamian soils are so poorly developed that in a normal classification they would either be left out, or put in a separate *Azonal* (that is 'without definition') or immature category. However, despite the limitations, The Bahamas does have a growing medium that can be recognised and classified, and the following is such a classification:

- Red clay soils
- Sedimentary soils
- Organic soils

RED CLAY SOILS

Originally it was thought that these clay deposits were residual soils, derived from impurities after the surface layers of the limestone had been dissolved (Land Resource Study, 1977). When limestone is dissolved, a small residue of its impurities is left behind - providing that these are, of course, insoluble. With Bahamian limestone usually 99%-99.5% pure, it would take a minimum of 30 metres of limestone to provide just 15-30 cms (6-12 inches) of residue, providing none of it was washed away!

Muhs[1] has now shown that the residual theory is quite inadequate to account for the thicknesses of red soils found in the Caribbean. What we see today was unquestionably derived from the Sahara, but was deposited on the surface of the limestone where we find it now. Most likely this occurred during the most recent glacials rather than the interglacials, as the Sahara was drier at these times.

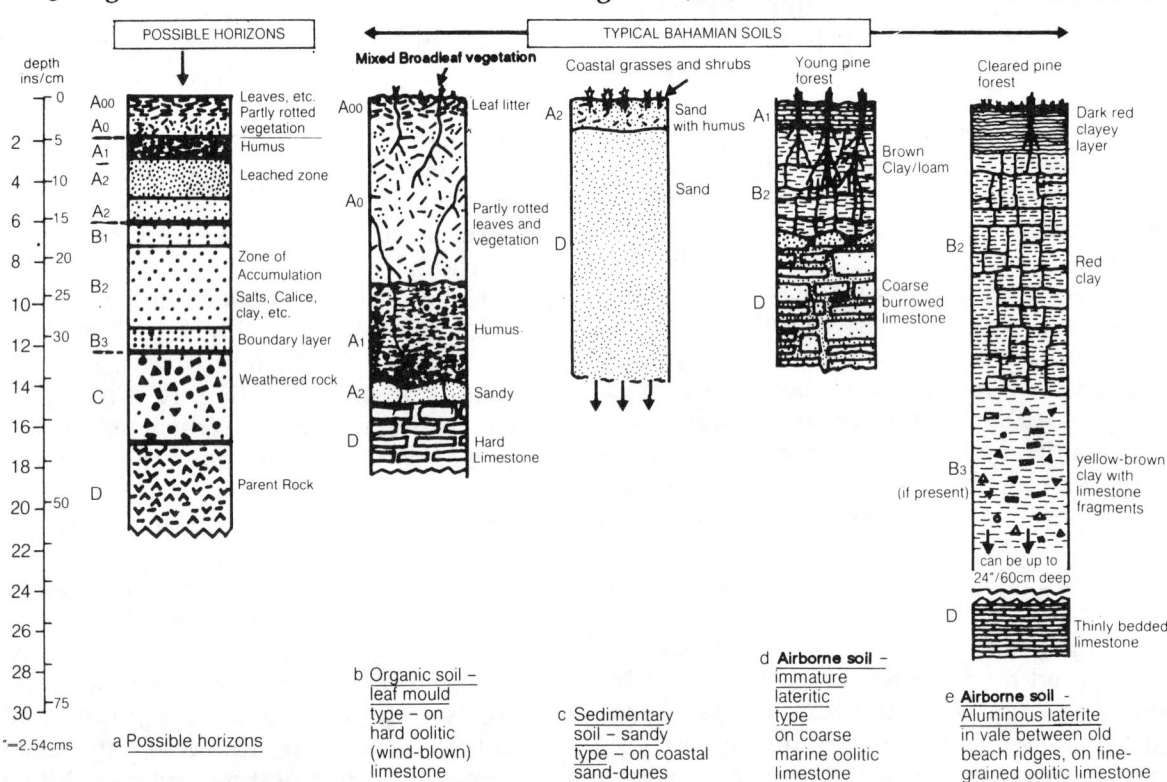

Figure 8.1 Bahamian soils

Figure 8.2 Soil that the Arawaks used! This is typical 'salt and pepper' or whiteland soil, at Pigeon Creek on San Salvador. Having been well used over the years, it is dark with humus.

In this case most of the red soil found in the Bahamas arrived here about 125 000 years ago.

The nature of this soil, mainly insoluble iron and aluminium oxides, is that of a *laterite*, but it is one that formed in the Sahara, not in the Bahamas. Apart from this there are some local conditions that affect the distribution of these soils. It has always been noted that the red soil was found in the vales between the ridges, or on the undulating surface of the older limestones as in Eleuthera. It seems likely that there has been some concentration in the hollows between high ground, much as might be expected from a wind-borne deposit. Also the older ridgeland landscapes will have accumulated more Sahara dust than the younger limestones, which rarely show any red soil concentrations.

Bearing these factors in mind, we can now consider the two types of soil that fall in this category:

■ *Aluminous laterite* (Bahamas red loam) (Figure 8.1e) This soil is a shallow red clay, containing a lot of free *sesquioxides* (a sesquioxide is an insoluble oxide) of iron (Fe_2O_3) and aluminium (Al_2O_3). It is the high aluminium content that gives them their name, and they are in fact cousins to the *bauxites* of Jamaica which may have had the same origin. It occurs in small basins, pockets, on the lower slopes and the vales between ridges, and on the upland formed by coalescing ridges. Humus is totally absent, and nutritionally the soil is virtually sterile. Although the clay swells with water, it does not release it easily and so it is not readily available to plants. When the clay is dry it becomes brick-hard and unworkable, so it is best mixed with sand or a sedimentary soil to improve both porosity and tilth. Although it occurs on most islands, it is best seen on the ridgelands of Eleuthera, Cat Island, San Salvador, New Providence, and between the old beach ridges of the northern section of Abaco. Local farmers plant a wide range of crops in this soil, especially in Eleuthera. The reason for this is not the fertility, which is poor, but the relative absence of calcium carbonate and phosphates, and the free sesquioxide conditions, all of which are necessary for the most popular crop, pineapples.

■ *Immature aluminous laterite* (Bahamas stony loam) (Figure 8.1d) This appears as a shallow dark brown clay and pebble mixture which is considerably more weathered than any of the other types of soil. The upper horizon contains fair amounts of organic matter, and the lower horizon has large amounts of free sesquioxides in a hard, dry and crumbly texture. Unfortunately the soil is never consistently deep enough, even over very small areas, to provide an adequate rooting depth for agricultural crops. In its original state and when covered by coppice vegetation it has, and can be, farmed by traditional shifting cultivation methods. It may be suitable for modern farming if the underlying rockland can be broken and crushed sufficiently to give a greater depth to the soil.

In central Abaco it is associated with weathered beach ridges in the Norman's Castle area near Treasure Cay. As the beach deposits contain more shelly and organic deposits than the oolite, the weathered limestone produces a better artificial soil when crushed, and this area has been much used for farming. The immature laterite is simply ploughed in with the limestone.

SEDIMENTARY SOILS

These belong to a group of soils in which the rock itself is still in an unconsolidated form. However, a sand or any other sediment cannot become a soil until at least some degree of organic matter has been added to it, and these soils vary according to the amount of vegetation that is growing on them. Usually the darker they become the better they are.

■ *Sandy soils* (Whiteland) These are based on geologically recent (Holocene) marine calcareous sands. The upper layer is usually grey or greyish-brown, although reddish-brown is also possible. The depth of this layer is normally less than 12 inches and the rest is pure mineral sand. This soil is commonly found as a narrow discontinuous strip along the coastline, especially on the windward side, of nearly all of the islands. It is often referred to locally as 'whiteland'. The landscape is coastal and varies from short, steeply sloping sand dunes to gently rolling, almost flat, land. In Abaco and Eleuthera a certain amount of agriculture is undertaken in the more sheltered areas where the organic content of the upper horizon is high and where fresh water is available close to the surface (Figure 8.1c and 8.2).

■ *Sandy soils with caliche nodules* There are a variety of these soils, according to the concentration and depth of the nodules. They are exclusively found in the south-eastern islands with the single exception of Treasure Cay, Abaco. They are a development of the sandy soils in a drier climate. It appears that dissolved calcium carbonate is not washed through the soil, but is drawn to the surface by evaporation, where it is redeposited as a crust or as nodules within the sand. These nodules can vary from as small as peppercorns to as big as footballs (Figure 8.3). If they are well below the surface this soil can be farmed, as it is in Acklins and Inagua. The presence of a mantle of leaf litter is important to fertility, as the lower layers are raw sands and infertile. In most cases the surface layer contains a grey cemented sand which has little fertility, and in areas such as Long Island and Cat Island is unlikely to be of any value.

■ *Limesilt* This is scarcely a soil at all, although it usually supports a thicket type of vegetation. Basically it consists of raw deposits of calcareous silt, often mixed with

Figure 8.3 Nodules from the soils of the south-east Bahamas. They can vary greatly in size, can be extremely numerous, and eventually may link up to form a hard pan.

limestone blocks. It is only known in the far south-western islands.

ORGANIC SOILS

To some extent these soils can be seen as the opposite of the sedimentary soils. In the latter case the soil was largely mineral and lacked organic matter, but in this case there is an organic deposit with no mineral depth. The extreme case occurs in swamps where many feet of pure peat may form.

■ *Leafmould soil* (Black land, Provision land) This is the typical soil of the rockland. It most often consists of a very variable depth of humus over less than 15 cms of humic sandy earth. This in turn covers the irregular and often outcropping parent limestone rock (Figure 8.4). It is by far the most common soil in The Bahamas and accounts for more than 90% of the surface area of some islands. However, there is a great deal of variation in the depth of the profile and the irregularity of the limestone surface underneath. Karstic weathering has produced solution holes often referred to as *banana holes,* wherever there is sufficient water and organic material in them to allow the planting of bananas or other crops. Other holes are known as pot holes and give rise to the term 'pot hole farming', which typifies the nature of the soil as a patchy medium at best.

In some flat areas such as parts of Eleuthera, the surface of the limestone is only a few feet above the water table and with the aid of the potholes allows permanent farming of suitable crops, such as tomatoes. In the extensive flat areas of the pine islands this soil may occur in association with immature laterite, and in many cases the underlying limestone is suitable for mechanical crushing to provide an artificially improved soil over 22.5 cms (9 inches) deep. It is only in such a combination of circumstances that the leafmould soil can provide a continuous cover on which modern mechanised farming can be successfully practised.

Figure 8.4 A ridgeland soil profile. Note that only the horizons of solid rock and weathered rock are present. The 'soil' is in fact the organic debris trapped among the rock fragments. Nevertheless this is enough to support a typical coppice vegetation.

■ *Muck soils* These are deep peaty soils which occupy wide hollows. They are subject to periodic flooding and are usually waterlogged to within a foot of the surface. They cannot be used on their own, but by adding crushed rock and sand they can be 'reclaimed', a practice which has been quite successful on a small scale in Exuma. At Mount Thompson fresh-water ponds have been reclaimed using sand from nearby dunes. This has proved to be the basis of the most intensive small-scale farming seen in the Bahamas.

In conclusion it will be realised that outside of traditional shifting cultivation Bahamian soils are rarely used in their natural state. They are poor in nutrients and require heavy fertilisation. Mechanised agriculture is restricted by the shallowness of the soil and the frequent outcrops of bare rock. Although the deeper sandy soils do not have this limitation they have the additional problem of high alkalinity. Salinity, calcification and leaching may be additional problems. In practice the soil that is farmed may well have very little to do with the normal properties of a soil. It is more likely that the extent of flat land, availability of fresh water, depth to the water table, and nature and porosity of the bedrock will be the prime considerations.

WATER RESOURCES

Rainfall is the sole source of fresh water in The Bahamas. Other countries in addition may have large reserves underground and receive further supplies from rivers, lakes, glaciers or snowfields. There is also only one means of storing water naturally, in underground *lenses* (Figure 8.8). Without rivers to replenish them the many lakes are both shallow and brackish.

It therefore follows that the study of water resources must first examine the factors affecting the amount of rainfall, then its percolation into the bedrock, and finally its preservation, pollution or extraction while underground (Figure 8.9).

RAINFALL - HOW MUCH, AND WHERE DOES IT GO?

The amount of rain that falls at any place can be quite variable. It depends on the following factors: (See also Chapter 9)

■ *Nearness to North America* When cold winter air leaves the USA, it arrives in The Bahamas as a *cold front*. Such cold fronts bring rain, and the colder the front the more rain there is likely to be. However, these fronts are warmed up rapidly as they move south-eastwards across The Bahamas, and so it is the northern islands that receive the most rain, and the south-eastern the least of all. This rainfall is particularly important as it falls during the winter dry season. (See Figure 8.5, and p.115)

■ *Size of the islands* In summer, the trade winds are laden with moisture and very unstable. Any disturbance leading to the uplift of air can cause rain of a *convectional* type. This may be due to heat rising off the land, or to uplift and turbulence caused when the winds cross the coast or ridges of high land. Often it is a combination of both that leads to rain.

Obviously it is the largest islands that generate the most heat and create the largest convection currents. The largest islands are:

Table 8.1 Size of largest islands

Island	Area (sq kms)	Area (sq miles)
Andros	5 980 sq kms	(2 300 sq miles)
Abaco	1 690 sq kms	(649 sq miles)
Inagua	1 550 sq kms	(596 sq miles)
G. Bahama	1 380 sq kms	(530 sq miles)

No other island exceeds 560 square kilometres (200 square miles), and most of them are long and narrow like central Eleuthera. Under these conditions any heating (probably little) and turbulence (probably a lot) that produces rain is of limited value, because the winds pass over these islands so quickly that the rain falls in the sea on the leeward side. However, if the island is broad from east to west, as in North and South Eleuthera, and Mayaguana, for instance, the rainfall may be significant and good fresh water lenses can develop.

■ *Hurricanes* These generate considerable amounts of rain over a very large area, often as much as 320 kilometres (200 miles) from their centre. The Bahamas can expect to receive about a quarter of its rainfall from tropical storms or hurricanes in any one year. Unfortunately, as hurricanes are unpredictable, this is a very unreliable source. In severe hurricanes the damage from too much water- flooding will outweigh the advantages.

As a result of these factors we can conclude that the northern and larger islands will have the most rain, and the south-eastern and smaller islands will have the least (Figure 8.5). When the rain falls and it is measured we get an indication of the amount that has actually landed on the Earth's surface. Of this only a small part, 25% or less, will actually be collected in a fresh water lens. This is because:

- Some water will *evaporate* from the surface. Evaporation will be high in areas bare of vegetation (no shade) and from lakes. Man-made surfaces such as roads also increase evaporation.

- Where there are plants, water will be transferred from the soil to the foliage and *transpired* into the atmosphere. As evaporation and transpiration both result in the loss of water back to the atmosphere they are often considered together, and the loss is known as *evapotranspiration.*

- Some water *runs off* the surface into the sea, but as there are no rivers in The Bahamas this is not a big problem.

- Some water that reaches the fresh-water lens also runs into the sea. It flows across the surface of the fresh water lens, through the pores and passages in the limestone, until it reaches the coast. The narrower the island the shorter the distance to the sea and the thinner the lens is likely to be. Lenses in the narrower islands are often only 3 to 6 metres thick while in the larger islands they may be between 15 and 30 metres thick, and one lens in Andros is reported to exceed 30 metres in thickness (see Figure 8.10).

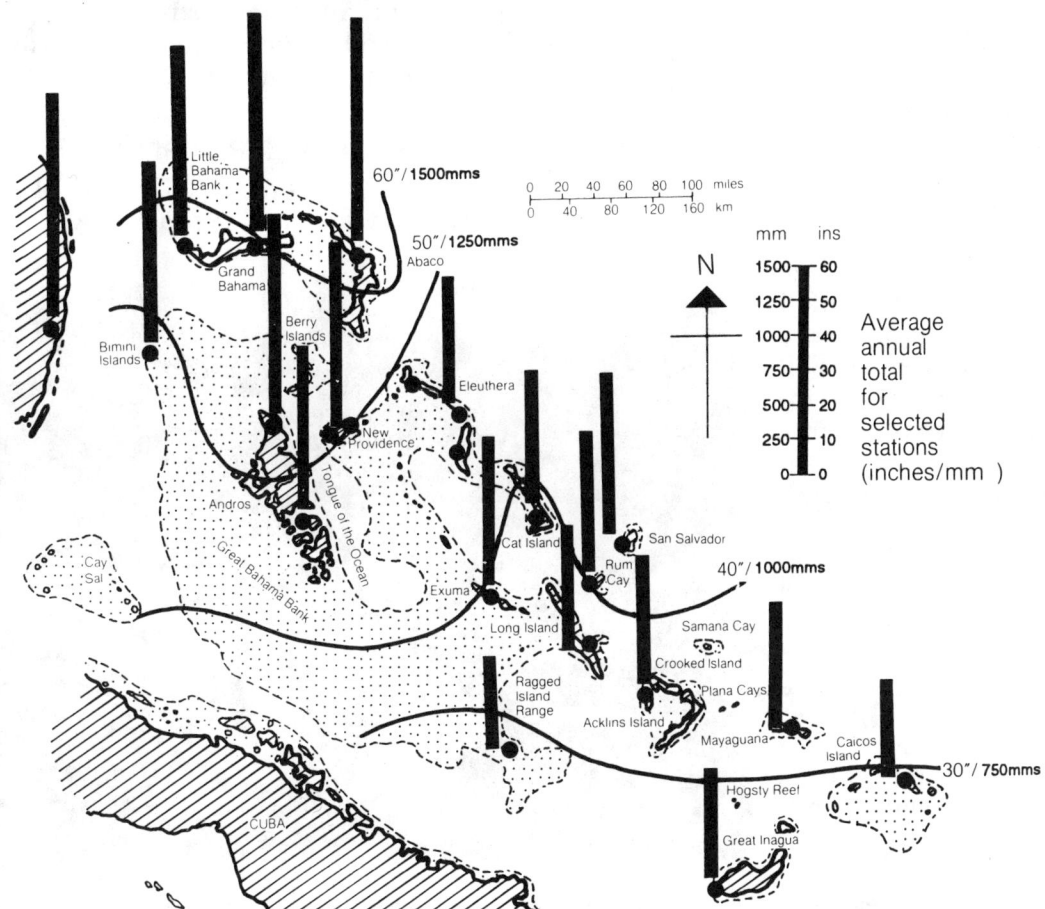

Figure 8.5 Rainfall distribution over The Bahamas

Table 8.2 Impact of evapotranspiration on rainfall totals.

REGION	APPROXIMATE RAINFALL (mms/inches)	POTENTIAL EVT* (mms/inches)	IMPACT ON FW LENSES
Large Northern Islands			
The Pine Islands	1 250-1 500/50-60	1 250-1 375/50-55	In balance
North Central Islands			
Eleuthera, San Salvador, Central and S Andros	1 000-1 250/40-50	1 250-1 375/50-55	Small loss
South Central Islands			
Exumas, Long Is, Acklins & Crooked Is, Mayaguana	750-1 000/30-40	1 375-1 500/55-60	Large loss
South-eastern Islands			
Inaguas, Turks & Caicos	625-750/25-30	1 500-1 875/60-75	V. large loss

* Potential EVT is the amount of evapotranspiration that would take place if it rained enough

THE BALANCE - ENOUGH OR TOO LITTLE?

Evapotranspiration, as well as being a loss, varies from one island to another. It is greatest in those islands with the highest temperatures and most sunshine, such as small islands or cays and those in the south-east. Unfortunately, as we have seen, it is already these islands that are getting less rain in the first place, and so they are doubly affected - less in, and more out. If we combine the effects of rainfall and evapotranspiration for the whole of The Bahamas it will be seen that not only does rainfall decrease towards the south, but evapotrans-piration increases. Even if the rainfall were the same for all the islands, the amount retained and stored would be much less in the smaller south-eastern islands.

We can summarise these two conflicting effects as follows:

Assuming no interference from man, only the northern islands have enough rainfall to support a full growth of vegetation appropriate to these latitudes. As we go further south the pine trees are replaced by the hardwood coppice which contains much smaller trees, and farther south again these become stunted. Eventually the hardwood forest itself is replaced by a desert scrub of thorny bushes, cacti and wiry grasses.

LIVING WITH THE WATER SUPPLY

The *fresh water lens is* actually part of a bigger body of water, and in practice we can

Figure 8.6 A typical trench collection system for domestic water on New Providence. Pumps abstract the water from the trenches, which allows easier access to the fresh water than wells.

say that it floats on top of *salty* water from which it is separated by a less salty, or *brackish* layer. (Figure 8.8). Just what is meant by these terms is shown below:

Table 8.3 Salinity values for ground water (parts per million chloride content)

Fresh water	*30-400
Brackish	400-1 200
Saline	1 200-12 000
Sea water	20 000+

*600 ppm is the World Health Organization limit

Rainwater will have 0-10 parts per million (ppm) chloride content, acquired from salt in the air. Thick lenses in the Pine Islands may have fresh water with as low as 30 ppm, while official samples taken in New Providence range from 200-500 ppm chloride content. All Bahamian water will also be *hard,* that is, it will contain calcium carbonate in the range 200-400 ppm carbonate content. Only rainwater will be soft.

Fresh water is taken from the top of the lens, and as long as the amount extracted does not exceed the ability of the rainfall to replace it, the lens will stay intact (Figure 8.9). The problems arise when the lenses are small, or the demand is high, causing the lens to shrink and the *saline layers to rise.* Normally the depth of the water table will remain the same, while the saline water will rise until eventually a well will start sucking brackish water. If, indeed, the fresh water has been totally removed it will be a long time before the lens can be re-established. Observation of the wellfields on some of the eastern islands has shown that they will recharge at about 300 mms (12 inches) per year. On New Providence it took 30 years for the Blue Hills wellfield to return to its original state after becoming brackish.

Figure 8.7 A modern version of an old idea, catching rainwater. The government rainwater rewservoir at Abraham's Bay, Mayaguana

In areas of shortage there are several alternatives towards improving the supply, of which the most important are:

■ *Transferring water* If there is a water shortage in one place but a surplus exists in others, then it may be relatively simple to transfer water from one area to another. For instance, the central part of Eleuthera between Glass Window and Tarpum Bay has small lenses, but a lot of settlements. Larger lenses exist in the broader areas of the north

Table 8.4 New Providence water supply 1971-1992 (Million imperial gallons per year).

SOURCE	1971	1975	1980	1985	1990	1992
Corporation wellfields	1 255	885	845	1 270	1 375	1 170
NP Development Company	665	550	470	575	555	495
Other fields	30	95	85	0	0	0
Wellfield Total	1 950	1 530	1 400	1 845	1 930	1 665
Desalination plants	65	390	130	0	0	0
Barging (Andros)	0	0	290	555	1 060	975
Total	2 015	1 920	1 820	2 400	2 990	2 640

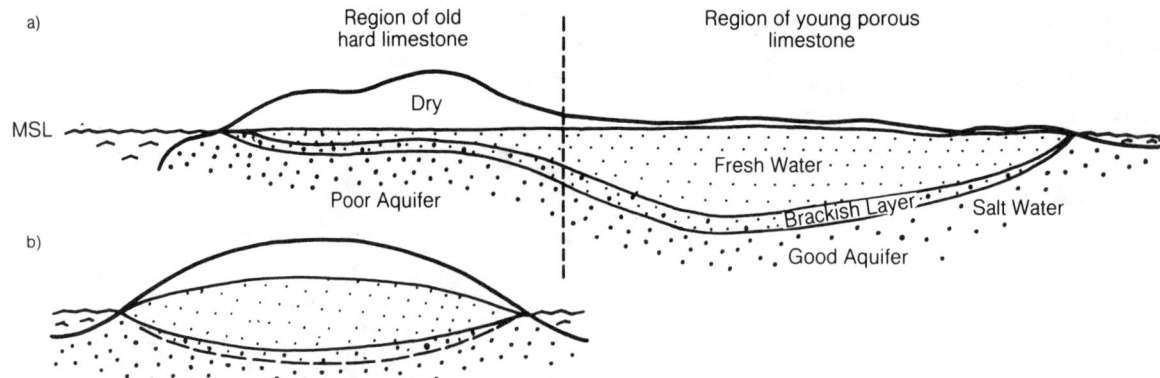

Figure 8.8 a) A typical lens on a large island. Differences in the rock's porosity will affect the thickness of the lens. Over 90% of the fresh water will be below sea level, and hilly areas will need deeper wells. b) Simplified but misleading sketch of a lens - Bahamian lenses are much more complex.

and south, and a pipeline from these now serves the central settlements as well. North Eleuthera supplies water by pipeline to Spanish Wells.

The largest fresh water lenses in The Bahamas are in North Andros, while the largest concentration of population is on the small island of New Providence. Since 1978, water has been sent by barge from Morgan's Bluff to Arawak Cay and fed from there into Nassau's water system (Figure 8.4 and 8.9). As the table shows, about 20% of Nassau's water now comes from Andros (Table 8.4).

■ *Catching more water* In Bermuda it is the law that all houses have a roof constructed with guttering to collect rainwater, which is then stored in a rainwater tank at or below ground level. This is a common method still in the Bahamas, although a large number of rainwater tanks are disused and the majority of new houses and other buildings do not even have guttering. As outside of the three large northern islands all the water lenses have a significant amount of salt in them it makes sense to catch rainwater whenever possible, as it will be salt-free. This is healthier and the plumbing is not subject to corrosion. It is usually rainwater that the water-bottling companies use as a basis for their purified drinking water.

Another method is to use a natural slope to collect water and direct it into tanks. The eastern slope of the famous Rock of Gibraltar has been entirely cemented over and is used for this purpose, and a similar but smaller system was constructed by the US Navy for their base at Graham's Harbour in San Salvador. This is still in use today by the present occupants of the old base, as indeed are the systems on other old bases in Eleuthera and Mayaguana.

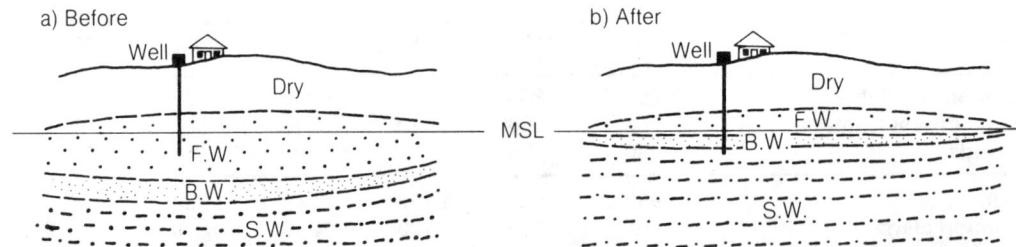

Figure 8.9 Effect of over-using a freshwater lens. Because excessive amounts of water have been taken from lens a), it has 'gone salt' and shrunk to the size of lens b). Saline water is now drawn into the well.

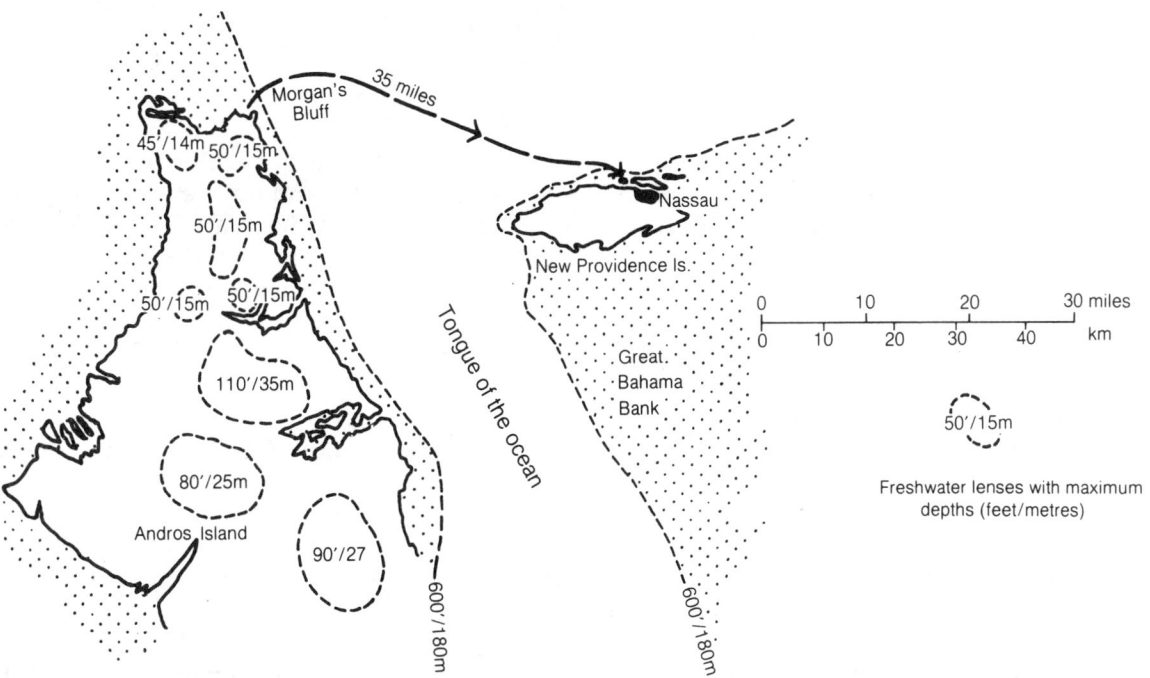

Figure 8.10 Nassau is on the small island of New Providence which nevertheless has to house over half the population of The Bahamas. In order to provide enough water, wellfields in North Andros are linked to the small port of Morgan's Bluff by pipeline, and from there the water is shipped to Nassau in barges. It should be noted that Andros has some wellfields as big as Nassau, but only a small population (6 000).

Figure 8.11 The village well often serves as a social centre as well as a source of drinking water. Many communities still depend on an open well like this one at Red Bays in Andros

■ *Purifying the water* - desalination. Salt is the most difficult impurity to remove from water.

Sediment can be filtered, bacteria can be chlorinated, and hardness (due to calcium carbonate) can be removed with the aid of salt, although it is not such a serious problem, affecting the plumbing more than the drinker. If salt is to be removed, then there are really only two ways this can be done on a large scale: by *evaporation*, usually known as *distillation*, as the water is first boiled and then the distilled, pure, water taken off; and *reverse osmosis*, in which a special membrane acts as a chemical filter and extracts the salt.

Unfortunately such desalination plants are expensive to build, to run, and to maintain. They require fuel for heating the water or pumping it through the membrane, and the salt is extremely corrosive so that stainless steel or other resistant metals have to be used throughout.

Over the last 20 years several desalination plants have operated in New Providence. (Table 8.5)

After 1974 the cost of fuel rose enormously and was the main factor in the closure of the later two plants. Several smaller plants operate to supply small cays, as on Cat Cay in the Biminis and on Walker's Cay in the Abaco chain. In addition certain private companies have their own supplies, notably Bacardi and Aquapure, both in New Providence, and a reverse osmosis plant producing 750 000 gallons/day serves some of the hotels on Paradise Island. Another one was built next to the Cable Beach Hotel in the late 1980's.

■ *Conservation techniques* By conservation we mean making better use of the water we have. Most of us are familiar with the ways of saving water at home, and the same ideas have to be applied to water lenses if the best use is to be made of them.

One of the most common losses is by evaporation. This can be reduced by the construction of ditches and drains in built-up areas so that the rainwater will run underground rapidly and not lie in puddles to be evaporated away. Such a scheme to channel and collect water has been established at the Nassau International Airport. The soil is another medium from which water can be evaporated, and it will also draw it up to the surface from the water table. A bare soil surface encourages evaporation, and care should be taken not to allow unnecessary ground clearing. Trees will shade the soil and provide an insulating cover of leaf litter. They will reduce evaporation by a much greater amount than they will transpire water.

Another area of loss is due to uncontrolled extraction. It has been noted that a water lens can only supply as much as it receives. If too much water is taken from it the brackish layer will rise and pollute the fresh water zone. If water is only taken out of the lens at known points via metered wells a close watch can be kept to see that this does not happen. If wells or trenches are dug independently it is not possible to plan the use of the lens, and water may be taken out very unevenly, causing lateral flows of water across the lens. Excess withdrawal will go unnoticed until the water turns brackish. It has been estimated that there are from 12 000 to 20 000 private wells in New Providence.

Loss of water once it is in the distribution system is another problem. Unfortunately, this is very high in The Bahamas,

Table 8.5 Desalination projects. Capacity in million imperial gallons per day

Location	Water Supply	Operational Period	Capacity (mgpd)
Clifton Pier	Sea water	1961-71	1.2
Blue Hills	Brackish ground water	1972-77	2.0
Airport	Lake Killarney	1977-80	0.5

Figure 8.12 An irrigation bore hole.

with unaccounted losses estimated at 46% of the water supplied in New Providence alone.

Prevention of pollution is the last main area for conservation. Pollution is likely from six main sources - sewage; industrial wastes; agricultural products; leaking fuels; the natural sulphur cycle; and by brackish or salt water incursion. There are existing rules for the first two, ensuring that domestic and industrial wastes, if discharged into the ground, are far enough away from wells and the water lens so as not to cause pollution. Bacteria in the ground will normally take care of any organic wastes, as will sea water. The problem arises when the time needed for this to happen is too short for the quantities being discharged. With increasing population and the spread of settlements, sewage is often treated before disposal, as are some industrial wastes. A major sewage collection system has recently modernised and extended the network originally installed in Nassau in 1928. Disposal is in the deep well beneath Potter's Cay.

Pollution by fertilisers, pesticides, fungicides and herbicides is not prevalent in The Bahamas. However, the use of these products should be noted and controlled, especially as the areas of modern commercial agriculture are all in the Pine Islands where the largest fresh water lenses occur.

As the use of both water and agricultural chemicals is certainly going to increase, it is clear that this is a field where large-scale pollution could be a problem.

The problem of brackish water has already been discussed. Largely, this is a technical problem which is monitored at the pumping stations which control the rate and amount of extraction so as to keep the fresh water lens intact. There is no such control at domestic wells, however, and salt pollution is a common occurrence in New Providence in particular. The use of domestic wells also interferes with the pumping station's own controls, as they can only estimate what is going on outside their control. A related problem is the cutting of canals and docks for marinas. As these all connect to the sea they allow sea water to penetrate far inland at the surface. Seepage of salt water into the fresh water lenses is a serious problem in such cases unless the canals are lined, which is unlikely as this is expensive. The Grand Lucayan Waterway crosses Grand Bahama in the middle and is about 11 kilometres (7 miles) long with about another 32 kilometres (20 miles) of branches. It has been estimated that about 50 billion gallons of fresh water will be lost as a result (Figure

Figure 8.13 An irrigation pond on N. Eleuthera. A recently bulldozed trench has exposed the water table. The 'pond' created in this way will be used for the irrigation of about 2.5 Ha (10 acres) of recently cleared land. The water will be distributed by a portable pump and sprinklers.

Figure 8.14 The Grand Lucayan Waterway. This has been cut right across Grand Bahama with many branch canals. Full use of this development is a long way off and hardly compensates for the loss of fresh water it causes. In future such canals would be lined to prevent this.

8.14). By 1990 the effects of this loss were being noted on the adjacent golf courses, and new wells further away have had to be brought into service.

SALT

The Bahamas has long been noted for its natural salt lakes or ponds, and commercial salt production has been a feature in the economic history of the islands since their earliest settlement.

Records show that all the islands as far north as New Providence and the Berry Islands have been producers at some time or other, and a survey in 1802 listed 25 ponds in 17 of the islands. In 1982, commercial production was limited to the single island of Inagua, although this operation produces more salt than at any time in The Bahamas' past. Small-scale production for local consumption is still practised in a few islands such as Little Exuma, Ragged Island and Cat Island.

The capacity of sea water to produce salt has already been mentioned (p. 24). To some degree the process is a natural phenomenon, as described in the account of salt ponds (p. 72), but as time has gone on the technique of producing salt has come much more under human control. From a beginning of scraping the sides of natural salt ponds man came to creating his own ponds and dividing them into pans of about 0.2 hectares (0.5 acres) each, roughly what one man could rake on his own. Embankments contained the sea water, and canals with sluices were used to control the flow of the brine. Evaporation by the sun removed the water to leave salt crystals which were then raked, dried, bleached and stored. This type of solar production reached a peak just before the mid-nineteenth century, but the boom died when trade between the Northern and Southern States resumed after the end of the American Civil War in 1865. The coming of the industrial revolution to the USA hastened this decline until, by the end of the century, 'traditional' salt production had completely disappeared.

Table 8.6 Nineteenth century salt production (tonnes) for available years

Year	Tonnes	Island
1834	15 625	
1839	74 100	
1840	4 450	Rum Cay
1852	11 160	Rum Cay
1871	67 000	Inagua
1881	1 160	
1889	3 560	
1891	1 680	

By 1910 production was down to 500 tonnes. In this period the largest producing islands were those listed in Table 8.7:

Table 8.7 Area of salt pans, major islands in the nineteenth century

Island		
Rum Cay	260 ha	650 acres
Inagua	180 ha	450 acres
Long Island	123 ha	308 acres
Exuma	89 ha	223 acres

The Bahamas was, and is, not a salt producer by accident. A variety of conditions have favoured it in the past, and it is the best of these that favour Inagua today. The most important factors are:

- *Constant sunshine* Inagua averages more

Figure 8.15 *Morton Salt Company's ship loading salt for the USA at Matthew Town, Inagua. Photograph courtesy Morton Salt Company*

hours of sunshine a day than the more northerly islands.

- **Constant winds** aid evaporation, and this is a notable feature of Inagua (average daily wind is 8.5 knots) and the other southeastern islands, such as Long Island (10.0 knots), Rum Cay and San Salvador, where the trade winds are extremely reliable.

- **High temperatures** Average mean temperatures are 26.4°C (79.5°F) in Inagua, 25.9°C (78.7°F) in Exuma, and 25.8°C (78.4°F) in Long Island.

- **Purity of sea water** Obviously any sediment or chemical impurities will be left behind with the salt and will have to be removed later. With an absence of rivers and no fine clay particles on the seafloor the sea water is extremely clean, so that the salt produced in Inagua is 99.5% pure.

- **Flat land** availability for the salt pans. As has been explained, the nature of sedimentation on the banks gives rise to very flat marine deposits and coastal plains, all easily flooded to form large salt pans.

- **Low rainfall** As just one inch of rainfall will dissolve one-third of an inch of salt, a low rainfall is essential. Inagua averages 690 mms (27.5 inches) and Long Island 870 mms (34.7 inches) a year.

It must be recognised, however, that there are certain adverse conditions present in The Bahamas as well. As competition has increased, all the islands except Inagua have found that they cannot produce salt economically, and have had to close down their salt operations. Among the problems are:

Excessive rainfall

Three centimetres of rain will dissolve one centimetre of pure salt, and above all it was excessive rainfall that led to the closure of the Diamond Salt Company's works at Hard Bargain in Long Island. In 1978, the salt crop was destroyed by a freak storm, in 1979 Hurricane David brought 200 mms (8 inches) of rain to the island and dissolved all the salt in the crystallisers (the final stage in modern solar salt manufacture), causing the loss of 164 000 tonnes, and there was heavy rain again in 1980 during the harvesting period. The works closed in 1981 and a watch on the weather pattern over the next few years was instituted.

Hurricanes

The Rum Cay works were shattered by a

severe hurricane in 1853 which left the pans, canals and docks in ruins. In 1866, and at the turn of the century, notably in 1908, more hurricanes caused severe damage which the declining industry could not afford to repair. Many islands such as Ragged Island and Rum Cay never recovered. Even Inagua suffered from floods in 1880, and eventually went out of production.

However, it was the economic situation that prevented the repair of the physical damage, and not the damage itself that caused the collapse of the industry. Competition came in the form of mined salt in the developed countries. In past geological time conditions existed which gave rise to the formation of evaporite deposits, hundreds, and in some cases thousands, of metres thick. With industrialisation these countries did not need to import salt, and, in fact, often prohibited or taxed its entry in order to protect their own mines from competition. Consequently any modern production of salt must be very efficient, if it is to be cheap enough to be sold abroad, and this is the case with the American owned Morton Salt Company in Inagua.

In Inagua both technique and scale are nineteenth century, and some 75 000 hectares (30 000 acres) of salt pans can produce over one million tons of salt in a year. This is one of the largest solar salt works in the world! Nowadays, evaporation is started in a series of 16 reservoirs, known as *evaporators*, through which the sea water is progressively moved as it becomes concentrated into a thicker and thicker brine. When this brine is ten times as concentrated as sea water it is led into a final set of pans where the salt will be crystallised out. There are 59 of these *crystallisers*, and the salt will be raked out when it has reached between 7 and 15 cms thick on the bottom of the pan (Figure 8.17). In this way a kind of factory production line is formed with each stage of the process being separately controlled. It also means that as soon as the crystallisers have been raked out, a fresh supply of *brine* is ready to be put in. In the old days fresh sea water would have been used to refill the pans, and the time between harvests was

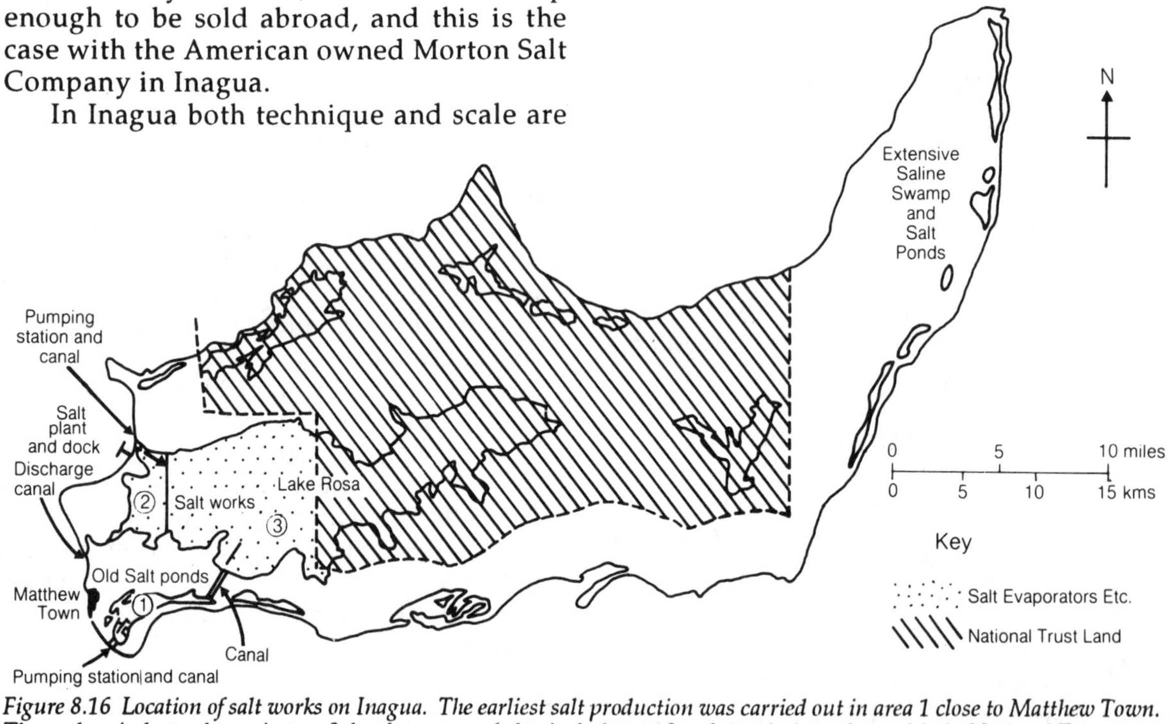

Figure 8.16 Location of salt works on Inagua. The earliest salt production was carried out in area 1 close to Matthew Town. The modern industry began in area 2, but later expanded to include area 3 as far as the boundary with the National Trust land. Area 2 is now devoted to crystallising and area 3 to reservoirs and evaporation.

consequently much longer. In this way salt can be raked virtually all the year round, weather permitting.

Table 8.8 Salt production (tonnes) in The Bahamas

Year	Production	Exported
1956a	138 000	18 000
1960	73 000	231 000
1965	394 000	470 000
1970b	342 000	710 000
1976	1 178 000	1 239 000
1980	668 000	573 000
1985	n/a	1 122 000
1990	n/a	1 299 000

It has already been pointed out that an impervious mat of algae forms on the bed of natural salt ponds (p. 72). This is, of course, also true of artificial reservoirs, and is an important part of the solar salt operation. If the carpet of algae did not form a waterproof seal, the salt water could leak out whenever the water table fell, which it would probably do every year in the dry season. In fact Lake Rosa used to be a seasonal lake, but it is now wet all the year round. When it dried up there was no food for migrating birds, including the flamingoes, but since 1971 there has been a great increase in both food and birds. Once again algae have come to the aid of The Bahamas.

Once the right amount of salt has been deposited, the brine, now known as *bitterns,* is drained back into the sea through a canal (see Figure 8.17). This is to prevent the precipitation of any other salts such as calcium sulphate, potassium and especially magnesium salts. Some of these have already contaminated the crude salt, so it has to be washed, and although some salt is dissolved in this process it is worth it in order to maintain the purity. Rain on the stockpiles also washes away any remaining magnesium salts, hence a small amount of rain is beneficial.

There are still some problems, however, including excessive and variable rainfall. Although the average is 687 mms (27.5 inches) per year, in 1960 Inagua received 1 470 mms (59 inches), but in 1963 only had 575 mms (23 inches). Very dry conditions can also affect the quality of the brine and the purity of the salt. Another problem has been the formation of a gel, believed to be produced by saccarites secreted from mangroves. This clogs up the salt pans and

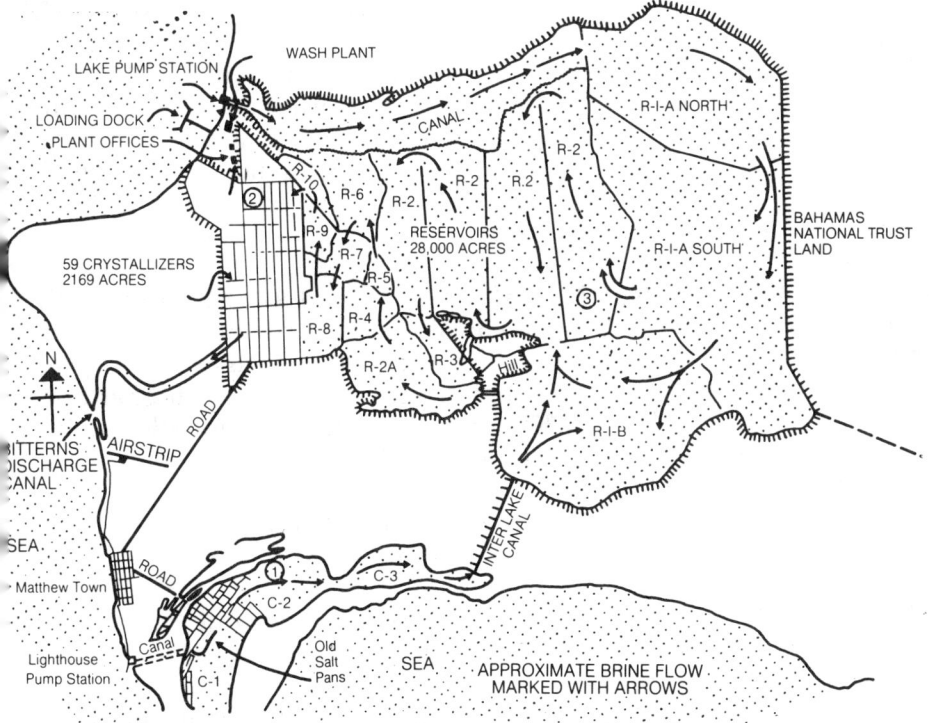

Figure 8.17 Layout of Morton Bahamas' Solar Salt operations on Great Inagua

is costly to remove. Fortunately it was found that if brine shrimps were put in the pans they would eat up the gel, and so the problem has been solved.

The value of Bahamian salt lies in its purity, cheapness of production, and closeness to North America. Most of the salt, which costs about US$8.00 per ton, is sent to paper and chemical companies along the Eastern Seaboard of the USA, but the coarsest grained salt, about 20% of the total, is exported for use as a water softener. The ideal conditions found in Inagua are not really found anywhere else in The Bahamas, and in 1983 it was announced that the Long Island salt works had been sold for marine shrimp farming. Other Caribbean producers such as the Turks and Caicos and Anguilla are both small and farther away from the USA, and unlikely to provide competition. On the other hand, it would be difficult to expand the operation on Inagua without interfering with the flamingo breeding grounds on Lake Rosa. However, northeastern Inagua also has extensive salt flats and an even drier climate, and it is possible that an entirely new salt works could be set up there.

ARAGONITE

Although always referred to as 'aragonite', what we are actually dealing with is *oolitic sand.* Modern industry requires large amounts of limestone in many of its processes - the manufacture of iron and steel, glass, cement, fertiliser, chemicals, and various uses in the building trade, being the most notable - and, indeed, it is probably the most widely quarried, mined or dredged mineral in the world.

Essentially what industry requires is simply *limestone*, or calcium carbonate. It does not have to be aragonite, or calcite. As limestone is an extremely common rock we must identify the particular advantages of Bahamian aragonite sand before we can understand its development as a mineral resource. Below is a typical analysis of the aragonite sand after it has been screened and washed for shipment:

Table 8.9 *Typical analysis of Bahamian aragonite sand from Bimini area*

$CaCO_3$	97.0%	Fe_2O_3	0.025%	NaCl	0.25%
$MgCO_3$	1.5%	AlO_3	0.15%	SrO	0.80%
SiO_2	0.08%	SO_3	0.20%		

It should be noted that the product is very pure in $CaCO_3$, and compares favourably with quarried limestone on the mainland of North America, the latter only averaging 74% purity after crushing. This degree of purity is significant and means:

- that, up to a certain distance from Bimini, aragonite sand will be a more economical material than local limestone in the USA, despite its transport costs. This is the case for virtually the whole of the US Eastern Seaboard and the Gulf of Mexico, from New York to Houston. Crushed limestone rock often includes silt, sulphur and phosphorus which have to be removed. Oolitic sand is additionally used for beach replenishment and play sand.

- that it can be used as a chemical in the chemical and related industries - such minerals being known as *chemical grade* - and can therefore fetch a higher price than its use in, say, cement allows. It is widely used in the glass industry for optical, auto and float glass; glass containers; and specialty glass including laser lenses.

- it needs no crushing and exists in an extremely uniform grain size.

The history of the development of this resource has been well recorded elsewhere.

Studies of The Bahamas banks in the 1950's identified four areas of oolitic sand deposits (Figure 8.18). These were estimated to contain 50-100 billion tonnes, enough to supply the whole world (at two billion tons per year) for the next 25-50 years!

The fall in production in the mid-1980's has been due to intense competition from a large Mexican operation working similar deposits off the Yucatan coast (an area of banks almost identical to The Bahamas). This has particularly affected the Gulf Coast markets.

In 1994, aragonite sand was worth about US$3.00 a tonne, so clearly it is a resource that is only going to be profitable in very large quantities. The key to realising a profit lies especially in the handling and transport, and in this respect the following points should be considered:

- The Bimini site is very close to the USA (compared with the Schooner Cays, for instance).

- As oolite is a natural deposit which forms near the bank edge, the working area is quite close to deep water. Only a short channel (over 13 metres /42 feet deep) had to be dredged to reach the Florida Straits.

- The water is shallow, which allows economical dredging.

- An island of about 38 hectares (95 acres) had to be built, equipped with a dock, airstrip, accommodation, power, and all other domestic and technical facilities. No natural island or cay was available, and everything including labour had to be shipped in.

- The marine environment always provides an element of risk, such as from hurricanes. In 1982, a freak wind totally wrecked the multi-million dollar loading equipment and blocked the harbour, and in 1992 Hurricane Andrew passed right over the cay causing immense damage and requiring $5 million in repairs.

Table 8.10 Production of aragonite sand 1980-93

1980	3.7 million tonnes
1985	2.0 million tonnes
1990	1.3 million tonnes
1993	1.2 million tonnes

The deposit around *Ocean Cay*, as the man-made island is called, extends for 35 kilometres (22 miles), and is about 3 kilometres (2 miles) wide and 3.5 metres (10-15 feet) thick (Figure 8.18). It probably contains about one billion tonnes, and at the present rate of extraction, it will obviously last for some considerable time. However, it will be necessary to construct new 'islands' from time to time. (See also p. 25, Figure 2.5)

A recent development has been the mining of calcite-rich limestone rock from the sea floor. This is sent to New Orleans where it is used in the production of calcium oxide.

Virtually all of the oolite is exported to

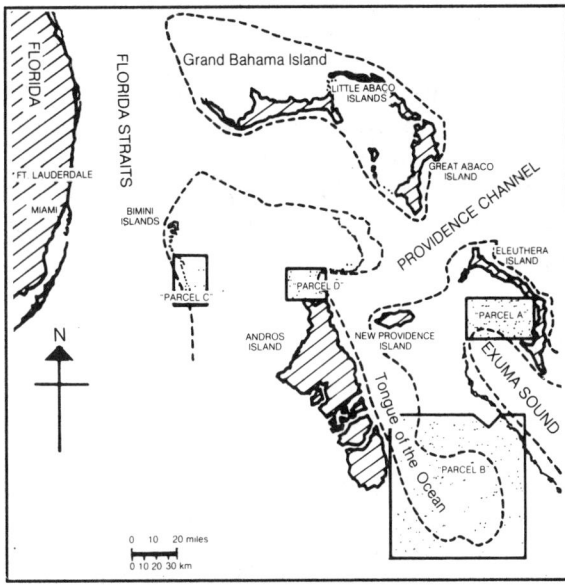

Figure 8.18 Aragonite concession areas. Only parcel 'C' is worked at present. The sites are: A Schooner Cays, B Southern Tongue of the Ocean, C Southern Biminis, D Joulter Cays

Figure 8.19 Ocean Cay in the Biminis. This man-made island has a dock, loading jetty and airstrip, and serves as the stock pile for aragonite sand (centre of picture). Suction dredgers pump it on to the island from where it is loaded on to ships via the conveyor belts and travelling gantry.

the United States, but an increasing amount is now being sent to Latin America.

Oolite is not the kind of resource that encourages manufacturing, so it is likely, like salt, to remain a basic export commodity. It is too low in value, and too easily shipped in bulk, to generate much in savings by producing a finished product at the source. The main uses are in the major manufacturing industries well-established abroad.

PETROLEUM

No commercial quantities of petroleum have yet been discovered in The Bahamas, but the likelihood that they will be found is good. Serious prospecting has been in progress for the last 50 years and is as active today as it ever was. The recent revival of interest began in the early 1980's, and continues into the 1990's, with a variety of exploration licences issued to international companies, and some drilling taking place. It is, therefore, worthwhile examining, as far as possible, the reasons for this optimism (Figure 8.20).

On a larger scale, it is the nature of The Bahamas platform that attracts interest, for geologically there are great similarities to the rich oil-bearing regions of Eastern Mexico and the Persian Gulf. In the latter case, the *source* beds are marine carbonate muds, and the *reservoir* rocks are porous limestones and dolomites, all of which are present in abundance in The Bahamas. It will be apparent from this that certain geological conditions must exist if there is to be any chance of oil being found. These are:

A SOURCE ROCK

This can be any rock in which some organic content can be altered to form *hydrocarbons*. In The Bahamas, hydrocarbons can be produced from the organic content of the shallow marine carbonate muds deposited on the banks. The best deposits of this type date from the Late Jurassic and Early Cretaceous periods (about 135 million years ago).

These lie below 4 575 metres (15 000 feet) of rock, but may be from 1 830-3 050 metres (6 000-10 000 feet) thick. Another source could be deep-water carbonates which are rich in fossils, and are associated with ancient coral reefs. These may exist along the Atlantic edge of the Bahamas' platform.

A RESERVOIR ROCK

The hydrocarbons, which form as minute globules of oil, need to migrate and collect in a *porous* rock from which they can be recovered in quantity. This is what will be known as the *oil field*. Again, it is in the deeper layers of rock that the most favourable conditions exist. Problems that have to be avoided are that the hydrocarbons may have migrated into the sea, or that the reservoir rocks may have been subject to marine erosion. These are the main reasons why the deeper layers are considered to be the most important, for in the late Cretaceous period (about 75 million years ago) the upper platform was divided into its present components. In particular the south-eastern Bahamas was fragmented, and the various deep-water channels were created. All along its north-eastern edge the platform has been open to the Atlantic Ocean, and sea water has invaded the rocks right down to about 4 575 metres (15 000 feet). Below this the strata are believed to have been capped by a barrier reef, and another 6 100 metres (20 000 feet) of possible oil reservoir rocks exist, at present largely unexplored.

A CAP ROCK

This is needed to create a trap in the reservoir rock. It has to be a rock through which the oil cannot flow - in other words it must be *impermeable*. Although most of the rocks are limestone, and are permeable, there is one group that can act as a cap very efficiently - the *evaporites*, especially *salt* and *anhydrite*. Fortunately the Bahamian past has often had conditions that led to these being formed, and so the last requirement is satisfied.

The problem of oil production is therefore limited to two situations:

- Do these three conditions exist *together*, and, in particular, was the cap in place to stop the oil escaping?
- If these conditions exist, can we find out where they exist? Will it be possible, given the great depths, to extract the oil?

Some direct evidence of oil does exist. In the Suniland region of South Florida eight small oilfields were discovered in the 1940's, seven of which still produce oil. These are all in Jurassic sediments belonging to the same sequences that exist in The Bahamas, at about 3 500 metres (11 500 feet) (see Figure 1.1). However, in The Bahamas these sediments are found at much greater depths. In addition, small oil seeps and oil fields exist along the northern edge of the Cuban coast.

In 1979, much farther north, in the Baltimore Canyon 160 kilometre (100 miles) off the New Jersey coast, natural gas was discovered at a depth of 3 875 metres (12 700 feet). It appears that there is an ancient coral reef off the eastern coast of the USA which stretches from Canada to The Bahamas, and it may be that oil and gas will be found anywhere in this region at depths of 6 100 metres (20 000 feet) or more, such as on the Blake Plateau.

In The Bahamas itself many oil-stains have been found, indicating that oil was once present but has escaped. The shallowest find was in young limestone at a depth of 1 300 metres (4 300 feet), and stains are quite common at depths greater than 1 900 metres (6 300 feet). The ultimate conclusion is that although oil existed in these shallower layers, it has long been lost due to sea water invasion. This can happen if sea water penetrates the porous rocks and flushes out the oil; or if it dissolves the evaporite beds which would otherwise have trapped the oil. This has been found to be the case as deep down as 4 400 metres (14 500 feet) below Long Island, and at lesser depths farther north. A total of five wells have been drilled.

Traces of actual oil and high-pressure gas have been found in some of the deeper salt-water flooded strata, such as around 5 200 and 5 500 metres (17 000 and 18 000 feet), and in one case the salt water contained dissolved petroleum gases. A 1986 drilling programme on the Cay Sal Bank was abandoned after reaching 4 250 metres (14 000 feet) without success.

As far as finding and extracting the oil is concerned, the economic advantages of location are very much in The Bahamas' favour. The Eastern Seaboard of the USA and Canada is the greatest consumer of oil in the world, and there would be no other source of oil closer than The Bahamas. On the other hand, the problems of drilling in depths of over 6 100 metres (20 000 ft), and the shallowness of water over the banks on which

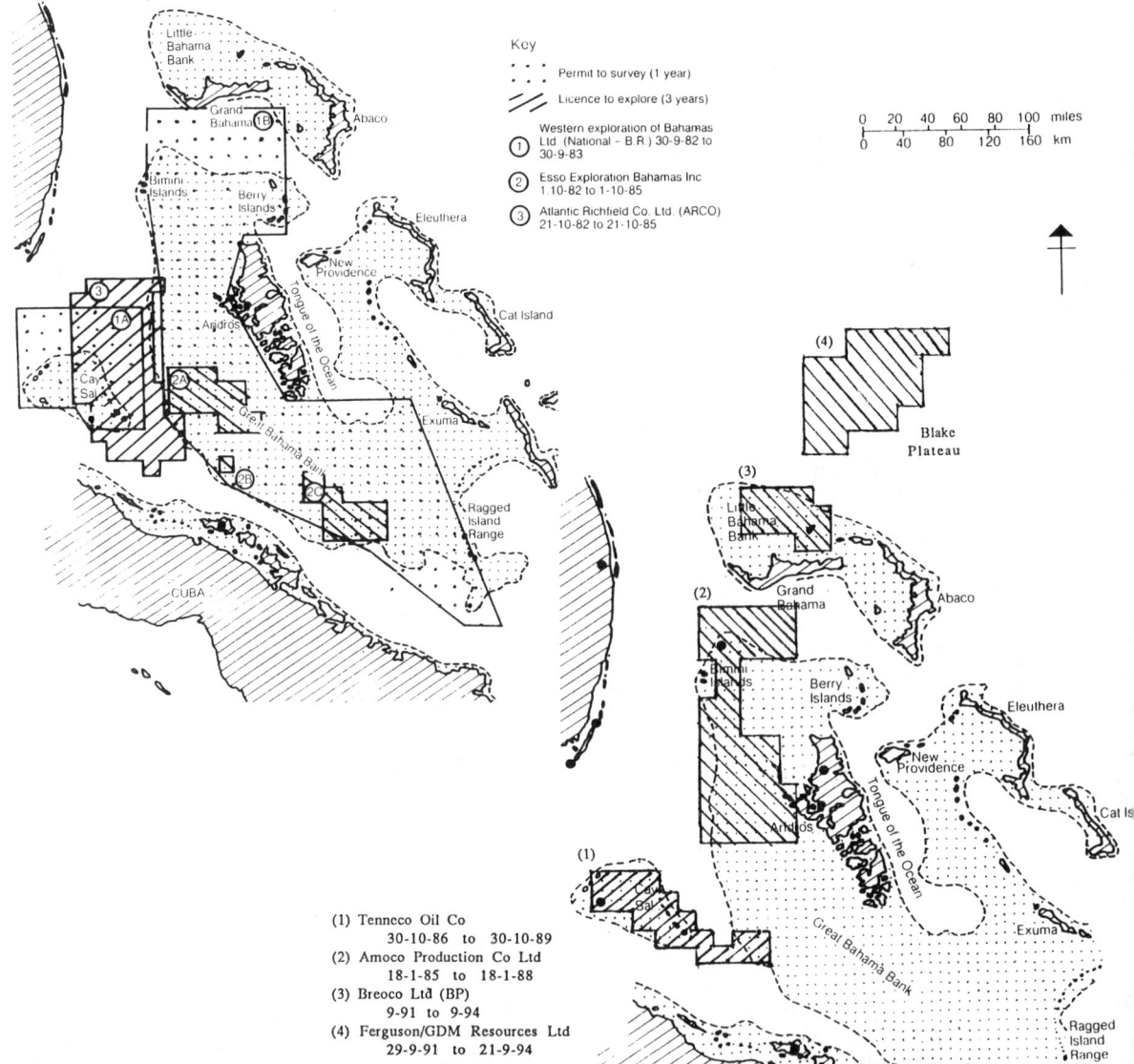

Figure 8.20 The search for oil. Activity from 1982 to 1985 is shown on the left, and from 1985 to 1994 on the right.

Figure 8.21 The Chiles Yucatan *drilling rig being towed into position on the Cay Sal Bank in 1985. Photograph courtesy of The Nassau Guardian.*

the rigs may have to work, greatly increase the expense of drilling. In addition, seismic surveys are not always very successful in showing the best places to drill. This is because the limestones of the Bahamian platform do not vary very much, and show up poorly on the recording equipment. This is even worse when the rocks are saturated with sea water. Nevertheless, in the 1990's major companies still have licences to drill on the Cay Sal Bank, and all along the western part of the Great Bahama Bank opposite the Cay Sal bank. A newer development has been the spread of interest northwards to the Little Bahama Bank and to the Blake Plateau, where the water is over 1 000 metres deep. (Figure 8.21)

There is little doubt that The Bahamas and its adjacent deep-water margins are regarded most seriously as a source of deep oil for the future.

CONCLUSION

Other mineral resources exist and are used on a small scale. About 100 000 tonnes of *building sand* are dredged up off Rose Island every year for use in the construction industry. It is mainly made up of skeletal grains and sells for about US$6.00 a cubic yard, making the industry worth about US$1.0 million a year (Figure 8.22). About 10 000 tonnes of silica sand are imported each year for use in jobs where calcareous sand is not suitable.

At one time the Bahamas Cement Company in Freeport produced cement using local marine *limestone* dredged from Freeport Harbour during its construction.

On a much smaller scale *clay* was used by the Lucayan Indians, and is used by modern-day craftsmen to produce pottery. The main source is the lateritic soil which is the only material to have a clayey texture. Crushed conch shell was used by the Indians as a temper to extend and strengthen the clay. *Conch shells* have also been used to reclaim land, for example along East Bay Street in Nassau, but this was done mainly to dispose of the unsightly and smelly shells that had accumulated in the harbour. It would not normally be economical to use these as a building material.

The local limestone has been used as

Figure 8.22 The stockpile of building sand at Malcolm Park, Nassau. Several times a day a dredger brings sand for the waiting builder's trucks. The length of the line of trucks is a virtual barometer of the country's economic health.

building stone everywhere, and this is particularly noticeable in the Family Islands. However, there are no commercial quarries at present, and little appears to be used today. This is a pity as the hard, dense limestone found in the older ridges could be used widely in place of cement blocks in larger buildings. The few buildings using this material, such as the now demolished Royal Victoria Hotel, show that, if professionally cut and laid, local stone is an attractive and durable product.

Possibly there are many more natural resources in The Bahamas that only advances in technology and man's ingenuity will find a use for. There may be others yet to be discovered. The uniqueness of the Bahamian landscape lends itself to extremes, and the difference between worthless rock and a valuable resource is only man's desire to use it. Who knows what the future may bring?

[1] Muhs, Daniel H et al. Geochemical Evidence of Saharan Dust Parent Material for Soils Developed on Quaternary Limestones of Caribbean and Western Atlantic Islands. *Quaternary Research*, 33, 1990, pp 157-177.

9 THE CLIMATE OF THE BAHAMAS

In a simple, classical, division of the earth into temperature belts (Figure 9.1) we can note that The Bahamas lies on the boundary between the temperate and tropical zones. This boundary is not a definite line, but a transition zone, and it is generally referred to as the *sub-tropical zone*.

For this reason it can be said that the climate of The Bahamas is *sub-tropical*. In fact, this is a bit simplistic, as although The Bahamas is certainly sub-tropical in that it does not get any great extremes of temperature, it does not really explain what the climate is like. A more precise description can be found by relating the Bahamian climate to each of its neighbouring temperate and tropical zones. If we do this we can say that **the Bahamian climate is sub-tropical, experiencing a warm temperate winter regime and a tropical summer regime.**

This will give us a feeling for the temperature, but we also need to describe the rainfall. This can also be described in terms of winter and summer, with The Bahamas experiencing wetter summers and drier winters. This wet/dry regime is typical of tropical regions, but we must note that The Bahamas, being a maritime country, does in fact receive rainfall all the year round, with twice as much falling in the summer season as in the winter.

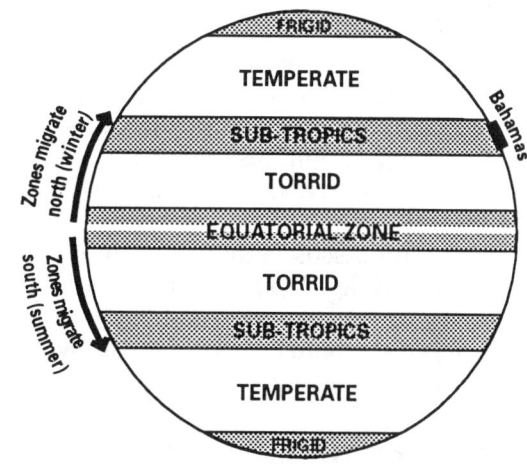

Figure 9.1 A modified classical view of the earth's climatic belts. Ptolemy divided the earth into Frigid, Temperate and Torrid zones, to which were later added the sub-tropics and equatorial belt. The Bahamas clearly lies in the northern sub-tropical zone.

It should also be noted that The Bahamas has a *trade wind climate*, in that it lies in the path of the *north-east trade winds* which blow all the year round. However, these winds are interrupted from time to time by disturbances, most notably by *cold fronts* from North America in winter, and by *hurricanes* from the Atlantic in summer.

Finally, we should recognise that The Bahamas covers a great latitudinal extent, stretching from 21°N to 27.5°N, a distance of some 730 kilometres (450 miles). This means that within The Bahamas the climate varies, most notably from north to south. The northern Bahamas has cooler winters than the south, while the southern Bahamas is drier than the north.

FACTORS AFFECTING THE CLIMATE

The main aspects of climate that are of importance are:
- Temperature
- Rainfall and humidity
- Wind
- Storms

In addition a study of *pressure* can tell us a lot about these other features, although unlike them it is not something we experience directly in any way. Locally we might also want to consider *visibility, cloud cover, sunshine,* and *evaporation*.

This chapter discusses the four main aspects of the climate in detail. Despite their variation during the year and across the country, they are nevertheless the product of global forces, which are first explained below.

LATITUDE AND THE ANGLE OF THE SUN

The division of the world into temperature belts (Figure 9.1) was based on the fact that the amount of heat received by the surface of the earth depends on the directness of the sun's rays which hit it. If the earth's axis was not tilted, it would simply be hottest along the equator and in the tropics, and progressively colder towards the poles, all the year round. However, because of the tilt, these temperature belts migrate north and south during the course of the year and give us our seasons. (Figure 9.3)

In The Bahamas the tropical belt moves north to cover the country in summer, and everywhere a typical tropical maritime climate is experienced - it is hot and humid throughout The Bahamas.

In winter the tropical belt recedes, and in the northern Bahamas especially it is replaced by the southern (warm) portion of the northern temperate zone. Consequently there is a drop in temperature and a more disturbed weather pattern, with the perennial trade winds being frequently disrupted by cold air travelling south from North America.

It is therefore the latitude of The Bahamas, and the changing relative position of the overhead sun, that gives us our two different seasons.

CONTINENTALITY

It is well known that land and sea heat up at different rates. As a result of this the continents and the oceans absorb, and lose, the sun's radiation at different rates. Continents in the temperate zone tend to get very hot in summer and very cold in winter. The oceans, however, do not vary so much.

The climate of a place also depends on where it is located relative to large land and water masses. An island in the ocean can be expected to have a smaller *range* of temperature than a place in the same latitude in a continental interior. It will be less hot in summer, and less cold in winter. It is said to have an *equable* climate.

Table 9.1 Average and extreme maximum and minimum monthly temperatures for Nassau, 1961-1990* (°F)

	J	F	M	A	M	J	J	A	S	O	N	D
Extreme Maximum	86.4	88.7	87.8	91.2	92.3	93.2	93.4	95.0	93.2	91.8	90.0	86.7
Average Maximum	77.3	77.5	79.7	81.8	84.6	87.3	89.1	89.3	88.4	85.4	81.8	78.7
Average Minimum	62.1	62.5	63.8	66.2	69.8	73.3	74.7	74.8	74.4	71.9	68.0	63.8
Extreme Minimum	41.4	45.8	44.6	48.6	55.5	59.0	64.2	64.4	59.5	56.0	51.0	41.5

*For clarity only Fahrenheit units have been used in this table. To obtain values in Celsius, subtract 32 and multiply by 0.556

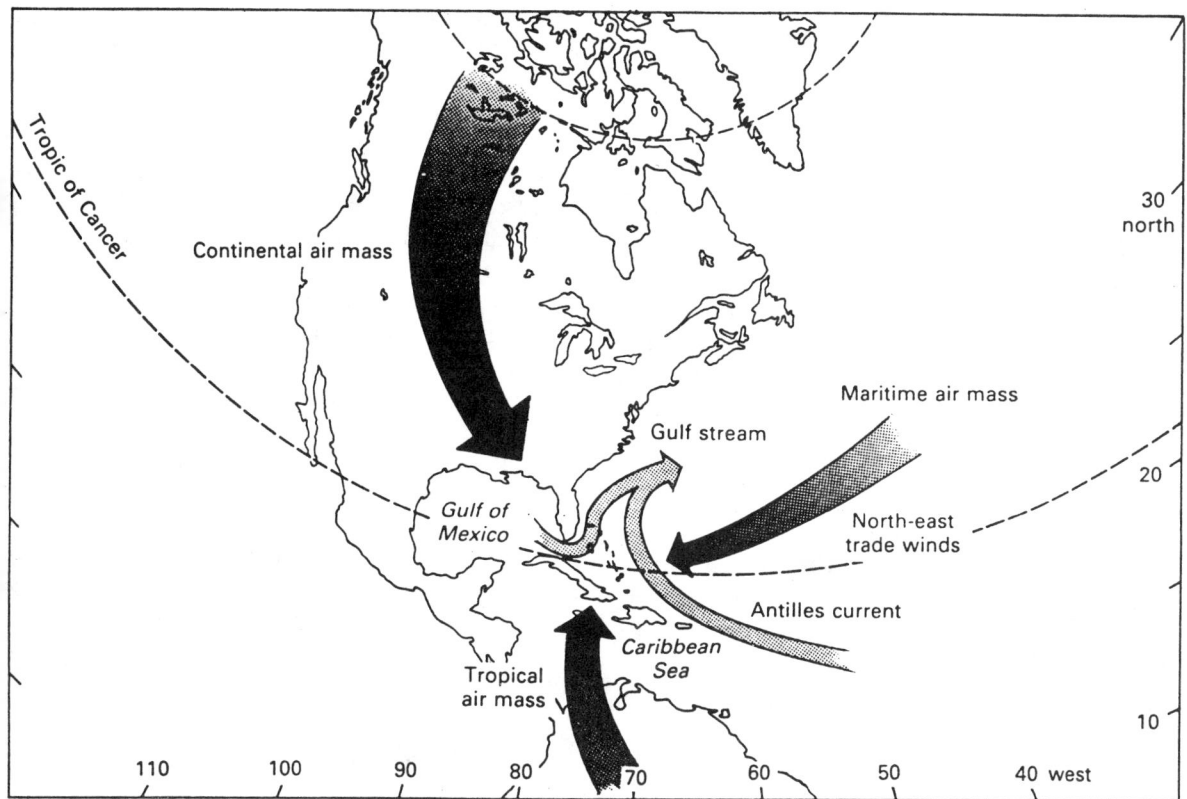

Figure 9.2 *Air masses (winds) and ocean currents affecting The Bahamas. The direction of the winds is approximate. The cold air masses from North America may arrive from a northwesterly direction as shown, or from the north or west. The Northeast Trade Winds curve around and blow from the east or southeast in summer, towards the southern USA.*

This is typical of a *maritime* climate. In addition, as islands are surrounded by water they are more humid than continental interiors, and can expect to have a wetter climate.

All of this applies to The Bahamas. It has a maritime climate with high to very high humidity all the year round (Figure 9.4). There is rain in every month. Similarly it has no great extremes of temperature. In Nassau the daily temperature has never exceeded 35°C (95°F) nor fallen below 4.5°C (40°F) (Table 9.1).

Even though The Bahamas is in an oceanic environment, the influence of North America must not be neglected. In winter extremely cold masses of air collect over the northern part of the continent, and being dense they travel south under the warmer, lighter air of the sub-tropics. These *cold air masses* often reach Florida and The Bahamas, and may even travel as far south as Cuba and Jamaica. In The Bahamas these cold air masses are known as *cold fronts*, this being the meteorological name given to the advancing edge of the air mass. Cold fronts arrive as often as twice a week during the middle of winter. This outburst of cold air is in fact exactly the same as a *monsoon*. Although monsoons are usually thought of as Indian, or Asian, in reality all the temperate continents have them.

In summer the North American continent heats up, develops low pressure, and tends to 'suck' air in. This is the opposite of the winter situation. In Asia this 'sucking in' of air creates the summer monsoons, which bring the well known torrential monsoon rains. In North America, a smaller continent, the effect is less, but even so it is enough to bend the NE Trade Winds round so that they blow from the southeast across The Bahamas on their way into the continent (Figure 9.2). (This is discussed further under winds on p.119)

It is important to note that the deflection of the NE Trade Winds does not create the SE Trade Winds. These **never** affect The Bahamas and never blow further north than Trinidad.

THE PLANETARY WIND SYSTEM

The Bahamas lie in the NE Trade Wind belt. Above all this dominates the climate of The Bahamas throughout the year.

The trade winds are a product of solar energy. As the equatorial belt is heated (Figure 9.3) the hot air rises, and within the troposphere this creates a three-dimensional circulation known as a *Hadley Cell*. At the surface of the earth a *thermal* wind is created blowing towards the equator, i.e. a northerly wind in the northern hemisphere and a southerly wind in the southern hemisphere. If the earth did not rotate this would be the end-result, but it does and creates a *planetary* wind which we experience as a wind from the east. The thermal wind created by solar energy, and the easterly wind created by the earth's rotation, combine to form the trade winds, divided into the NE Trade Wind and the SE Trade Wind belts respectively.

The trade winds are actually *systems* of winds. They are the largest and most consistent winds on earth. Being located within their influence ensures a uniformity of climate rarely experienced anywhere else on earth. Little can disturb them (only the monsoon effect is significant) so that day after day, month after month, the weather remains constant. As the trade winds we experience cross the Atlantic before they reach us, they are generally moist (more so in summer), and their temperatures are equable.

Despite this predictability, the NE Trade winds are nevertheless a system of winds. Within them are disturbances such as hurricanes, which is the end result of a progression from a tropical wave through a tropical storm to a hurricane. Travelling waves, or *easterly waves* as they are known, are another minor disturbance that frequently result in intense rain in the summer. There are also times when continental influences deflect the wind direction (Figure 9.2) so that the NE Trade winds may actually blow anywhere between NNE and SSE. Only occasionally are they displaced entirely by other air masses.

OCEAN CURRENTS

As we have seen the ocean itself is a great equaliser. However, whether the sea water is warmer or cooler than the adjacent land is also important. The map (Figure 9.2) shows clearly that The Bahamas is sandwiched between two warm currents, the Gulf Stream and the Antilles Current. Consequently they will warm any air masses crossing them. The NE Trades have to cross the Antilles Current, which is an extension of the North Equatorial Current. The Bahamas will never experience 'cold' trade winds. Similarly any wind from North America, such as is associated with a cold front, has to cross the Gulf Stream, the earth's most powerful current. This has an even greater impact on temperature than the Antilles Current, and when temperatures are below 0°C (32°F) in Florida they may well be over 10°C (50°F) in the northern Bahamas, only 160 kms (100 miles) away.

These warm currents are an additional cushion to our comfort, ensuring that even in the severest conditions The Bahamas does not experience freezing weather. This is why a number of

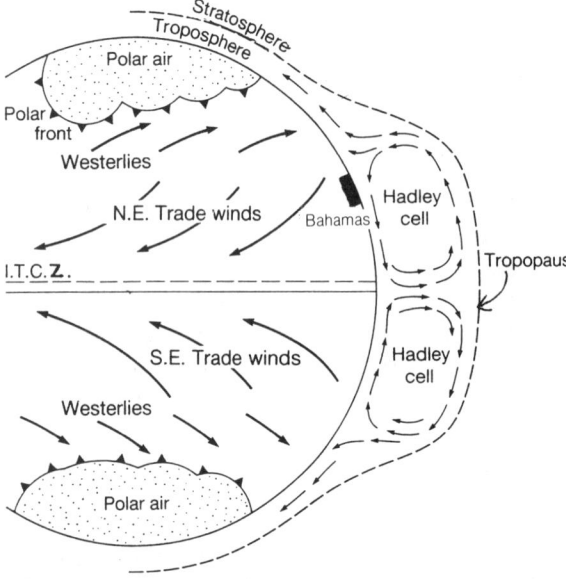

Figure 9.3 The Planetary Wind System. This shows the position of the Trade Winds in spring and Autumn. In winter the northern Hadley Cell will be over the equator, and in summer the southern Cell will take its place. It will therefore be clear that in winter The Bahamas is under the descending portion of the cell (dry), and in summer under the ascending portion (wet).

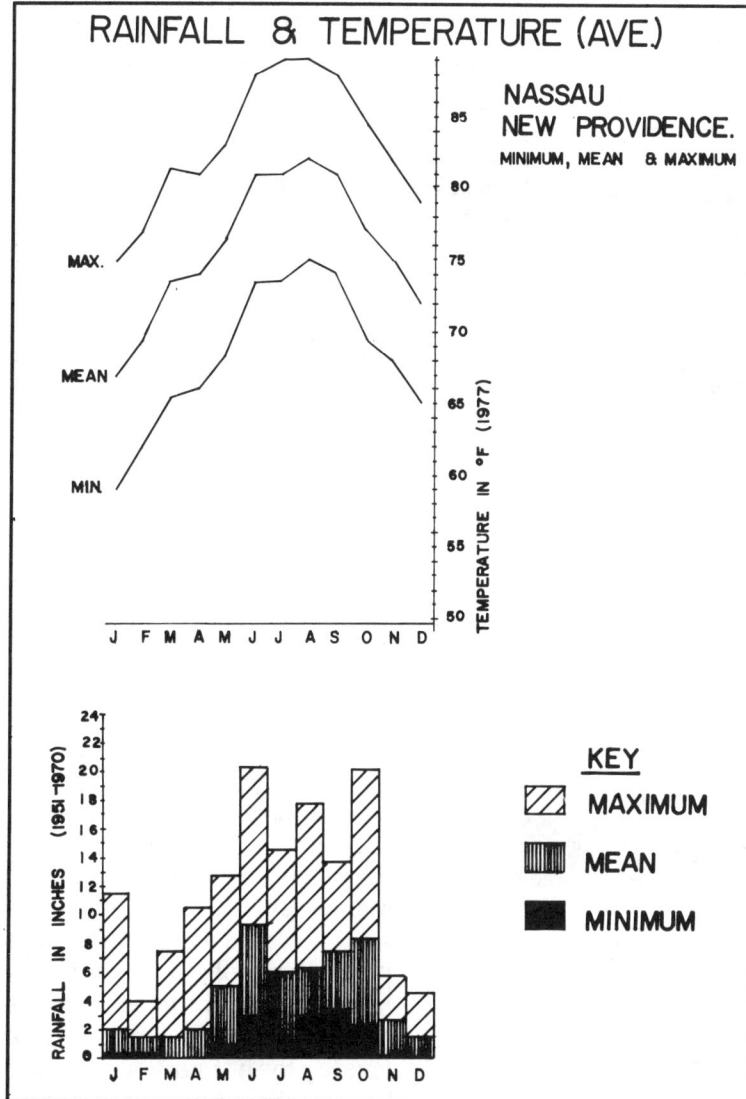

Figure 9.4 Mean, maximum and minimum monthly temperature and rainfall data for Nassau.

Florida farmers have set up additional citrus fruit farms in the northern islands.

TEMPERATURE

The compound graphs (Figures 9.4, 9.5) show how the temperature of The Bahamas varies throughout the year and across the country. It should be noted that in summer most of the country has virtually the same temperature, it being just as hot in Abaco as in Inagua. In winter there is a significant difference, with Grand Bahama and Abaco being distinctly cooler than the rest of the country. The simple exercise on page 115 will illustrate this.

It would be misleading to think of the temperatures being the same day after day. In summer this is largely true, but in winter there is much variation hidden in the averages, especially in the northern Bahamas.

WINTER CONDITIONS

The most likely conditions are:

■ *The normal trade wind weather.* Temperatures will be in the low 20's °C (70's °F) at midday, and fall to about the mid teens °C (60's °F) at night. It is sunny during the day, no rain.

■ *After a cold front* the daytime temperatures may stay in the teens °C (60's °F), occasionally lower, and at nightfall to the 10's °C (50's °F). Although it may be rainy near the front, it is usually sunny after its passage.

■ *The wind is from a southerly direction*, indicating an air mass blowing up from the Caribbean, perhaps from as far away as the Amazon Basin. This air mass will have crossed very warm seas and will be hot and humid. Temperatures will be in the high 20's °C (70's °F) and may reach 30°C (86°F). At night temperatures will drop to the mid-teens °C (60's °F), but as it will also be very humid there will be a heavy dew. The high humidity gives a particularly 'muggy' or summer feel to the atmosphere.

'Spring' and 'Autumn'

Although winter and summer have been regarded as the only two significant seasons, it would be a mistake to think that early (April and May) and late (September and October) summer were alike. Anyone living in The Bahamas will vouch for the fact that the former is more pleasant because the temperatures, especially at night, are lower, as shown in table 9.2.

Table 9.2 Average Temperatures (°C/°F) for spring and autumn

	Minimum	Maximum
April	19/66	28/82
May	21/70	29/84
September	24/75	31/88
October	22/72	30/86

As the sun is at its highest in June it might be expected that early summer would be hotter than late summer, but hot, humid days persist until the first cold fronts arrive at the end of October.

Sea temperatures and warm ocean currents

The reason for the above disparity lies in the sea temperatures. (Table 9.3)

Having a maritime climate means that the air temperature is very much conditioned by the temperature of the sea it crosses. In spring the sea is still cool from the impact of the winter's cold air masses (average $25°C/77°F$), and so the warm air crossing it is pleasantly cooled, and has its humidity lowered. In autumn the sea has been heated to its highest level by the hot summer sun, and being water it retains this heat long after the land has started cooling down (average sea temperature $28°C/83°F$). The air that reaches The Bahamas is thus heated up, and is humid. Only when the sea starts to cool down do we feel the onset of 'winter'.

Even if there were no warm ocean currents the sea would modify the Bahamian climate, by exchanging heat with the cold air passing over it in winter. However, as the winter progressed the

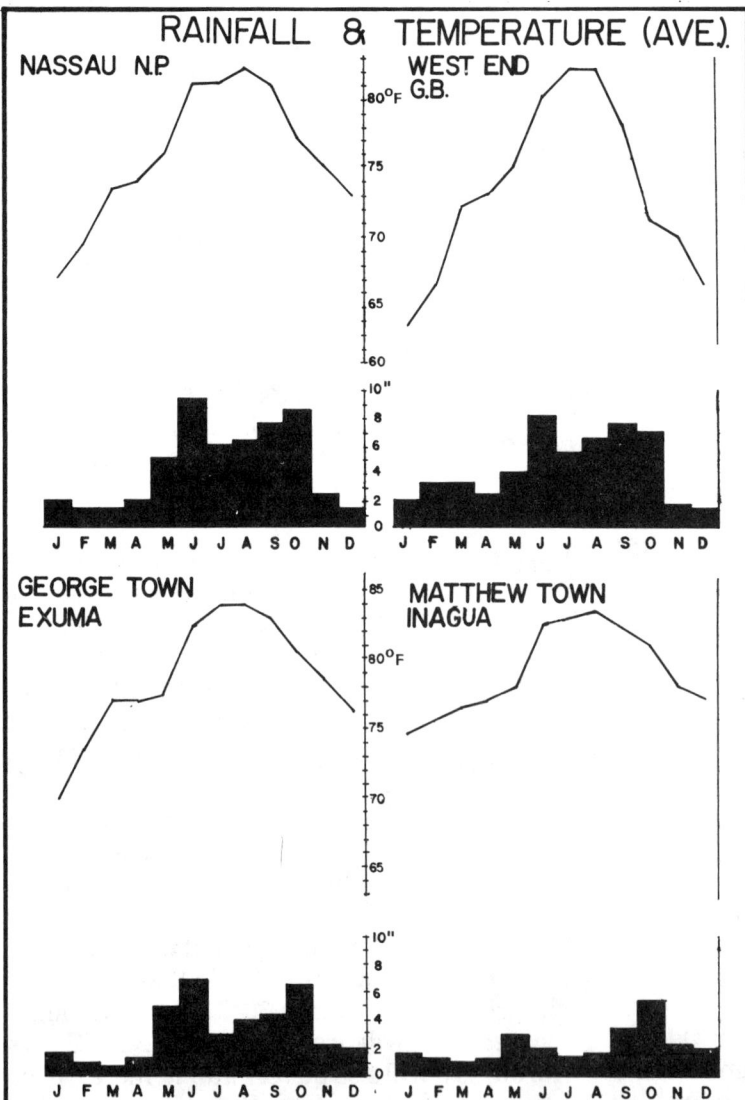

Figure 9.5 Combined temperature graphs and rainfall histograms ('climographs') for four stations in The Bahamas.

Table 9.3 Mean monthly sea surface temperatures for Nassau and Hope Town, Abaco.

		J	F	M	A	M	J	J	A	S	O	N	D
Nassau	°C	23.7	23.6	23.9	24.4	25.8	27.2	28.4	29.1	28.8	27.6	25.9	24.7
	°F	74.7	74.5	75.0	76.7	78.5	81.0	83.1	84.3	83.8	81.7	78.6	76.5
Hope Town	°C	23.6	23.2	23.3	24.2	25.3	26.9	28.1	28.6	28.2	26.9	25.7	24.4
	°F	74.5	73.8	74.0	754.5	77.5	80.5	82.5	83.5	82.7	80.4	78.2	76.0

sea would cool down gradually, and the heat exchange would become less pronounced. Cold fronts would then be less affected as they crossed the Florida Straits, and The Bahamas would experience a cooler winter climate.

In fact the enormous mass of water that makes up the Gulf Stream is very resistant to cooling. As each cold air mass cools the surface water this layer sinks down, to be replaced by warmer water at the surface, which continues being carried northwards across the Atlantic. As far away as Norway temperatures in winter are approximately 22°C (40°F) warmer than they would be without the Gulf Stream. The Gulf Stream is replenished by warm water from the equator, which passes through the Caribbean Sea and the Gulf of Mexico. At an average rate of four knots the entire mass of water between The Bahamas and Florida is replaced every two days. Despite this the Gulf Stream does become somewhat cooler during the winter. This is because cold fronts travel down the central USA and out into the Gulf of Mexico (New Orleans has an average maximum of only 15.5°C (60°F) in January compared with 25°C (77°F) for Nassau). The Gulf Stream cools down by about 5°C (9°F) in winter.

The Antilles Current also helps to keep Bahamian temperatures stable and warmer in winter, but as the trade winds are never cold, and the Antilles Current relatively slow, the impact is much less than for the western side of the country.

RAINFALL AND HUMIDITY

The histograms (Figure 9.5) show the seasonal pattern of rainfall for a variety of island locations. There is no doubt that summer is wetter than winter, by a ratio of 2:1, and that the southern islands are drier, also in the ratio 2:1. Both of these phenomena need explaining.

THE WET AND DRY SEASON

Summer is the wet season, and as it is the hot season it is logical to expect that the higher temperatures increase convection, and therefore create convectional rain. Certainly this

---

TEMPERATURE EXERCISE
Using Figure 9.5, place a ruler across the graph and read off the maximum and minimum temperatures for each of the four islands. Then complete this table:

Location	Maximum (Summer)	Minimum (Winter)
West End		
Nassau		
Georgetown		
Matthew Town		

Then answer the following questions:

1. What is the difference in temperature (the *geographical range*) between West End and Matthew Town in a) winter and b) summer?

2. In each case explain why the range is high or low.

3. Which town has the greatest *annual range* of temperature throughout the year? Why?

happens, and most of the rain that occurs is convectional. Nevertheless, as the southern Bahamas only gets half as much rain as in the north, but has the same or even slightly higher temperatures, it cannot be the complete explanation. Why is it drier in the southern Bahamas?

It is also the case that there are many hot days during the winter, and convectional currents are certainly active over the larger islands, but it does not usually rain. Why not?

In both cases the answer lies in the humidity of the atmosphere - it cannot rain if there is not enough moisture in the air with which to form rain. Therefore the air (the NE Trade Winds, in effect) must be drier in winter, and drier over the southern Bahamas than over the northern Bahamas in summer.

Inspection of Figure 9.3 shows that this is indeed the case. During the winter the trade wind belt shifts south, and only the northern limits of the NE Trade Winds affect The Bahamas. This is air that has already released most of its moisture far to the south of us, and is now *descending* (the opposite of a *convection current*) which stabilizes it. As summer approaches the trade wind belt migrates northwards, and eventually the wet zone reaches the southern Bahamas. As a result we should expect to see the southern Bahamas start its wet season first as the wet weather travels north. Equally, at the end of the wet season, the rains should last longest in the south. An examination of the rainfall data for Inagua, Exuma, and Grand Bahama shows that this is in fact the case.

Table 9.4 Rainy season in The Bahamas

	Inagua	Exuma	G Bahama
Start	May 7	May 15	May 25
End	Oct 25	Oct 20	Oct 15
Length	6m 18d	6m 5d	5m 20d

THE DRIER SOUTHERN BAHAMAS

The southern Bahamas does actually have a longer rainy season, but less rain, than the north. The wettest month in Inagua is October, with 112 mms (4.5 inches) of rain compared with 275 mms (11 inches) in Freeport. For rain to occur by convection there must be some surface heating, so it might seem that the larger islands of the north generate more heat than the smaller islands in the south. There is certainly some truth in this, but the fact is that Inagua at 1 550 square kilometres (600 square miles) is bigger than Grand Bahama at 1 370 square kilometres (530 square miles). There is no doubt that the air is moist, as rainfall is very heavy along the mountainous coasts of Cuba and Hispaniola, immediately to the south of the southern Bahamas. This matter deserves further investigation as it is not easily explained. At present the logical explanation is that there is increased convection in the north due partly to the larger islands, but also partly due to the wide extent of shallow water on the Little and Great Bahama Banks. The bank water, being shallow,

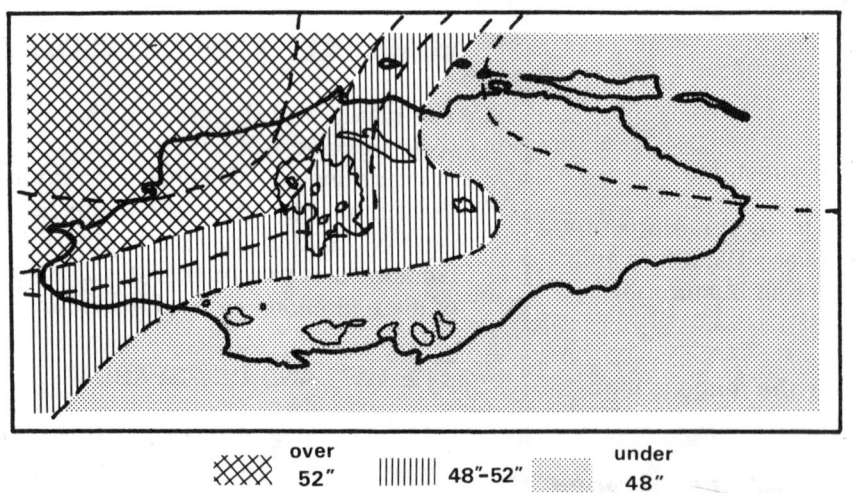

Figure 9.6 Rainfall distribution on New Providence Island. On average the west is wetter than the east.

over 52" |||||| 48"-52"   under 48"

Table 9.5 Average annual rainfall (1951-1970) and number of rain days per year for 15 Bahamian stations.

STATION	RAIN(mms)	RAIN DAYS
West End, GB	986	110
Cherokee Sd, Ab	836	119
Alice Town, Bim	556	93
Airport, NP	1 234	137
Harbour Is	800	89
Rock Sound, El	793	99
Kemps Bay, And	632	79
The Bight, Cat	669	74
Georgetown, Ex	607	101
Clarence Town, LI	718	80
Cockburn Town, SS	828	91
Colonel's Hill, Cr	644	92
Abraham's Bay, May	935	104
Matthew Town, In	631	70
Duncan Town, RI	607	101

Figure 9.7 Convectional cloud building up over New Providence in June 1990.

responds rapidly to solar heating, and so creates its own convectional currents, in turn producing rain over the islands on those banks. In the south there are no large banks, and the water remains cooler around the more widely separated islands, thus discouraging convection.

TYPES OF RAINFALL

Four types of rainfall may be recognized in the Bahamas (Table 9.6)

Table 9.6 Rainfall distribution by type in The Bahamas

Distribution/ Season	Local	Regional
Winter	RELIEF	FRONTAL
Summer	CONVECTIONAL RELIEF	TROPICAL STORM EASTERLY WAVE

Convectional rain

This is caused by a combination of solar heating on the larger islands and shallow-water banks, and the high summer humidity of the NE Trade Winds.

It is most common during the passage of easterly waves which increase the humidity, and allow convectional uplift to be more effective at producing rain (Figure 9.7). At these times it may rain continuously for one or more days, and remain overcast. These conditions are most common at the beginning and end of the rainy season (May/June and October), and local flooding is common (Figure 9.8). Without the presence of easterly waves a summer's day is much drier, and three or four days without rain is not uncommon. When it does rain showers are local and late in the day, although they may be very heavy and develop into thunderstorms. July and August are generally drier than the other summer months.

Orographic or relief rain

There are no mountains in The Bahamas and the significance of relief rain is debatable. Until the matter is fully researched by extensive rainfall monitoring, it may be reasonable to say that uplift is enhanced by the long ridges common to most islands, and roughly perpendicular to the prevailing winds. The long narrow eastern islands commonly have a parallel band of cloud over them, but somewhat downwind. In very humid conditions even the small uplift caused by crossing the ridges may be enough to create condensation, which will also be prompted by convection.

Figure 9.8 Early summer flooding in the eastern part of Nassau, 1988.

Easterly waves and tropical storms

Easterly waves are extremely humid low pressure belts travelling within the NE Trade Winds. Rainfall at sea is common under these conditions, but is amplified by convectional and orographic influences. Whenever an easterly wave is present convectional rain is increased.

Easterly waves may develop into tropical disturbances, tropical storms, and hurricanes. These systems often generate huge amounts of rain which affect everywhere in their path. As the diameter of a tropical storm may be as much as 800 kilometres (500 miles), it is reasonable to assume that some part of The Bahamas will be affected by them at least once during the year. Anything from 100-500 mms (4-12 inches) of rain may fall as they pass. Consequently some 5-25% of the annual rainfall may be accounted for by storm activity in or near The Bahamas. In 1979, for instance, Hurricane David added 225 mms (9 inches), and immediately after that Hurricane Frederick passing to the south added another 250 mms of rain. In that year 575 mms (23 inches) of rain were accounted for by summer tropical disturbances. Generally the amount of rain received from one of these systems depends on the speed at which it is moving. There was much less rain from Hurricane Andrew which crossed The Bahamas at 15 knots in 1992.

Frontal rain

This is the rain associated with the passage of a cold front, and it is the most important source of rain during the winter. Frontal rain can in fact be caused by a variety of types of fronts, but the most common situation is shown in the diagram (Figure 9.9). The actual amount of rain received as a front passes can vary greatly, and the following points should be noted:

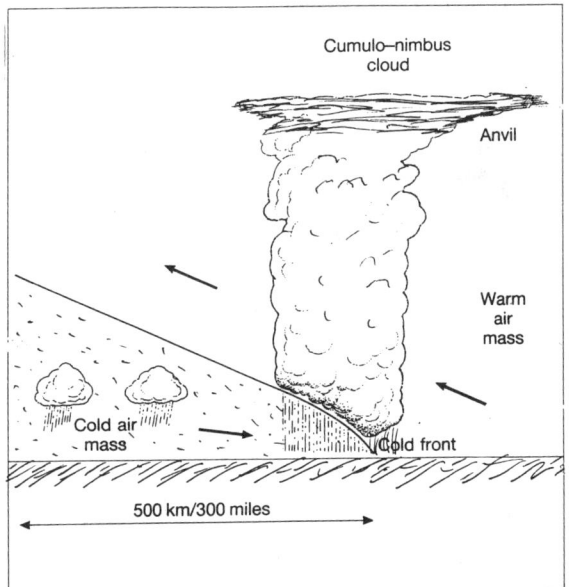

Figure 9.9 Cross-section of a cold front. The warm air mass will be the NE Trade Winds, and the height of the anvil might be as much as five kilometres. The diagram is greatly exaggerated vertically. (From Sealey, Caribbean World, *1992)*

Figure 9.10 Hailstones from the passage of a cold front at Treasure Cay, Abaco, in April 1983. Note the one cent coin for scale. The largest hailstone was 4 cms (1.5 inches) across.

- More rain is likely as the temperature differential between the two air masses increases. Very cold fronts are likely to create more rain, as they will cause a greater degree of condensation along the zone of contact and mixing.

- If the uplifted warm air mass is hotter and more humid than usual, the rainfall will be greater. This occurs when The Bahamas is covered by an air mass from the south (as opposed to the NE Trade Winds). Southerly winds are not uncommon in winter and represent warm moist air from the Caribbean. (See p.113)

- The intensity of the rainfall will increase with the speed of the advancing front. A rapid advance causes violent uplift and mixing. Thunderstorms and even hail are likely. (Figure 9.10)

- If the front becomes stationary, cloudy and possibly wet conditions will persist in the frontal area. The amount of rain may be quite low if there is little temperature difference, but if the opposing air mass is from the tropics then continuous rain is possible.

- As the cold air mass crosses the Gulf Stream it is warmed up, and it continues to be warmed and weakened as it crosses the warm waters of the Bahamas' banks. This means that the islands closest to Florida receive the most frontal rain, and explains why fronts may not even reach the central and southern Bahamas.

WINDS

As the wind roses show (Figures 9.11, 9.12) the wind can blow from any direction, but easterly is most common. In fact easterly winds (from NE, E or SE) account for 77% of the frequency in August, and 46% in February, averaging 63% over the whole year. The NE Trade Winds, which these statistics represent, are therefore the most common, or *prevailing*, winds in The Bahamas. Wind from the other directions can be accounted for by:

- Cold air masses in winter. These arrive from

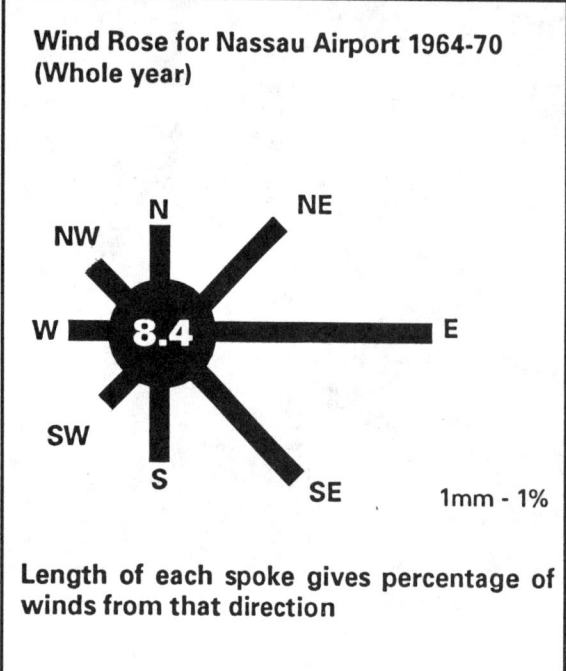

Figure 9.11 Average annual wind directions at Nassau Airport, 1964-1970. The central figure is the percentage of calms.

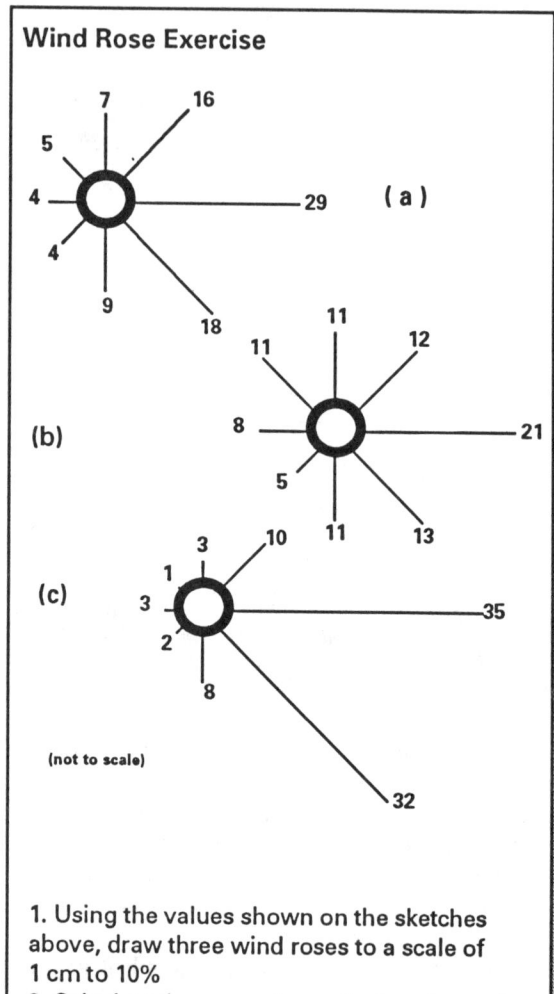

1. Using the values shown on the sketches above, draw three wind roses to a scale of 1 cm to 10%
2. Calculate the percentage of calms for each period.
3. With aid of the wind roses in Figure 9.12, identify the periods represented by the roses you have drawn.

the USA and therefore are mainly north-westerly, but can blow from the north or west as well. In February they account for 30% of the wind. These winds are cooler and drier than the Trade Winds.

- Southerly winds from the Caribbean occur 9% of the time. These are warmer and more humid than the Trade Winds.

- Various disturbances, such as winter depressions crossing the Gulf of Mexico, and tropical storms including hurricanes, will generate winds from any point of the compass.

Finally it should be remembered that cold air masses do not affect the southern Bahamas as much as the northern Bahamas, and therefore they will experience fewer northwesterly winds, but more southerly ones.

Tropical Storms and Hurricanes

The storms and hurricanes that affect The Bahamas usually form in the Atlantic Ocean between 10°N and 20°N. It is possible for storms in the Caribbean to reach The Bahamas after crossing Cuba, or for those formed in the Gulf of Mexico to arrive after crossing Florida. Never-

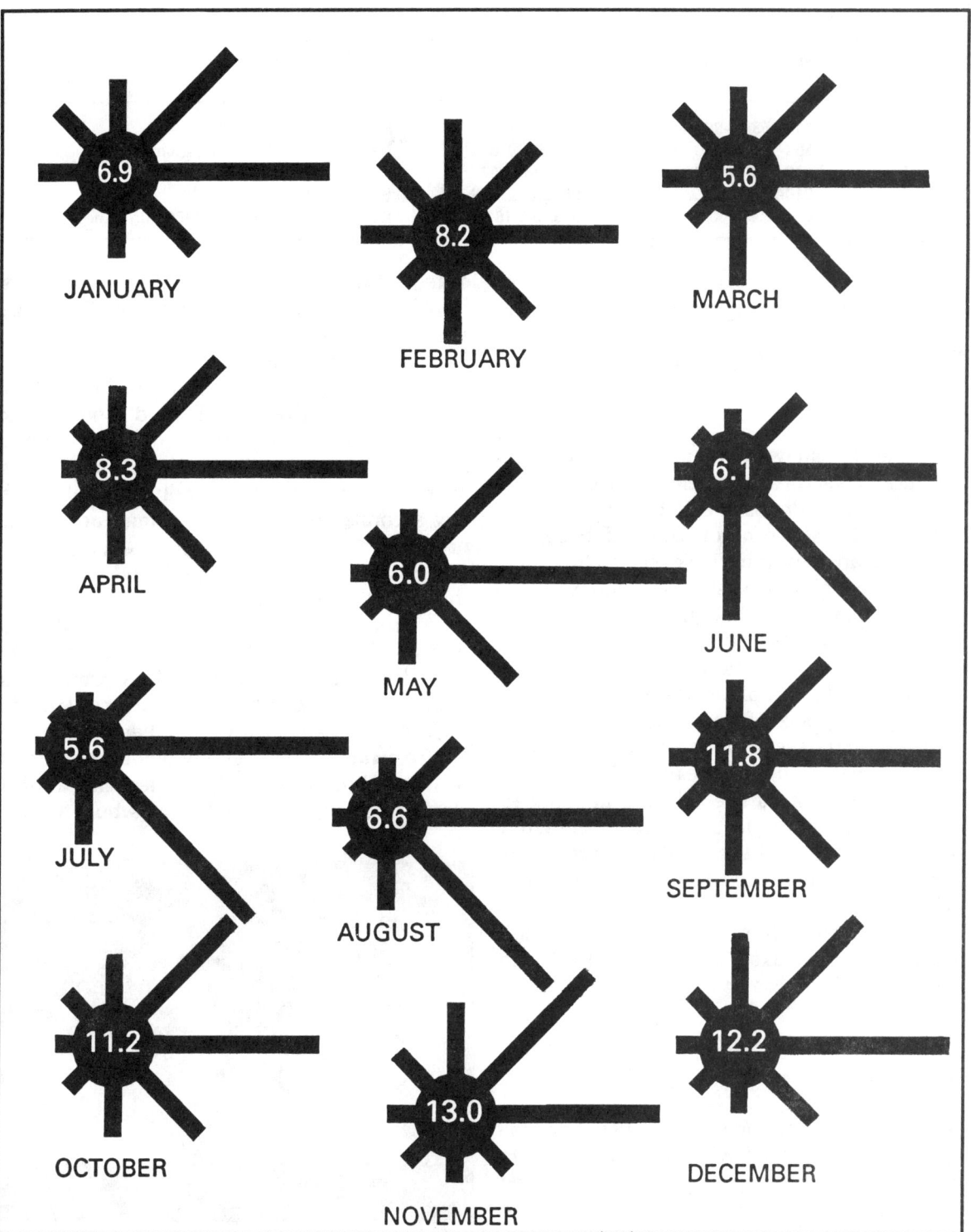

Figure 9.12 Average monthly wind directions at Nassau Airport, 1964-1970, same scale as in Figure 9.11.

Table 9.7 *The Saphir-Simpson Hurricane Scale*

CATEGORY	WIND SPEED (Km per hr/mph)	SEA SURGE (Metres/Feet)	DAMAGE
1	119-153/74-95	1.2-1.5/4-5	Minimal
2	154-177/96-110	1.6-2.4/5.1-8	Moderate. H. David in Bahamas, 1979
3	178-209/111-130	2.5-3.7/8.1-12	Extensive. H. Betsy, 1965
4	210-243/131-150	3.8-5.5/12.1-18	Extreme. H. Andrew, 1992
5	Over 243/150	Over 5.5/18	Catastrophic. Probably 1926 hurricane

theless, the serious storms of the last 40 years (see Figure 9.15) have all originated in the Atlantic.

FEATURES OF A HURRICANE

Wind Speed

The table (9.7) shows that hurricanes have five classifications according to sustained wind speed. The *sustained* wind is one that has been maintained for at least one minute. A wind speed that lasts less than one minute is a *gust*. In Hurricane Andrew the highest sustained wind was recorded at 138 mph, although the highest speed may have been more as the wind recorder broke at that reading. Gusts reached 175 mph in Eleuthera and 115 mph in Nassau.

The wind speed affecting the ground varies according to the sector of the hurricane in which you are situated. In the case of Andrew, which was travelling across The Bahamas at about 15 mph, this speed has to be added to the wind speed of rotation in the northern part of the hurricane, but subtracted from it on the southern side.

Consequently, Nassau, on the southern side of the eye, was not as seriously affected as North Eleuthera, which was on the northern side.

Tornadoes, waterspouts, and microbursts.

When Hurricane David struck in 1979 two 'tornadoes' were reported in Nassau. From time to time tornadoes have apparently been spawned by hurricanes, but in 1994 they were also recorded in the Berry Islands during February. In this case they were part of bad weather associated with a cold front. Similar occurrences have been reported from around The Bahamas, such as on Ocean Cay in the Biminis, Long Island, and South Andros.

These are not always traditional tornadoes with the distinctive funnel cloud and a track many kilometres long. In recent years some of these phenomena have been termed *microbursts* by meteorologists, and generally they only last a few seconds and affect very small areas. At present these severe winds, varying from 40-150 mph or more, are believed to form in the middle of thunderstorms, and are in fact an extremely powerful down-blast of cold wind. (They are related to the *wind shear* feared by aircraft). As thunderstorms are a common feature of hurricanes and cold fronts, microbursts may occur within them.

Tornadoes are extremely powerful vortices of wind, recognised by their menacing funnel cloud. They occur in The Bahamas, but are most

Figure 9.13 *Waterspout in its early stages, Montagu Bay, Nassau, April 1994. (Photograph courtesy Florence Bryden)*

common over the sea, where they look the same but are known as *waterspouts* (figure 9.13). They are most common during rainy weather in the wet season.

The storm surge

During Hurricane Andrew the worst damage was created along the south-facing shores, where a storm surge (probably combined with high waves) reached 7 metres (23 feet) at The Current in Eleuthera. Generally (Table 9.7 Saphir-Simpson Scale) the storm surge increases with wind speed, but it can also be increased if the sea is trapped or funnelled into a bay. In fact the shape of North Eleuthera does create a large south-facing bay, and it was here that the storm surge was greatest, taking sea water inland for 1.5 kilometres (1 mile). Any property within four metres of sea level and close to the coast is at serious risk from a storm surge.

Rainfall

This was discussed on p.118. Generally the slower-moving storms generate the most rain, but all hurricanes can be considered as great sources of rain, and may create extensive flooding in low-lying areas.

HURRICANE TRACKS

These can be very unpredictable, and the ability to predict exactly where a hurricane will strike has not improved greatly this century. However, the ability to spot the start of a hurricane early, and to track its progress, has improved immensely, so that all those in the danger zone can make the necessary preparations. Hurricane

Figure 9.14 In October 1991 a hurricane off the New Jersey coast of the USA generated huge waves that caused considerable damage to the Bahamian coastline. On Eleuthera the island was (from the top) a) washed-over at several points near the Glass Window b) public services were disrupted c) The Glass Window bridge was displaced by more than one metre d) the coast road north of Governor's Harbour was washed away.

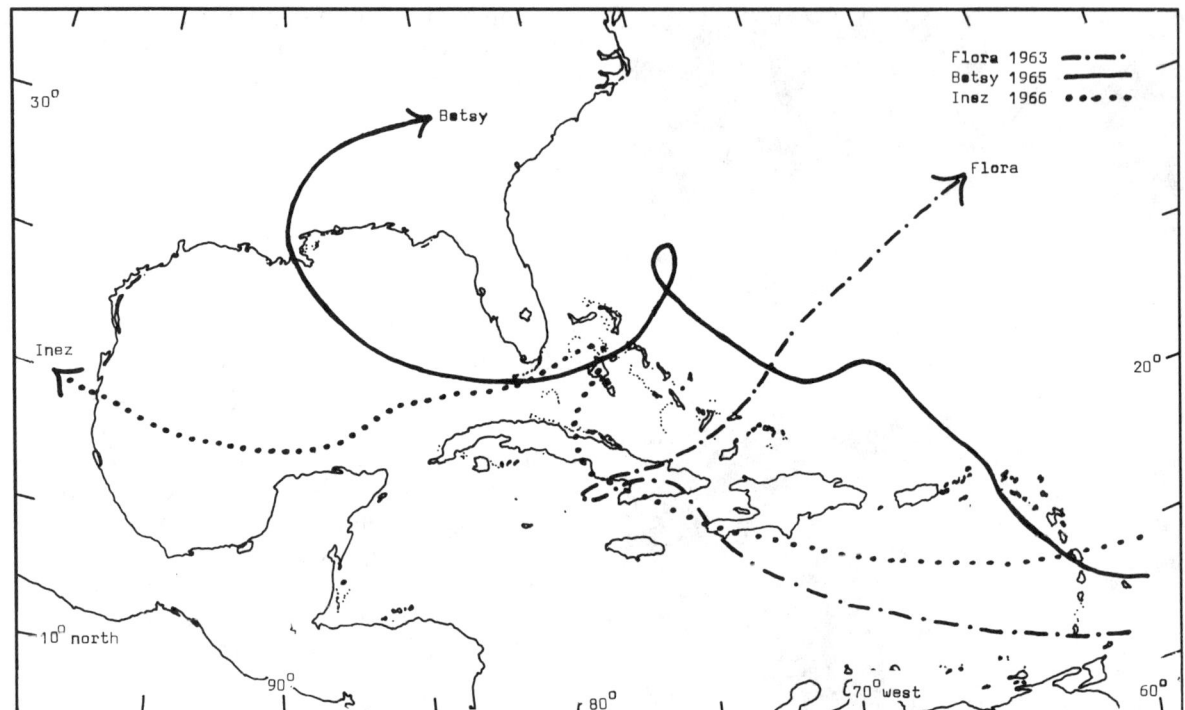

Figure 9.15 a) Three hurricanes that affected the Bahamas in the 1960's. Flora only affected the southern Bahamas; Betsy scored a direct hit on Nassau; and Inez was an October hurricane.

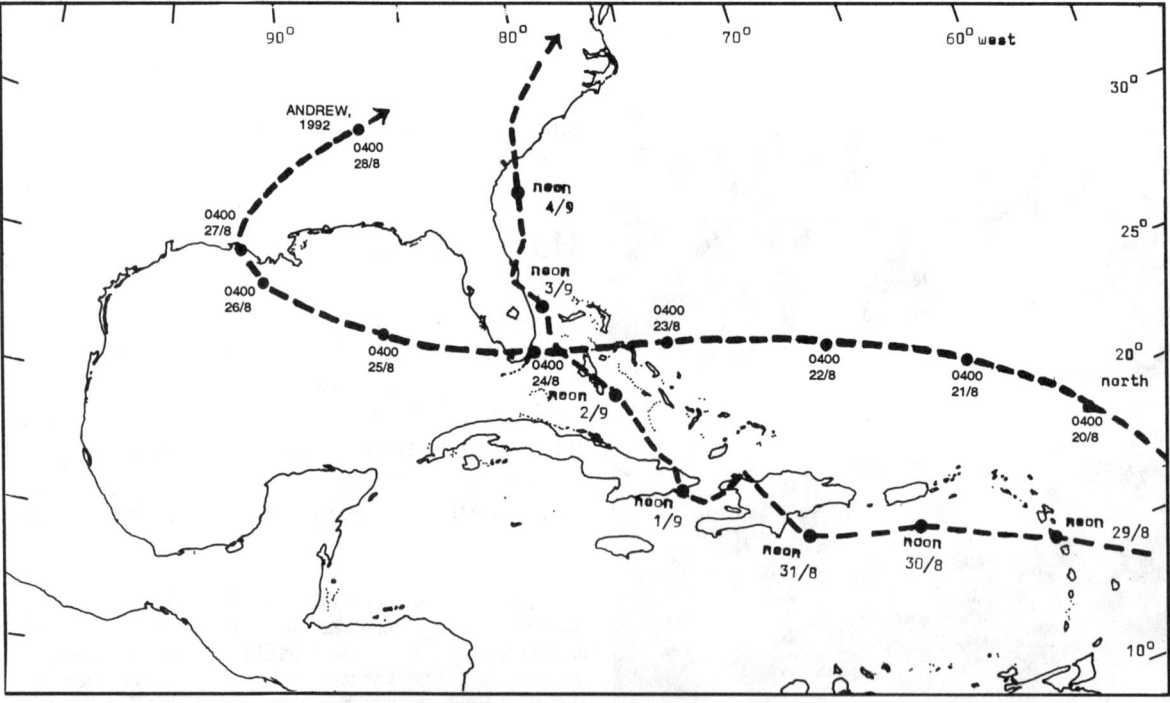

Figure 9.15 b) The tracks of the last two hurricanes to hit The Bahamas. Hurricane David lost much of its strength after crossing Hispaniola, and was downgraded from Category 4 to Category 2 by the time it reached The Bahamas. Andrew did not reach hurricane strength until about midday on 22nd August.

Hugo at first seemed much more of a threat to The Bahamas than it eventually was, and for two days was just 12 hours away. Hurricane Andrew appeared to be travelling harmlessly northwards in the Atlantic, but changed course and arrived very quickly from the east.

Observation of the behaviour of hurricanes suggests the following trends:

■ Small hurricanes may change course and speed quickly, while large hurricanes tend to maintain their course and speed.

■ Hurricanes formed in the Atlantic may do one of three things:
  ● Travel more or less due west until they hit the Central American coast. e.g. Hurricane Gilbert. They are not usually a threat to The Bahamas.
  ● Travel northwards up the Atlantic.
  ● Travel west but then turn and take a northerly course. e.g. Hurricane David, which turned northwest when it was south of the Dominican Republic; and Hugo, which turned northwest south of the Virgin Islands. These are always a threat to The Bahamas.

Meteorologists suggest that all hurricanes try to travel north, but that various conditions in the upper atmosphere prevent them, and force them westward instead. It may therefore be realistic to think of a westward-tracking hurricane as trying to turn north as soon as it can.

■ Hurricanes forming in the Caribbean Sea and in the Gulf of Mexico usually occur late in the season when these water bodies have heated up, and are not usually a threat to The Bahamas.

■ All hurricanes are subject to indeterminate atmospheric forces and may take totally unprecedented courses. e.g. Hurricane Betsy in 1965, which had passed the Bahamas and was travelling north, but turned around and came back to cause serious damage in Nassau. **No hurricane in the region can be considered to be without some degree of threat to The Bahamas.**

Table 9.8 Hurricane occurrences for all The Bahamas, Northern Bahamas, and New Providence, 1886-1993

	May	June	July	Aug	Sept	Oct	Nov	Total
All Bahamas	1	*2	3	17	26	17	5	69
Northern Bahamas	0	28	3	14	17	14	5	53
New Providence	0	0	1	2	7	2	0	12

* The two June storms are not universally agreed to have been of hurricane strength

This chapter incorporates much information and some illustrations from *The Climate of The Bahamas*, by M Halkitis et al, published by the now defunct Bahamas Geographical Association. The author, who was also editor of that publication, gratefully acknowledges the use of this important earlier publication, which has long been out of print.

BIBLIOGRAPHY

The following works will provide both additional information on the topics dealt with in this book, and lead eventually to a much greater depth of knowledge about The Bahamas as a whole.

GENERAL GEOLOGICAL ACCOUNTS

- H. Gray Multer - *Field Guide to Some Carbonate Rock Environments in the Florida Keys and Western Bahamas.* 2nd edition 1977. 400pp. Kendall/Hunt. About $20.00.
An excellent collection of important papers organised in the style of a field guide to the marine environments. Numerous photographs, maps and other illustrations, and a list of over 500 references.

- John E. Hoffmeister - *Land from the Sea.* 1974. 140pp. University of Miami Press. About $12.00
A layman's account of the geology of South Florida. As this is often very similar to The Bahamas (and the author discusses this), it is well worth studying.

- R. W. Adams *et al.* Donald T. Gerace, Editor - *Field Guide to the Geology of San Salvador.* 3rd edition 1983. 172pp. Available from The Bahamian Field Station, San Salvador, The Bahamas. About $20.00.
A collection of six studies on the geology of San Salvador, which, in fact, covers many of the features common to all of the islands. Well illustrated and easy to read. The Bahamian Field Station publishes many excellent studies on The Bahamas, and a list of these may be obtained from the Director.

- R E Sheridan *et al* - Geology and Geophysics of The Bahamas. In *The Geology of North America, Vol 1-2, The Atlantic Continental Margin: US.* The Geological Society of America, 1988, P329-363
A comprehensive survey of the relationship of The Bahamas to the North American plate, together with a summary of the main features of the country's geology.

MAJOR CONTRIBUTIONS TO THE GEOLOGICAL LITERATURE

- Norman D. Newell and J. K. Rigby - Geological Studies on the Great Bahama Bank. *Bulletin of the Society of Economic Palaeontologists and Mineralogists,* Special publication No. 5, 1957, pp. 15-72.
The classical study of The Bahamas, yet to be superseded.

- Leslie Illing - Bahamian Calcareous Sands. *Association of American Petroleum Geologists Bulletin,* **38,** No. 1, 1954, pp. 1-93.
A major study of Bahamian sediments, and the starting point for much of the more recent work.

- Robert S. Dietz *et al.* - Geotectonic Evolution and Subsidence of The Bahama Platform. *Geological Society of America Bulletin,* **81,** 1970, pp. 1915-1928.
A sound study of the geophysical evolution of The Bahamas, starting with the formation of the Atlantic.

- Wolfgang Schlager and Robert N. Ginsburg - Bahamian Carbonate Platforms - The Deep and the Past. *Marine Geology,* **44,** 1981, pp. 1-24.
A good modern summary of present knowledge which pays particular attention to the deep water troughs. Both writers have written many papers about The Bahamas which are all worth reading, and this is an excellent introduction to their work.

- P. Garrett and S. J. Gould - Geology of New Providence Island, Bahamas. *Geological Society of America Bulletin,* **95,** 1984 pp. 209-220.
A geological history of the island which reconstructs its past geographies.

- R N Ginsburg *et al* - The Growth Potential of a Bypass Margin, Great Bahama Bank. *J of Sedimentary Petrology,* 61, No 6, 1991, pp967-987.

- F Whitaker and P L Smart. Active Circulation of Groundwaters in Carbonate Platforms. *Geology,* 18, 1990, pp200-203.

- John E Mylroie & James L Carew - 'The Flank Margin Model for Dissolutional Cave Development in Carbonate Platforms. Ch 15, in: *Earth Processes and Landforms.* 1990. pp 329-363.

GEOGRAPHICAL AND GENERAL SCIENTIFIC PUBLICATIONS

Several organisations produce journals and other publications likely to be of interest to readers of this book.

- *The Bahamas Journal of Science.* Published three times a year by Media Enterprises, PO Box N-9240, Nassau, The Bahamas. By Subscription, $29.00 per year. This journal started in 1993 aimed at those persons who wished to know more about the Bahamian environment from a scientific point of view. Articles vary widely in topic and level. Some examples from the first issues include:

Edward N Rappaport & Fred C Sheets. *Hurricane Andrew.* (Oct. 1993, pp. 2-9)

Paul J Hearty and Pascal Kindler. *An Illustrated Stratigraphy of the Bahama Islands.* (Oct. 1993, pp. 28-45)

Neil E Sealey. *Early Views on the Geology of The Bahamas.* (Feb. 1994, pp. 27-30)

K M Sullivan et al. *Abundance Patterns of Stony Corals on Platform Margin Reefs.* (May 1994, pp. 2-11)

William L Wilson. *Morphometry and Hydrology of Dean's Blue Hole, Long Island, Bahamas.* (Oct. 1994)

- *Bahamas National Trust*, Village Road, PO Box N4105, Nassau. The Trust occasionally publishes the *Bahamas Naturalist*. The following are some relevant articles from earlier issues:

J. L. Carew et al. *Bahamian Caves and Sea Level Changes.* (Winter 1982, pp. 5-13)

Neil E. Sealey. *Conservation and the Coast.* (Winter 1982, pp. 29-34)

Stephen J. Gould. *Cerion, Snail of Many Shells.* (Spring 1980, pp. 2-3)

Rod Attrill. *The "Drop-Off".* (Spring 1980, pp 11-15)

- *Lands and Surveys Department*, Bay Street, PO Box N592, Nassau.

Complete set of topographical maps at 1:25 000 (Bimini 1:10 000). $1.00 per sheet.

Various large scale maps and plans, e.g. 1:12 500, 1:2 500.

General map of The Bahamas, 1:1 million, paper folded or laminated, $4.00 and $10.00. Hydrographic chart of The Bahamas at 1:1 250 000.

Vertical air photographs of the whole of The Bahamas, at about 1:10 000.

- *International Oceanographic Foundation*, 3979 Rickenbacker Causeway, Virginia Key, Miami, Florida 33149, publishes *Sea Frontiers* six times a year. This journal frequently publishes short illustrated articles of relevance to The Bahamas. Annual subscription is $20.00. Some examples are:

E. A. Shinn. *Atlantis: Bimini Hoax.* May/June 1978, pp. 130-141.

Steven D. Bach. *The Ecology of Coral Reef Algae.* March/April 1979, pp. 99-104.

Steven D. Bach. *Calcareous Algae.* May/June 1976, pp. 138-142.

Kathleen Mark. *Coral Reefs, Seamounts and Guyots.* May/June 1976, pp. 143-149.

J. E. Reynolds. *The Dry Tortugas* (Florida Keys). March/April, 1983, pp. 66-75.

- *The Land Resource Study of The Bahamas* was carried out from 1969 to 1976 by a team of specialists from the British Ministry of Overseas Development. It studied the land and water resources, including soils, rocks, landforms, shore-lines, climate and vegetation, and the past and present agriculture. The first eight volumes covered all the main islands except New Providence and San Salvador. Unfortunately, these are not available to the public. However, a summary and the volume on the pine forests were made available to the public:

a) B. G. Little et al. *Land Resources of The Bahamas: A Summary* No. 27. 1977. 133 pages plus maps.

b) P. W. T. Henry. *The Pine Forests of The Bahamas* No. 16. 1974. 178 pages plus maps. These two volumes provide the only major study of the geography of The Bahamas. They are available at libraries and the Lands and Surveys Office.

- Robert Palmer - *Blue Holes of the Bahamas.* Jonathan Cape, 1985, pp184.

Robert Palmer - *Deep into Blue Holes.* Unwin Hyman. 1989, pp. 164.

Two books dealing with the underwater exploration of blue holes in The Bahamas, with specific reference to Grand Bahama and Andros

- David Campbell - *The Ephemeral Isles.* Macmillan. 1979. About $15.00 paperback. A sound introduction to the natural history and ecological landscapes.

- Neil E Sealey - *Caribbean World.* Cambridge University Press, 1992. About $20.00 paperback. A geographical survey of the physical and human geography of the Caribbean, with substantial discussion of The Bahamas in this context.

- Neil E Sealey, *Bahamas Today.* Macmillan Caribbean, 1990. About $12.00. A companion volume to this book, dealing with the human and economic geography of The Bahamas.

Index

Abaco 60, 87-8
Age of The Bahamas 9
Ages of rocks 7, 28-9
Aggregates 26
Agriculture 55, 62, 97
Air masses 111, 120
Airborne soil 86-8
Algal mats 69-70
Aluminous laterite 87
Amino acid racimization 43-4
Andros 63, 67, 71, 82, 95
Antilles Current 111-5
Aquifer 94
Aragonite crystals 19, 24, 51
Aragonite sand 102-5
Arches 76
Atlantic Ocean 9-10, 31, 115
Atlantis 49, 83
Atoll 17, 38
Attrition 23

Banana hole 49
Bank scalloping 15-6
Barging water 93-6
Bat guano 59
Bauxite 87
Bay-head beach 80
Beach cusps 79-80
Beaches 79-80
Beach deposits 47, 60, 79-82
Beach rock 47, 82-4
Bedding planes 40
Bimini 29, 48, 96, 103-4
Bimini Embayment 13, 34-5
Bio-erosion 77
Blake Plateau 14-5, 107
Blanket deposits 26
Blow holes 76
Blue holes 50, 63-7
Boreholes 9-10, 18, 58
Brackish water 93, 98
Brine shrimp 102
'Bucket' theory 17
Building sand 108

Cable Beach 80-2
Calcareous green algae 19-21
Calcite crystals 19, 51, 104
Calcium carbonate 19, 24-5, 51-2
Caliche 88
Carbonate platform 6-9
Cat Island 54, 87
Caves, caverns 56-9, 75-6
Cay Sal Bank 107
Cement 102
Cementation 18, 50-1
Cerion morphology 42-5
Channels 16, 31-7
Clay 19-20, 108
Cliffs 46-7, 74-5
Clouds 117
Coastal erosion 46-7, 74-7
Coastland 74-84
Cold fronts 111-3
Continental Drift 6-7, 14
Continentality 110
Convectional rain 90, 115-7

Coralgal sediments 18, 20-24
Coralline algae 22
Corals and coral reefs 18-24, 45
Cross-bedding 40-1
Cryptocrystalline grains 19
Current bedding 48

Dating (geological) 28-9, 42-9
Dean's blue hole 62-4
Deep well disposal 58, 98
Deposition 77-84
Desalination 96
Diagenesis 50-2
Dolomite 52
Dripstones 58
Dune ridges 53-5

Easterly waves 112, 118
Eleuthera 19, 55, 67, 75, 87, 89, 123
Erosion 46, 74-7
Evaporation 24, 91-2
Evaporites 18, 24
Evapotranspiration 91-2
Exumas 29-30, 55, 75

Faecal pellets 20-1, 26
Faults, fault lines 7, 15, 33, 66-7
Flamingoes 102
Flank margin caves 57
Flooding 118
Florida Keys 14
Foraminifera 19
Fossils 42-5
Fresh water lenses 67, 93-4
Frontal rain 118-9

Glass Window 123
Grand Lucayan Waterway 98
Grapestone 21, 26, 28
Gravity measurements 11-2
Gulf Stream 111-5, 119

Hadley Cell 112
Hail 119
Halimeda 19-21
Hamilton's Cave 56
Hard water 93
Hatchet Bay Cave 57, 59
Headward erosion 16, 36
Hidden troughs 13-5, 34-36
Hogsty Reef 70
Honeycomb weathering 62, 75, 78
Humidity 115-9
Hurricanes 80-1, 90-1,100, 104, 120-5
Hydrocarbons 105
Hypersaline ponds 72

Ice Ages 6, 38-45, 63
Inagua 99-102
Irrigation 97

Joulter Cays 27

Karst 60-2

Lagoons 71-3
Lake Rosa 102
Lakes 73-4

Lateral accretion 15, 34-5
Laterite 87
Leaching 86
Leafmould soil 89
Limestone crust 48, 67-8
Limestone for building 108
Limestone types 18, 51-2
Long Island 54, 67, 80
Longshore drift 79-80
Lumps 23, 26-7

Magnetic measurements 16-7
Mangrove swamp 69-74
Mars Bay blue hole 65
Marshes 69-74
Mayaguana 45, 93
Microbursts 122-3
Mineral resources 98-108
Mixing zone 93-4
Monsoon 111
Muck soils 89
Mud 21, 27-8

Ocean Cay 103-5
Ocean currents 111-5
Ocean holes 63
Offshore bars 80-2
Oil exploration 106-7
Ooids 19-21, 24-6
Oolite, oolitic limestone 18, 24-7
Oolitic sand 24-7
Organic soils 89-90
Orographic rain 117

Parrot fish 21-3
Peat 19, 29, 48-9, 89
Pedalfers 86
Pedocals 86
Pellets 20-1, 26
Penicillus 19-21
Petroleum deposits 105-7
Pine Islands 60, 91-2
Pineapples 87
Pink sand 19
Planetary wind system 112
Plate tectonics 9, 14
Pollution 97-8
Ponds 71-3
Porosity 61
Pothole farming 89
Preacher's Cave 76
Protosols 86
Provision land 89

Rainfall 90, 100, 115-9
Rainwater tanks 96
Raised beaches 47
Recrystallisation 51-2
Red soil 86
Research submarines 33-5
Residual soils 86
Reverse osmosis 96
Rhizomorphs 44, 76-8
Ridgeland 53-9
Ridges 53-9
Rift valleys 33
Ripping 68
Rockland 53, 60-4

Sahara dust 68, 86-7

Salinity 25, 93
Salt 24-25, 98-102
Salt and pepper soil 87-8
Salt Pond Cave 59
Salt ponds 71-2, 99
Samana Cay 81
Sand dunes - fossil 53-6
Sand dunes - modern 56, 77-9
San Salvador 42, 48-9, 53, 84, 87
Sea caves 75-6
Sea level changes 38-49, 63-4
Sea surface temperature 23, 114-5
Sea urchins 22-3
Sea water 24
Sedimentary soils 88-9
Sediments 7, 16, 18-30
Seismic measurements 13-4
Sewage 98
Sinkholes 61-4
Skeletal sediments 19-24, 26
Soft water 93
Soil fertility 86-90
Soils 85-90
Soil use 86-90
Solar salt production 98-102
Solution weathering 56-7, 60-4
Spits 80-2
Sponges 22-3
Stacks, stumps 76
Stalactites, stalagmites 50, 58-9
Stargate blue hole 66-7
Storm beaches (berms) 81-2
Storm surge 122-3
Straits of Andros 13, 34-5
Stromatolytes 29-30
Submarine canyons 31-36
Subsidence 11, 46, 49
Swamps 69-74

Temperature 99, 110, 113
Tidal creeks 70-1
Tidal flats 69-70
Tombolos 80-2
Tongue of the Ocean 15-6, 33-7
Tornadoes 122-3
Trade Winds 110-2
Transpiration 91-2
Tropical storms 118-22
Troughs 16, 31-37
Turbidites 32
Turbidity currents 16, 32, 35-6

Underground drainage 56-8, 63

Water conservation 97-8
Water lenses 93-4
Water resources 90-8
Water table 57, 62-4, 93-4
Waterspouts 122-3
Wave action 48
Wave-cut platform 48
Wellfields 93
Wetland 69-74
Whiteland 88
Winds 99, 119-23